Date Due

M

CHRISTIANITY AND NATURALISM

CHRISTIANITY AND NATURALISM

..

ESSAYS IN CRITICISM
SECOND SERIES

. .
.

BY ROBERT SHAFER

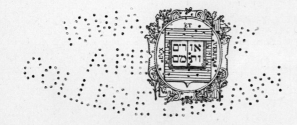

NEW HAVEN
YALE UNIVERSITY PRESS
LONDON, HUMPHREY MILFORD, OXFORD UNIVERSITY PRESS
1926

TO
PAUL ELMER MORE

PREFACE

This volume, like its predecessor (*Progress and Science*), is not a systematic treatise, but a series of essays. The first six essays were originally written for delivery as a course of Ropes Lectures, which I had the honour of giving before the University of Cincinnati in the spring of 1924. These essays have since been revised, and in several cases entirely rewritten.

I am indebted to the officers of the University—and in particular to Dean Louis T. More and to Dean Frank W. Chandler—not only for their kind invitation to give a course of Ropes Lectures, but also for my appointment to a permanent fellowship which has enabled me to complete the present work under unusually favourable circumstances, and to look forward hopefully to the early execution of several other literary projects. Too many of our colleges and universities, despite the volume of printed matter which issues from them annually, have become institutions of lecturing rather than of study and intellectual inquiry. The wise policy of the University of Cincinnati, directed against a false economy which dries up the springs of informed and fruitful thought, deserves the gratitude and support of our patrons of learning.

I am obliged to several publishers for permission to quote from a number of books: *The Idea of a University, Parochial and Plain Sermons, Oxford University Sermons, Loss and Gain,* and *Verses on Various Occasions,* by Cardinal Newman, the *Letters and Correspondence of John Henry Newman,* edited by Anne Mozley, and the *Life of Cardinal Newman,* by Wilfrid Ward (all published by Messrs. Longmans, Green, and Company); *Science and Hebrew Tradition, Science and Christian Tradition, Method and Results,* and *Evolution and Eth-*

ics, by T. H. Huxley, and the *Life and Letters of Thomas Henry Huxley,* by Leonard Huxley (Messrs. D. Appleton and Company) ; *The Fair Haven, Evolution Old and New, Life and Habit, Unconscious Memory, The Way of All Flesh,* and *Notebooks,* by Samuel Butler (Messrs. E. P. Dutton and Company) ; *Poems, Essays in Criticism,* First and Second Series, *Culture and Anarchy,* and *Literature and Dogma,* by Matthew Arnold, and the *Letters of Matthew Arnold,* edited by George W. E. Russell (The Macmillan Company) ; *Unpublished Letters of Matthew Arnold,* edited by Arnold Whitridge (Yale University Press) ; *The Dynasts* and *Collected Poems,* by Thomas Hardy (Messrs. Macmillan and Company, Ltd.) ; *Creative Chemistry,* by E. E. Slosson (The Century Company) ; and *Lectures and Essays on Natural Theology and Ethics,* by William Wallace (Oxford University Press).

The dedication of these essays to Mr. Paul Elmer More commemorates a relationship which dates from my undergraduate days. It was then one-sided and unknown to him. In more recent years it has happily become a friendship marked by good offices on his part for which I have much reason to be grateful.

I owe more than I can attempt to say to my friend Professor Charles W. Hendel, jr., of Princeton University, and to my wife for reading my manuscript and making suggestions which have resulted in its marked improvement. My wife has also read the proofs and compiled the index. Finally, I cannot omit to mention my debt to the staff of the Yale University Press for full coöperation and the careful performance of their responsible work.

R. S.

Graduate School,
  University of Cincinnati,
    14 January, 1926.

CONTENTS

E quel consiglio per migliore approbo
che l'ha per meno, e chi ad altro pensa
chiamar si può veracemente probo.

DANTE

CHRISTIANITY AND NATURALISM

I.

RELIGIOUS THOUGHT IN ENGLAND IN THE XVIITH AND XVIIITH CENTURIES

I.

NATURALISM is as old as philosophy. In the sixth century B.C., in Ionia, civilization had reached a high level. There was sufficient wealth for leisure, and the arts of life had so far developed as to provide men with the means of refined and delicate enjoyment. In Miletus, at least, life was pronouncedly secular in character. The crude religious beliefs of immemorial tradition could no longer be taken seriously and were practically abandoned, though stories of the gods, of course, still furnished material for both poets and artists. The decay of primitive religion, however, disclosed a problem, which was perhaps accentuated by the refinements of wealth. As life became fuller and richer, increased and more varied experience taught men that they lived in a world of decay and death, while by reason of the same experience the gods who had given stability to the scheme of things were become incredible. What, then, was the eternal reality underlying the incessant change of the sensible world?

This was the question which Thales, the earliest of the Milesian philosophers, asked himself, in complete independence, apparently, of bankrupt tradition. Of his teaching practically nothing is known save that he regarded water as the abiding element of which all things are made, and that he said 'all things are full of gods.' By the latter statement he may have meant, if we can judge from his followers, that since water was the ultimate reality, it must have been water in various of its manifestations to which people had previously given divine names, and that, since all things were formed from water, all must contain 'gods.' He may, on the other hand, have meant nothing so definite as this; but it is hardly doubtful that he lived in an atmosphere of implicit naturalism, and that this he made explicit by transforming what had been a religious question into a scientific question. He thus brought both philosophy and science into the world. His associate or disciple, Anaximander, was thoroughly naturalistic in his outlook, as can be seen beyond doubt from trustworthy reports of his teaching which still survive:

Anaximander of Miletus, son of Praxiades, a fellow-citizen and associate of Thales, said that the material cause and first element of things was the Infinite, he being the first to introduce this name for the material cause. He says it is neither water nor any other of the so-called elements, but a substance different from them which is infinite, from which arise all the heavens and the worlds within them. . . . He says that this is eternal and ageless, and that it encompasses all the worlds. . . . And into that from which things take their rise they pass away once more, "as is ordained; for they make reparation and satisfaction to one another for their injustice according to the appointed time," as he says in these somewhat poetical terms. . . . And besides this, there was an eternal motion, in the course of which was brought about the origin of the worlds. . . . He did not ascribe the origin of things to any alteration in matter, but said that the oppositions in the substratum, which was a boundless body, were separated out. . . . Rain was produced by the moisture drawn up from the earth by the sun. . . . The sea is what is left of the original moisture. The fire has dried up most of it and turned the rest salt by scorching it. . . . He says that the earth is cylindrical in form, and that its depth is as a third part of its breadth.

. . . The earth swings free, held in its place by nothing. It stays where it is because of its equal distance from everything. Its shape is convex and round, and like a stone pillar. We are on one of the surfaces, and the other is on the opposite side. . . . Living creatures arose from the moist element as it was evaporated by the sun. Man was like another animal, namely, a fish, in the beginning. . . . The first animals were produced in the moisture, each enclosed in a prickly bark. As they advanced in age, they came out upon the drier part. When the bark broke off, they survived for a short time. . . . Further, he says that originally man was born from animals of another species. His reason is that while other animals quickly find food by themselves, man alone requires a lengthy period of suckling. Hence, had he been originally as he is now, he would never have survived. . . . He declares that at first human beings arose in the inside of fishes, and after having been reared like sharks, and become capable of protecting themselves, they were finally cast ashore and took to land.[1]

However some of these passages may appear in the light of present-day knowledge, there is every reason to believe that none of Anaximander's teaching was merely fanciful. It was grounded on and controlled by such observation of the phenomenal world as was possible in his day, without regard for commonly received opinion. Concerning his theory of the origin of living creatures Professor Burnet says: "It is clear . . . that Anaximander had an idea of what is meant by adaptation to environment and survival of the fittest, and that he saw the higher mammals could not represent the original type of animal. For this he looked to the sea, and he naturally fixed upon those fishes which present the closest analogy to the *mammalia*. The statements of Aris-

[1] Quoted from Burnet, *Early Greek Philosophy*, 2d ed., where further passages containing fragmentary reports of Anaximander's teaching are also translated.

totle about the *galeus levis* were shown long ago by Johannes Müller to be more accurate than those of later naturalists, and we now know that these observations were already made by Anaximander. The manner in which the shark nourishes its young furnished him with the very thing he required to explain the survival of the earliest animals.''

It is impossible, of course, to know how far or how definitely Anaximander worked out his naturalistic speculations, but it is evident that his view embraced the universe as a whole in all its phenomenal appearances without distinction, and that he regarded these as varied manifestations of a single element which was the sole abiding reality underlying all processes of change. Phenomenal worlds thus formed a self-sufficient system beyond which there was no supernatural cause or reality, the elemental substance and motion being enough to account for everything. Human beings were natural products like any other sensible object, and were to be accounted for, with all their characteristics, on the same principles. They might be said to partake of eternal life as one might say the same thing of a tree, or of the earth itself. Human beings and trees both were composed of indestructible or eternal substance which remained after their periods of individual existence what it had been before those periods. Plainly Anaximander's speculations were thoroughly naturalistic. He is reported, it is true, to have termed the infinite underlying substance divine, and likewise the infinite world-systems formed from it; but, as Professor Burnet has observed, it was this use of the word 'god' which caused the Greeks to regard the philosophers as atheists.

It seems well briefly to recall these beginnings of philosophy because there is a widespread popular impression that naturalism has become a formidable power only as a result of the development of modern science, and in particular as a result of the general acceptance of the theory of evolution in the latter half of the nineteenth century. Echoes of the battle between science and religion precipitated by the theory of evolution still ring in our ears, but many are now seeking to assure us that this was a temporary and mistaken struggle. We are told that there is no real antagonism between the two, but that on the contrary they supplement each other in a common effort to make the world a better place in which to live. Thus a recent theological writer says: "In the relation of religion and science three successive phases may be roughly distinguished. The first may be designated the period of theological dominance: the second, that of independence and conflict: the third, of mutual respect and co-operation."[2] Similar statements are nowadays familiar to most of us, but they distort the facts, both past and present.

For naturalism, as I began by saying, is as old as philosophy. It is one of two rival interpretations or estimates of the character of life which have existed side by side in continuous hostility since the dawn of conscious thought. And naturalism has ever been a powerful foe of religion, nor had it to await, for this purpose, the development of modern science or general acceptance of the theory of evolution. This can be seen in a period as recent as the eighteenth century, as it is one object of the present essay to show. Moreover, the age-long quarrel between religion and naturalism is by no means settled, nor can it be settled by any compromise or 'peace without victory.' Undoubtedly that particular phase of the conflict which helped to make vivid the later years of the nineteenth century has now passed, but this is not

[2] A. Alexander, *The Shaping Forces of Modern Religious Thought*, p. 204.

because all the questions at issue have been resolved. It is rather because active controversies have their day and pass from the centre of the stage whether they are settled or not. Our capacity for attention is limited. If we cannot promptly answer a hard question very many of us can bear to let it go unanswered; for life is short and, meanwhile, there are many diverting possibilities which tempt us to the exercise of our right to the pursuit of happiness.

This, however, should not confuse us. It shows neither that there is no fundamental hostility between religion and naturalism nor that the two have coöperatively joined hands with mutual respect for each other. It does show that naturalism, or science, has gained a temporary victory; and as a matter of fact only those who desire the victory of naturalism are satisfied with the present situation. Naturalism and science are not, of course, for all purposes exactly equivalent terms, but in the present connexion they may legitimately be so used. Naturalism is simply the statement in philosophic form of the assumptions on which science is based and of the meaning of its revelations. So far as science is incomplete, naturalism is the more inclusive term, but science cannot dissociate itself from naturalism without ceasing to be science, and such an abdication will never come unless forced by external pressure. It is sometimes said that science and religion occupy different spheres and that each can and should pursue its own proper activity without disturbance from the other. But actually science has been continually widening its sphere, and it is at one with naturalism in claiming for its province the whole world of experience. This leaves for religion's sphere the world of the imagination, which is a thinly veiled way of saying that religion has nothing to do with reality—a contention which no religious man could for a moment

admit. For religion so conceived would have ceased to
be religion.

This is one way of stating the deep opposition which
exists between the two; and it has the advantage of indicating that religion does not properly have any quarrel
with knowledge, of whatever kind, so far as knowledge
is attainable by man, but only with the claims of science
and with the naturalistic philosophy which speaks in the
name of science. This understood, it is still fair to say
that he who is not for religion is against it. For the
divergence between religion and naturalism goes to the
root of things, so that no one can manage to avoid taking
one side or the other. The mere attempt to remain neutral
is itself a decision of one kind; because, practically, he
who attempts neutrality finds himself ranged alongside
the man who has concluded that modern science has dealt
religion a blow which, if not fatal, is at any rate serious
enough to sanction the unreflective pursuit of immediate
pleasure so far as that is compatible with respectability.

It is this consideration, the unescapable fact that
each individual must somehow take sides in this quarrel,
whether consciously or unconsciously, whether deliberately or by evasion, will-he nill-he, which leads me to
believe that a survey of some aspects of religious thought
in England in the nineteenth century may have an interest not merely historical in character. It should be obvious from the titles of the essays which follow that I do
not propose to attempt anything like an historical survey
of the period in the usual sense of the term. Rapid historical surveys which cover a broad field, however useful
or necessary they may be for some purposes, are inevitably superficial; and this is even truer, I think, in the
history of thought than in political or social history.
Consequently I shall discuss only a small number of
writers; but these are, I believe, representative figures,

so that consideration of them should carry us at least some way towards a real understanding of the religious situation in England in the last century. It is first necessary, however, rapidly to review the course of English religious thought in the seventeenth and eighteenth centuries, which is intimately bound up with the thought of the last century, and to this I proceed in the present essay.

II.

It is often said that the Protestant Reformation substituted an infallible Book for an infallible Church, and this is true as far as it goes; yet it is misleading unless we remember that the Catholic Church as well as the Protestant reformers regarded the Bible as divinely inspired. The real difficulty lay in the necessity, which neither Protestants nor Catholics could escape, of showing, first, how they knew that the Bible was divinely inspired, and of deciding, in the second place, what the Biblical message was. In denying the infallibility of the Church the Protestants repudiated one method of solving this difficulty, but thereby laid themselves under the necessity of discovering another.

The Bible was alleged to contain a direct revelation of God's will, but a revelation made in a former age, to men long since gone from earth; how could later generations be certain that the Book was all it professed to be, and not a fabrication? But even if men agreed in accepting the Biblical message as the truth, difficulties were not over. For, granting that we do have, collected into a book, the Word of God, an all-sufficient guide for the individual's conduct of his life upon earth if he is to save his soul and attain immortal life, still, the question inevitably arose what this Word of God practically meant, what beliefs and what actions it imposed on him who did whole-heartedly accept the book as given to men directly by the Deity. Here was the crux of the situation. Catholics asserted that the reality and truth of the Christian revelation were guaranteed entirely by the Church, which had been instituted for that purpose directly by Jesus Christ, and which had enjoyed a continuous life from that time. Likewise they asserted that the Church alone acting as a spiritual body politic had adequate authority to interpret God's Word and to translate it into articles of belief and a code of action.

This was a claim that because of the alleged divine origin of the Church, certain men who were its ministers could in each generation transcend universal human limitations and attain infallibility. This the Protestant reformers denied. They pointed out that the Church was composed of a body of fallible men who, as men, were liable to mistake and corruption like the rest of us. They were able easily to prove this by the many patent, grave, and even loathsome abuses in the practice of the Church which had long been notorious. They were then able to point out that the authority of the Church rested ultimately upon documents whose authenticity the Church used its authority to prove. But if this source of authority, resting in the end only upon such circular reasoning, was a delusion, where then was to be found an adequate basis for the beliefs of men? It was to be found, Protestants answered, only in the Bible itself, and to the Bible men must return. For better or worse, however, this apparently plain answer would not hold. Those obstinate questions still remained: How could men know that the Bible was divinely inspired?—and what did the Bible mean, what beliefs and practices did it really enjoin? And to answer these questions the reformers had finally to fall back on the position that religion was essentially a personal relation between man and his Maker, and consequently that each individual must be his own final authority for his beliefs and actions.

This was the profoundly significant point which slowly emerged from the heat of controversy. Protestantism was no merely negative movement. It became—not because this was what all leaders of the Reformation wanted, but, rather, in spite of the best efforts of so powerful a dictator as Calvin, it became the assertion of individualism in religion. Complete individualism is the denial of all external authority and is synonymous with anarchy, a condition regarded with equanimity only by those who have a perfect confidence in the goodness of human nature. When I say that Protestantism was forced by an unescapable logic into individualism I am, of course, characterizing a tendency, not describing an accomplished fact. Nevertheless the tendency was plainly evident from the beginning. The whole force of Calvin's genius was exerted throughout his career to make an end of Protestant anarchy in the only possible way—by calling into existence a second infallible church. But though Calvin's influence was great, and though all Presbyterians still pay him a sort of official homage, he failed in his aim. The multiplication of Protestant sects has continued from the sixteenth century to the present day. It is difficult, perhaps impossible, to ascertain how many there have been, for very many have been local and ephemeral. Many also have been extraordinary in their tenets, as is, to take a trivial instance, that still existing sect whose members fasten their clothes together with hooks and eyes on the ground that buttons are unbiblical. One may pardonably be amused by such a harmless eccentricity, but other practices and beliefs which the historian of Protestantism has to record are of a different order, and the situation in northern Europe and England in the seventeenth century was far from amusing.

The problem, indeed, of dealing with innumerable prophets, each claiming to be the channel of an infallible and divine inspiration, was one that shook the foundations of society. Accordingly the best energies of the century were expended in seeking a solution of the question where an adequate centre of authority for belief and conduct could be found outside of commonly received tradition.

It may be permissible to doubt whether any universally acceptable answer to this question will ever be found. Certainly none has yet been. But men in the seventeenth century were not hopeless. Perhaps mercifully, they could not see into the future, and they had on their side, passed on to them from ancient times through the great schoolmen of the thirteenth and fourteenth centuries, what may nowadays appear to be a singular trust in human reason as an organ of absolute truth. Philosophy had long been the handmaiden of theology; it was thought to be so still. William Chillingworth in the first half of the seventeenth century, the author of the great controversial work, *The Religion of Protestants a Safe Way to Salvation*, assumed, as he fairly could, that all Christians were agreed as to the authority of the Bible, but, if that were questioned, he did not hesitate for an answer: "If Scripture cannot be the judge of any controversy, how shall that touching the Church and the notes of it be determined? And if it be the sole judge of this one, why may it not of others? Why not of all? Those only excepted wherein the Scripture itself is the subject of the question, which cannot be determined but by natural reason, the only principle beside Scripture which is common to Christians."

As to the interpretation of Scripture, Chillingworth says: "Every man is to judge for himself with the judgment of discretion. . . . For if the Scripture (as it is in things necessary) be plain, why should it be more neces-

sary to have a judge to interpret it in plain places, than
to have a judge to interpret the meaning of a council's
decrees, and others to interpret their interpretations,
and others to interpret theirs, and so on for ever? And
where they are not plain, there if we, using diligence to
find the truth, do yet miss of it and fall into error, there
is no danger in it. They that err and they that do not err
may both be saved. So that those places which contain
things necessary, and wherein error were dangerous,
need no infallible interpreter, because they are plain;
and those that are obscure need none, because they contain not things necessary, neither is error in them dangerous.'' And the defender of Protestantism confesses:
''For my part I am certain that God hath given us our
reason to discern between truth and falsehood; and he
that makes not this use of it, but believes things he knows
not why, I say it is by chance that he believes the truth,
and not by choice; and that I cannot but fear that God
will not accept of this *sacrifice of fools*. But you that
would not have men follow their reason, what would you
have them follow?—their passions?—or pluck out their
eyes and go blindfold? No, you say, you would have them
follow authority. On God's name let them; we also would
have them follow authority; for it is upon the authority
of universal tradition that we would have them believe
Scripture. But then, as for the authority which you
would have them follow, you will let them see reason why
they should follow it. And is not this to go a little about?
—to leave reason for a short turn, and then to come to it
again, and to do that which you condemn in others?—it
being indeed a plain impossibility for any man to submit
his reason but to reason; for he that doth it to authority
must of necessity think himself to have greater reason
to believe that authority.''

These passages make Chillingworth's position clear.

The Bible's authenticity, if questioned, was to be determined by the use of man's natural reason; the meaning of the Bible also was to be determined by man's natural reason; and wherever the Bible was perplexing or
obscure men could safely conclude that the doubtful
points were not necessary for salvation. Only that on
which all men could agree was essential. In other words,
men needed to accept only that in the Bible which was
self-evidently true; and, moreover, if they went beyond
this to accept anything merely on the basis of prescrip-
tion they were making the perilous "sacrifice of fools."
Of course Chillingworth could not, at any rate as a defender of Christianity, have gone so far as this in drawing out to its logical conclusion the Protestant position
had he not been perfectly confident that the voice of
reason was everywhere one voice and the voice of absolute truth. And in this he is typical of the greater English divines throughout the century. Richard Hooker himself, at the close of the preceding century, had shared the
same confidence in reason, and in so doing was only following the lead of St. Thomas Aquinas.

From the period following Chillingworth many examples of essentially the same point of view could be in-
stanced. Benjamin Whichcote wrote a discourse on *The
Glorious Evidence and Power of Divine Truth.* "Truth,"
he said, "of first inscription is connatural to man, it is
the light of God's creation, and it flows from the principles of which man doth consist, in his very first make;
this is the soul's complexion." "Among other excellences
of divine truth," he affirmed, "this is none of the smallest
weight: that when it is declared it doth recommend itself
to and satisfies the mind of man concerning its reality
and usefulness. Men are wanting to themselves, that they
do not see with their own eyes; that they do not make a
particular search; that they do not examine; that they do

not consider; or, in a word, that they do not use the judgement of discerning. For we that are of the reformed religion, who deny the infallible visible judge, we do allow to every Christian a private judgement of discerning not only as his *privilege* that God hath granted him, but as his *charge.*" John Smith, in his discourse *Of the Excellency and Nobleness of True Religion,* said that men "are content and ready to deny themselves for God," but added, "I mean not that they should deny their own reason, as some would have it; for that were to deny a beam of divine light, and so to deny God, instead of denying ourselves for him." Those philosophers are right, he is sure, who say that to follow reason is to follow God.

III.

THESE liberal and enlightened divines did not see, of course, where man's natural reason was presently to lead him, nor did they realize that the very toleration and free inquiry for which they contended were soon to make possible a critical scrutiny of the reason itself, with an eye to its capacities, its limitations. I do not mean in saying this that, had they seen further, they would not have followed wherever the argument led, for the greater divines of seventeenth-century England were honest men; I mean only to point out that these men had no doubt whatever that the Christian revelation was rational in character, that its truth was strictly demonstrable.

But as early as the second quarter of the seventeenth century it was not impossible to see what the future held in store. For even thus early Lord Herbert of Cherbury, elder brother of "that sweet singer of the Temple," George Herbert, was saying that no historical revelation, no revelation save it were made directly to one's self, could be accepted by man; nor was a revelation even to one's self necessary in order to salvation. For all men by virtue of their very humanity had implanted within them certain common notions amongst which were the essential articles of religious belief. These, Lord Herbert thought, were elements common to all religions of whatever age or place, though in most positive religions they might be more or less obscured by varying overgrowths. The propositions universally held were five in number:

(1) That there is a supreme Being or God;

(2) That this Being should be worshipped;

(3) That the chief part of his worship consists in virtue or the proper use of our faculties;

(4) That impiety and crimes are to be atoned for by repentance; and

(5) That punishment and reward follow our deeds both in this life and in a life to come.

Since the comparative study of religions was still in its infancy in the early seventeenth century, I hardly need add that Lord Herbert's data were very imperfect and that nobody now supposes his five propositions to be, or ever to have been, universally received articles of belief. This, however, does not concern my present point, which is simply that Herbert's conclusion was that no proposition beyond these five could be essential to man's salvation, and that these essential propositions were naturally implanted in the mind of every normal man. This goes very far—further, indeed, than Herbert himself cared to insist—for his natural religion not only cuts away the necessity of the Christian or any other historical revelation, but really also denies the validity of any distinctively Christian beliefs.

It had been all very well for Christian Rome to regard herself, like pagan Rome, as the centre of the world, and to claim that Christianity was the world's one religion, as long as the known world was comprehended in the lands immediately surrounding the Mediterranean Sea. But the activities of Rome's own missionaries united with the larger and now better-known activities of explorers to make this pretension increasingly difficult of maintenance and finally ridiculous, or tragic, as one pleases. By the seventeenth century thinking men could no longer blind themselves to the problem created by the fact that there were millions upon millions of human beings who had lived and died in involuntary ignorance of the Christian revelation. Could a deity who was altogether just and righteous have possibly confined the truth essential to salvation in the beginning to one obscure and specially favoured people, and afterwards to those others who gradually in the course of time might by hearsay learn this momentous news? Nor was this the only difficulty; for men were also presently to see a gross incongruity between the supposition that God had framed us reasonable creatures, and the notion that then, through sheer perversity as it might seem, he had made our salvation to depend upon beliefs which were beyond reason or plainly contradictory to reason.

Lord Herbert of Cherbury is sometimes called the father of English deism, but the deistic movement itself is supposed to have begun with the publication in 1696 of a book by John Toland which was addressed specifically to the latter of the difficulties just mentioned. The book was entitled *Christianity not Mysterious, or a Treatise Showing that there is Nothing in the Gospel contrary to Reason, nor above it, and that no Christian Doctrine can be properly called a Mystery*. The book was in one sense harmless enough, as Toland professed to find nothing irrational in the Bible. Yet his book raised a storm because, whatever his actual words were, his general tone was thought to be hostile to Christianity.

He was thought, probably with justice, to have meant much more than he dared frankly to say. However, neither Toland's private beliefs at this time nor his later pantheism are now so interesting as his assertion of the supremacy of reason. "We hold that reason," he said, "is the only foundation of all certitude; and that nothing revealed, whether as to its manner or existence, is more exempted from its disquisitions than the ordinary phenomena of nature." "Religion is not to be modelled according to our fancies, nor to be judged of as it relates to our private designs." "Since religion is calculated for reasonable creatures, 'tis conviction and not authority that should bear weight with them. A wise and good man will judge of the merits of a cause considered only in itself, without any regard to times, places, or persons. No numbers, no examples, no interests can ever bias his solid judgement, or corrupt his integrity. He knows no difference between popish infallibility, and being obliged blindly to acquiesce in the decisions of fallible Protestants."

From Toland's position other deists argued more positively against Christianity. Not only were the so-called internal evidences of Christianity attacked, but also the evidence from alleged prophecies in the Old Testament and the evidence from alleged miracles in the New. Probably the most important book produced by the movement was Tindal's *Christianity as Old as the Creation*. Tindal did not argue directly that the Christian revelation was untrue, but merely contended that whatever in it was necessary for salvation must have been discoverable by all men at all times from the first appearance of humanity until his own day, simply by the use of natural reason. Thus, according to him, a particular historic revelation was wholly unnecessary, or gratuitous—though he did not deny that it might have taken place.

The orthodox were of course not idle when such opinions were being circulated, and indeed there was a widespread impression at the time that the deists were triumphantly argued down and defeated by the talented and learned men who were on the side of wealth, respectability, and the forces of tradition. The fact is, however, that the orthodox on the whole were committed to the supremacy of reason as fully as the deists. Toland had quoted on the title-page of his *Christianity not Mysterious* a sentence from one of Archbishop Tillotson's sermons which shows it plainly enough. "We need not desire a better evidence," said Tillotson, "that any man is in the wrong than to hear him declare against reason, and thereby to acknowledge that reason is against him."[3] Tillotson, of course, was merely maintaining a position which earlier defenders of Protestant Christianity had confidently taken up; while the deists were merely deriving an unexpected conclusion from the same premises. Thus the apparent differences between the two camps, being much greater than the real ones, tended to give a certain artificiality to the whole controversy. The true God, both sides agreed, was the God of reason; was the Christian revelation necessary for man's right relation with him?—or was it, as an act of favouritism, irrecon-

---

[3] Sermon LVI (*Works*, ed. of 1820, IV, 45), *The Excellency of Abraham's Faith and Obedience* (preached in 1686). Tillotson had studied Hobbes's *Leviathan* (for references to it see Sermon LXV, *Works*, IV, 233, and Sermon CLIII, *ibid.*, VII, 177), and in the sentence used by Toland was repeating what this arch-enemy had said. In Chap. XI of the *Leviathan* (p. 50, ed. of 1651) Hobbes had asserted that men, in basing their actions on precedent, are "like little children, that have no other rule of good and evill manners, but the correction they receive from their Parents, and Masters; save that children are constant to their rule, whereas men are not so; because grown strong, and stubborn, they appeale from custome to reason, and from reason to custome, as it serves their turn; receding from custome when their interest requires it, and setting themselves against reason, as oft as reason is against them."

cilable with God's goodness and justice, and hence to be regarded as, if not false, unnecessary?

The general result of the controversy was the decay of living religion. The God discoverable by reason was a vague and remote abstraction—the great Uncaused Cause. And when this First Cause had brought the world into existence and established its unalterable laws his active relationship with it had ceased. Thenceforward the world went its way automatically. The First Cause was demonstrably a perfect being. Consequently—as Shaftesbury and Bolingbroke and Pope agreed—"Whatever is, is right." The world is perfect, it seemed necessary to conclude, because its Creator is perfect. Common sense tells us that the world is not perfect. Even those who are most fortunate in the possession of natural endowments and worldly goods, and who are well satisfied with life as they find it, admit that there are some difficulties involved in existence which they would change if they could. However, the proponents of the new view had a reply to this objection. The appearance of evil in the world they readily admitted, but they contended that, since it is logically certain that the world as a whole is perfect, existing evils must be only apparent, not real. Man cannot see the world as a whole, but only its parts, and not more than a few of them; hence he should realize that what seems evil to him must be in reality only a lesser good, necessary in order that the whole may be a perfect harmony. "Whatever is, is right." This was the outcome of the religion of nature—a complacent optimism which preached the satisfied acceptance of things as they are. A more complete contradiction of the grinding, tragic world of actual experience cannot be imagined, nor a more complete denial of the foundation of religious belief.

IV.

SUCH was one result of the progress of free inquiry. Meanwhile Locke, towards the close of the seventeenth century, had begun to scrutinize reason itself. Those notions common to all men which Lord Herbert of Cherbury had catalogued struck him doubtfully and, in general, he considered that we might reason more securely if we first carefully determined what we are able to know— what is the province and competence of reason. The famous *Essay on the Human Understanding* determined the course of philosophical inquiry for a century. Locke, if one may state his conclusion in a couple of words, limited the sphere of knowledge to the field of possible human experience, and decided that even within this field there could be no science of reality. He was not entirely consistent and did not see all the implications of his premises. The completion of the line he took came, a generation or more later, in the work of Hume.

Hume was the one thinker of the eighteenth century who knew completely what he was about and who was not afraid to face his conclusions, whatever they were. And in Hume's hands reason became a wonderful and inexplicable instinct, adequate for our practical needs, but for nothing more. He showed that there could be no science of reality, because we can become acquainted only with the appearances of things. We can attain merely an empirical or provisional knowledge of the sequences of phenomena. There can, moreover, be no rational proof of the existence of God. All metaphysical speculation, in short, can be nothing other than *mere* speculation. Thus the sceptical attack upon the pretensions of rationalism came to a nihilistic conclusion which would have horrified Locke, and which swept the ground from under the feet of the oblivious theologians, absorbed in argument amongst themselves.

The separation of theology from philosophic thought which thus came about is significant. And, moreover, theology was for the most part as far from the realities of life as it was from grasping the meaning of the progress of philosophic inquiry. In general, eighteenth-century theology seems to have been hollow and vain, and it was, certainly, Christian only in name. A thinker like Shaftesbury found a deity a metaphysical necessity, and so he believed in God's existence. More than that, he conformed to the Church of England as by law established. And he tells us why. It was for the sake of social order. It was a duty to give an example of respect for law. Like many others, he believed that morality would suffer amongst the vulgar, unlearned multitude unless it were supported by the supposedly religious foundation of a belief in future rewards and punishments. But for himself he preferred a purer morality than that which he supposed Christianity to teach, and consequently in his private capacity he looked to the Stoics of pagan antiquity.

In many churchmen of the eighteenth century a roughly similar, though often less attractive, state of mind prevailed. These churchmen were servants of the state. As public-spirited subjects they exhibited an external profession of Christianity, which they believed to be necessary for social order and prosperity. In their actual teaching, however, they aimed only at the inculcation of worldly prudence. They dutifully took their starting-point from the Bible but their sermons were not expositions of the teaching of Jesus;—they were rather lessons in the means of explaining it away. Thus that excellent man, Samuel Clarke, though he nominally admitted the world's corruption, still conceived that an adequate piety made no unreasonable demands upon men. In this age, he told his flock, we are required "only to retrench our vain and sinful expenses; not to sell *all* and give to the poor, but to be charitable out of the super- fluity of our plenty; not to lay down our lives, or even the comfortable enjoyments of life, but to forsake the unreasonable and unfruitful pleasures of sin.''

In similar strain Bishop Atterbury warned his audi- tory that there might be poisonous extremes of righteous- ness as of other things—even charity might lead them into folly if they overdid it after the manner of some Catholic saints. He also told his contemporaries that we are not bound to spread Christianity at the risk of our lives, when we have no longer the power of working miracles, though he did add that it is not our duty to deride men whose honest zeal has carried them beyond this moderate point of view. And, again, the once-famous Hugh Blair cried out inspiringly: ''We call you not to renounce pleasure, but to enjoy it in safety. Instead of abridging it we exhort you to pursue it on an extensive plan. We propose measures for securing its possession and for prolonging its duration.'' Blair properly enough said that Christ is our great example; but, then, he ap- parently thought it was Christ's special merit that he indulged in ''no unnatural austerities, no affected singu- larities,'' but practiced those virtues ''for which we have most frequent occasion in ordinary life.'' In short, as Leslie Stephen says, ''Christ's deportment was unim- peachable.''[4]

These citations make sufficiently plain how far osten- sible Christianity had gone in forced accommodation of the teaching of Jesus to the spirit of worldliness. That

---

[4] *History of English Thought in the Eighteenth Century*, Chap. XII, Sec. ii, to which I am also indebted for the above quotations (in this and the preceding paragraph) from divines whose works are at present inacces- sible to me. In common with all other students of English thought, I owe much to Stephen's work, and take this opportunity of gratefully acknowl- edging my debt.

spirit was not in sole possession of eighteenth-century England, but it was in singularly complete possession of the upper and middle classes and of the dominant spokesmen in politics, in literature, and even in theology. It is not unfair to say that the typical man of the eighteenth century was comfortable, with more than a sufficiency of wealth, and was self-satisfied and materially-minded. His chief concern was the safe enjoyment of the pleasures of worldly life. Disturbing questions easily vexed him, and were simply to be dismissed. Self-knowledge, reflectiveness—what good lay in that direction comparable to the joys of the bottle and the chase?—comparable to the exhilarations of cultivated society and the flow of sophisticated wit?

V.

THE historian Gibbon, though far indeed from typical in his wide and accurate learning, in his intellectual grasp, and in his command of a brilliant if elaborate and formal style, may still be said fairly to represent the practical result of eighteenth-century life and thought. If one takes him as he is and asks no questions, his is a sunny, pleasant nature; and one may go far without finding a better companion for one's ordinary moments than the urbane and polished gentleman whom one meets in the pages of his *Memoirs* and of his *Decline and Fall of the Roman Empire*—both abiding classics in their kinds. It is necessary, however, here to ask questions; what were his beliefs, what his attitude towards life?—what was the spirit of the man?

The answers are plain. Gibbon was a man frankly pleased with life as he found it. He was pleased with himself, pleased with the cultivation of his age, pleased with the progress of reason. And what did reason mean to him? Well, in the first place he fully shared the eight-

eenth-century theologian's dread of being righteous over-
much; with the theologian he loathed enthusiasm, as they
all called it, or, as we should say, fanaticism. To that
passionate conviction which pushes a man to such ex-
tremities of action as we call heroic or insane, depending
on how the action itself affects us and our interests, Gibbon opposed an attitude calm, detached, sceptical, and
even, an unfriendly witness would say, supercilious. This
species of critical outlook condemned him to see everything that differed from his own age and its standards
from the outside, so that he observed only the surface
of life and grasped things only in their external relationships. But at the same time he did keep his head, as we
say, or his prejudices, as some would say, and his seren-
ity; he did remain self-possessed, and this was to be reasonable.

Preservation of a rational frame of mind also meant
that one must recognize the limitations of reason. What
was rational was true, what was irrational was false;—
this, of course, was the essence of rationalism, and here
there were no limitations whatever to diminish reason's authority. Yet it is also true that the progress of
rational inquiry through the century had steadily nar-
rowed the field wherein reason could work to any effect.
I have already pointed out how Locke attempted to narrow this field to the sphere of human experience and how
under Hume's dissolving analysis reason was shown to
be incompetent for all metaphysical inquiry. So things
had gone; and thus to be rational had come to mean that
one rested upon the merely empirical data of past experience—a sufficiently wide range still, it was thought, for
the happy conduct of life. Theoretical certainty or absolute knowledge was an impossibility in any direction, in
any subject; but practical guidance such as might be
derived from the range of human experience remained an

open field. An open field—though even here the rational mind had to accept novel limitations, as experience could guide us only in the profitable conduct of our present earthly lives, without reference to any possibilities beyond that circle. Hume himself obediently and consistently turned from philosophy to the writing of history. His own motives probably were mixed, but that makes his procedure none the less significant, as the change was perfectly in accordance with his philosophic conclusions. In all this Gibbon was completely at one with Hume, and this, then, is what a rational frame of mind meant to him.

How did it work practically? There are all the volumes of the *Decline and Fall* to answer that question, and in particular the famous fifteenth and thirty-seventh chapters, in which Gibbon treats of "The Progress of the Christian Religion, and the Sentiments, Manners, Numbers, and Condition of the Primitive Christians," and of "The Origin, Progress, and Effects of the Monastic Life." Gibbon's language about religion is, nearly always, outwardly polite, so that frequently his real attitude is conveyed by means of the irony so congenial to his temperament. Probably his most effective stroke against Christianity is his explanation of its early success.

We are naturally curious, he says, to learn the means by which Christianity obtained its remarkable victory over religions already established. An "obvious but satisfactory answer" is that it triumphed because of "the convincing evidence of the doctrine itself," and because of "the ruling providence of its great Author. But, as truth and reason seldom find so favourable a reception in the world, and as the wisdom of Providence frequently condescends to use the passions of the human heart, and the general circumstances of mankind, as instruments to execute its purpose; we may still be permitted, though

with becoming submission, to ask not indeed what were
the first, but what were the secondary causes of the rapid
growth of the Christian church. It will, perhaps, appear
that it was most effectually favoured and assisted by the
five following causes: I, The inflexible, and if we may use
the expression, the intolerant zeal of the Christians, derived, it is true, from the Jewish religion, but purified
from the narrow and unsocial spirit which, instead of
inviting, had deterred the Gentiles from embracing the
law of Moses. II, The doctrine of a future life, improved
by every additional circumstance which could give weight
and efficacy to that important truth. III, The miraculous
powers ascribed to the primitive church. IV, The pure
and austere morals of the Christians. V, The union and
discipline of the Christian republic, which gradually
formed an independent and increasing state in the heart
of the Roman empire.''

Doubtless this statement of causes would not be objected to by a Christian reader, were he able to take Gibbon at his word. But this, of course, Gibbon himself
makes impossible. It is clear that he gives no credit either
to "the convincing evidence of the doctrine itself" or to
"the ruling providence of its great Author," and that
for him the secondary causes of the rise of Christianity
are the real causes. If, then, the Christian reader begins
to ask questions about these causes, he quickly completes
his discovery that Gibbon's treatment of this subject depends upon certain assumptions very characteristic of
the eighteenth century. What, for example, supported
the inflexible and intolerant zeal of the early Christians?
To this Gibbon has in the end two answers; one was a
very popular mode of explanation in his day—people had
been fooled by the machinations of ambitious priests
eager for power. His other answer is that the Jews had
for some reason always been a race extreme in all things;

whatever they believed they believed passionately, de-
votedly, fanatically. The early Christians inherited the
bigotry of the Jews, while they discarded their jealous
disposition, which had prevented the Jewish religion
from spreading.

No one now, whatever his point of view, would consider these satisfactory answers to the question asked.
It is, I should suppose, universally recognized at present
that while religions create priests, who may or may not
then serve their religions scrupulously and self-sacrific-
ingly, priests do not create religions. And Gibbon's
second answer is at least a partial evasion. He is, in fact,
unable to account for early Christian zeal because he took
a wholly external view of Christianity and had decided in
advance that it had no legitimate foundation.

It is hardly necessary, for an understanding of his
attitude, to examine in detail Gibbon's explanation of all
of his five causes. It will be enough to pause over the
second, the doctrine of a future life. He points out "the
ignorance, the errors, and the uncertainty" of the wisest
and best instructed men of pagan antiquity with regard
to the immortality of the soul. Many armed themselves
against the fear of death with the melancholy reflexion
that the fatal stroke at any rate releases us from life's
calamities, and "that those can no longer suffer who no
longer exist." But, he says, there were a few Greek and
Roman sages who had a more exalted and perhaps a
juster conception of human nature, though it has to be
confessed that in this sublime inquiry "their reason had
been often guided by their imagination," and their imagination by their vanity. "When they viewed with complacency the extent of their own mental powers, when
they exercised the various faculties of memory, of fancy,
and of judgement in the most profound speculations, or
the most important labours, and when they reflected on

the desire of fame, which transported them into future
ages far beyond the bounds of death and of the grave;
they were unwilling to confound themselves with the
beasts of the field, or to suppose that a being, for whose
dignity they entertained the most sincere admiration,
could be limited to a spot of earth and to a few years
of duration. With this favourable prepossession, they
summoned to their aid the science, or rather the language, of metaphysics. They soon discovered that, as
none of the properties of matter will apply to the operations of the mind, the human soul must consequently be a
substance distinct from the body, pure, simple, and spiritual, incapable of dissolution, and susceptible of a much
higher degree of virtue and happiness after the release
from its corporeal prison.''

From these high principles, Gibbon continues, philosophers who followed after Plato drew the very un-
justifiable conclusion that the human soul not only was
destined to a future immortality but had already enjoyed
a past eternity, because it was, as they considered, ''a
portion of the infinite and self-existing spirit which pervades and sustains the universe. A doctrine thus removed beyond the senses and the experience of mankind
might serve to amuse the leisure of a philosophic mind;
or, in the silence of solitude, it might sometimes impart
a ray of comfort to desponding virtue; but the faint
impression which had been received in the schools was
soon obliterated by the commerce and business of active
life. We are sufficiently acquainted with the eminent persons who flourished in the age of Cicero, and of the
Cæsars, with their actions, their characters, and their
motives, to be assured that their conduct in this life was
never regulated by any serious conviction of the rewards
or punishments of a future state. At the bar and in the
senate of Rome the ablest orators were not apprehensive

of giving offence to their hearers by exposing that doctrine as an idle and extravagant opinion, which was rejected with contempt by every man of a liberal education and understanding.''

Since, consequently, the impartial historian says, ''the most sublime efforts of philosophy can extend no farther than feebly to point out the desire, the hope, or at most the probability of a future state, there is nothing, except a divine revelation, that can ascertain the existence, and describe the condition, of the invisible country which is destined to receive the souls of men after their separation from the body.'' But, he adds, the popular religions of Greece and Rome were very unequal to so arduous a task, and it was reserved to the ambitious priests of the ignorant barbarians in India, Assyria, Egypt, and Gaul, to inculcate this important truth. We might naturally expect that a principle so essential to religion would also have been revealed to the Jews, and, too, that it might safely have been entrusted to them. But no, he says, we can only ''adore the mysterious dispensations of Providence'' when we find that Moses knew nothing of the soul's immortality, that the prophets of Israel but darkly insinuated it, and that during the long period between the Egyptian and the Babylonian servitudes the Jews confined their hopes and fears within the narrow compass of the present earthly life. Even in the time of Jesus the Sadducees, because of their strict adherence to Mosaic law, piously rejected the notion of a future life. The Pharisees, however, being less strict, had recently admitted into their beliefs this and several other speculative tenets drawn from the philosophy or religion of the East. This doctrine so congenial to human desires, once it was admitted, they upheld zealously; but their zeal, as Gibbon notes, added nothing to its evidence, or even probability. Thus it was the authority of Jesus which alone made the doctrine a fundamental tenet amongst the early Christians, and amongst them it was very powerfully strengthened by an opinion which, as he puts it, "has not been found agreeable to experience." This was the opinion that the end of the world and the Kingdom of Heaven were at hand. He says: "The revolution of seventeen centuries has instructed us not to press too closely the mysterious language of prophecy and revelation; but, as long as, for wise purposes, this error was permitted to subsist in the church, it was productive of the most salutary effects on the faith and practice of Christians." Finally, he points out that the Christians joined to the doctrine of a future life the promise of eternal punishment for unbelievers, and urged this consideration with so much force that ignorant and credulous pagans were brought to conversion through their terror.

With like irony Gibbon treats the whole subject of the rise and triumph of Christianity. So far as, in this treatment, questions of historical fact were concerned, he was on firm ground and was well served by his scepticism. It had been argued for generations that, on the one hand, the company of early Christian martyrs had exhibited a depth of certitude that might in itself fairly command our own assent to their beliefs, and that, on the other, the swift success of Christianity in displacing the almost myriad religions of the peoples of the Roman Empire was a phenomenon so akin to the miraculous that this too could be accounted for only on the basis of divine sanction. But Gibbon showed, in a manner not seriously to be challenged save in unimportant particulars, that both the persecution and the numbers of the early Christians had been grossly exaggerated, and that there was nothing really extraordinary in the actual spread of Christianity —nothing that could not be completely accounted for by the conditions of the time and the operation of natural human motives.

This was wholesome and sound, but Gibbon of course went further. In deflating the pretensions of Christians regarding the early history of their religion he also attacked its claim to a divine origin and its fundamental articles of belief. The character and effectiveness of his attack I have sought to illustrate. Historic Christianity he considered to be a baseless fabric of superstition, and he lost no opportunity in the *Decline and Fall* to make this clear. He even commended Mahometanism at the expense of Christianity on the ground that it embodies a purer form of theism, less overlaid with superstitions in the shape of dogmas that carry us beyond the range of human experience. And he regarded the Christianization of Europe as a melancholy retrogression—a dark descent from the rational altitudes of thought attained by the best minds amongst the pagans of classical antiquity. This descent, moreover, he thought adequately explained by the ignorance, the credulity, and the vanity of barbarians.

Gibbon was not prepared for the outcry which was raised against his pages on their publication. He says in his *Memoirs:* "Had I believed that the majority of English readers were so fondly attached even to the name and shadow of Christianity; had I foreseen that the pious, the timid, and the prudent would feel or affect to feel with such exquisite sensibility, I might perhaps have softened the two invidious chapters [the fifteenth and sixteenth]. . . . But the shaft was shot, the alarm was sounded, and I could only rejoice, that if the voice of our priests was clamorous and bitter, their hands were disarmed of the powers of persecution. . . . Let me frankly own that I was startled at the first volleys of this ecclesiastical ordnance; but as soon as I found that this empty noise was mischievous only in the intention, my fear was converted to indignation, and every feeling of indignation or curiosity has long since subsided in pure and placid indifference.'' Gibbon probably remained, after his brief, youthful excursion into Catholicism, a believer in a First Cause, but this was hardly more than a conventional gesture, and it had no perceptible effect upon his rational, or worldly, outlook. His was eminently a safe, conformable personality, and he evidently believed he had done all that was necessary to conciliate his public in avoiding an open and direct attack upon a system of belief which it was still respectable to profess, but not to act upon. When, nevertheless, he was assailed, it never occurred to him that his opponents might have motives that were both sincere and worthy of respect. In other words, religion was really a closed book to him. The attacks surprised him, and roused in him a temporary curiosity concerning his fellow human beings, but left him on the whole indifferent as soon as he had made sure that they were to be only verbal and were not to endanger his personal safety. Probably, too, he was correct in his cynical estimate of the motives behind many, if not all, of the attacks levelled against him.

For, as I have said, Gibbon is fairly representative of the practical result of eighteenth-century life and thought. He is typical in his complacency, in his irreligion, in his sceptical rationalism, and in his frank elevation of selfish enjoyment as the only end for man to pursue. His estimate of life, thoroughly naturalistic in everything save in name, I have represented as the eventual outcome of English Protestantism. This, it seems to me, is the only conclusion which the facts make possible, but I must repeat that Protestant individualism and rationalism were the complete antithesis of what the leaders of the Reformation wanted. The individualism

and the rationalism made their appearance, and remained, despite all that Calvin and others could do to
prevent it, because they were implicit in the very nature
of Protestantism. And I am of course aware that other
factors of the utmost importance entered in as contribu-
tory causes—the humanism of the Renaissance, and the
inventions and discoveries which led Bacon and Des-
cartes to predict the indefinite progress of man in the
control of natural phenomena for his own purposes.
Nevertheless, these were what I have named them, con-
tributory causes. And Protestantism, acting as a principle of dissipation and working from the beginning to
discredit Christianity from within, powerfully helped to
open the English mind to their influence and provided a
congenial soil in which the influence could fruitfully grow.

II.

COLERIDGE

I.

In the eighteenth century religion had come to be centred in mere intellectual assent to a body of metaphysical doctrine which, by some, was thought to be susceptible of rational proof or, by others, was thought to be guaranteed by divine revelation. But at the same time the critical scrutiny of reason, of the Bible, and of history had undermined both of these contentions so deeply that metaphysics and religion tended to be dismissed together as mere dreaming and mere superstition. Again, religion had become so externalized in character and so attenuated in force that it could do no more than point to worldly prudence as the sum of its message to mankind. The philosophers agreed that practical wisdom was summed up in prudence, but pointed out that it needed no religious basis, because the esteem of prudence was sufficiently accounted for by its social usefulness. And the general result was that believers and unbelievers alike tended to rest in a point of view which we stigmatize with such a word as materialistic. It was a stagnant period, in which self-satisfaction and complacency reigned. Men took the solid comforts of life without apology, and found them good. If they had general views at all they regarded the universe as a mechanism, the deity, provided there was one, as the great master-mechanic, and themselves as small machines, and often very clever ones. Their conduct was determined mechanically, too, by self-interest, enlightened or otherwise.

There were of course exceptions; and at least two of them are of high significance, because both William Law —the author of a celebrated book, *A Devout Call to a Serious and Holy Life*—and John Wesley gave practical proof that there existed in human nature qualities entirely neglected by the intellectualists. Yet neither Law nor Wesley exerted any influence upon the course of eighteenth-century thought. Wesley, it is true, lived to count his adherents by the thousands, but his achievement was generally regarded as negligible, on the ground that it was the result of mere 'enthusiasm' or fanaticism aroused by preaching which could appeal only to the ignorant.

Despite the scepticism and worldliness of the eighteenth century, however, the public profession of Christianity remained a practically essential badge of respectability throughout the period, particularly at both of the universities. It was a characteristically English compromise, for the sake of which clarity was sacrificed and hypocrisy often encouraged, but which at least preserved the traditional forms of religious expression. That this, as I imply, had its good side no one is likely to deny in the face of present-day knowledge of the evils attendant upon sudden and violent revolutions. But of course it had its bad side also. Traditional forms of religious expression continued to exist apparently untouched and unharmed, while in reality life and thought were proceeding ever further upon an independent line of their own. It is remarkable that the great Wesleyan revival of religious emotion could create a new church of large proportions and could bring into being the Evangelical party within the Anglican Church, really without either disturbing or being touched by contemporary thought. It was a situation fruitful of confusion. No one, I suppose, ever succeeds in achieving a completely unified attitude

towards life, but, still, this is recognized as an aim worthy
of a man's utmost efforts. Yet the situation in England
not only rewarded men for holding fundamentally inconsistent beliefs but made it difficult or impossible for them
to detect them.

Everybody knows Matthew Arnold's eloquent description of Oxford as the chosen sanctuary of "lost causes"
and "impossible loyalties," and Cambridge in this matter was not far different. Striking instances of what was
possible there as late as the middle of the nineteenth
century are afforded by the cases of Leslie Stephen and
of Samuel Butler, the author of *Erewhon* and *The Way
of All Flesh*. Stephen professed Christianity as a matter
of course and while an undergraduate felt no influences
which opened his mind to a realization that there were
any serious difficulties in so doing; more than that, he
took holy orders, without conscious insincerity, as he
says,[1] and remained for several years a clerical fellow of
a Cambridge college before his misgivings became too
much for him. The very similar experiences of Ernest
Pontifex in Butler's *The Way of All Flesh* are, we are
told, a faithful picture, on the whole, of what Butler himself went through at Cambridge and afterwards.

One eminent case of unconscious self-contradiction,
which occurred about a century earlier and which, unlike
those just mentioned, was never resolved, is that of the
"excellent and pious" David Hartley, whose *Observations on Man, his Frame, Duty, and Expectations* was
published in 1749. This work consists of two parts. In
the first, Hartley treats of man's body and mind on a
basis of materialistic determinism. Yet Hartley never
doubted the real existence of God, and in the second part
of his work he undertook to prove it. "It is most notice-
able," as Coleridge remarks, that in this second portion,

[1] *Some Early Impressions*, p. 67.

"he makes no reference to the principles or results of the first. Nay, he assumes as his foundation ideas which, if we embrace the doctrine of his first volume, can exist nowhere but in the vibrations of the ethereal medium common to the nerves and to the atmosphere. Indeed the whole of the second volume is, with the fewest possible exceptions, independent of his peculiar system."

So Coleridge wrote in the *Biographia Literaria,* but he himself had not always realized that Hartley was profoundly inconsistent and that on the basis of his "peculiar system" all talk of man's duty was vain, and all belief in the existence of God delusory. Coleridge was born in 1772 and grew to manhood in the eighteenth century. It was probably while he was an undergraduate at Cambridge that he read Hartley's *Observations.* He was immediately carried away into eager discipleship. In 1796 he even named his eldest son after Hartley as a sign of veneration. Yet at the same time Coleridge was then, while a materialist and necessitarian in philosophy, a theist in religion. For Coleridge from boyhood to death never wavered in his belief in the existence of God, save for a brief period after reading Voltaire. And his allegiance to Hartley was a temporary aberration, which in time helped to open his eyes to the real bearings of empiricism, but which did not permanently colour his thought.

Coleridge said once, "Every man is born an Aristotelian or a Platonist. I do not think it possible that any one born an Aristotelian can become a Platonist; and I am sure no born Platonist can ever change into an Aristotelian. They are the two classes of men, beside which it is next to impossible to conceive a third. The one considers reason a quality, or attribute; the other considers it a power. I believe that Aristotle never could get to understand what Plato meant by an idea. . . . With

Plato ideas are constitutive in themselves.''² In this sense one may say that Coleridge was born a Platonist, and to that extent was born religious. He was bound sooner or later to revolt against the ''mechanical philosophy,'' whether that was masked by professions of belief in a deity or not, and he was bound so to do, not because of external influences, but because of the inner law of his nature.

The best source of information concerning Coleridge's early youth is a series of autobiographical letters which he addressed, beginning in 1797, to his friend Thomas Poole. In one of these letters there is a passage of the greatest importance which shows at how young an age he caught some vision of unseen, immaterial reality. In it he writes, it is true, in the language of his later thought, but there is no reason to doubt that he gives a faithful picture of his childhood self. ''I read,'' he tells Poole, ''every book that came in my way without distinction; and my father was fond of me, and used to take me on his knee and hold long conversations with me. I remember that at eight years old I walked with him one winter evening from a farmer's house, a mile from Ottery, and he told me the names of the stars and how Jupiter was a thousand times larger than our world, and that the other twinkling stars were suns that had worlds rolling round them; and when I came home he showed me how they rolled round. I heard him with a profound delight and admiration, but without the least mixture of wonder or incredulity. For from my early reading of fairy tales and genii, *etc., etc.,* my mind had been habituated *to the Vast,* and I never regarded *my senses* in any way as the criteria of my belief. I regulated all my creeds by my conceptions, not by my *sight,* even at that age. Should children be permitted to read

² *Table Talk,* 2 July, 1830.

romances, and relations of giants and magicians and genii? I know all that has been said against it; but I have formed my faith in the affirmative. I know no other way of giving the mind a love of the Great and the Whole. Those who have been led to the same truths step by step, through the constant testimony of their senses, seem to me to want a sense which I possess. They contemplate nothing but *parts,* and all *parts* are necessarily little. And the universe to them is but a mass of *little things.* It is true, that the mind *may* become credulous and prone to superstition by the former method;—but are not the experimentalists credulous even to madness in believing any absurdity, rather than believe the grandest truths, if they have not the testimony of their own senses in their favour? I have known some who have been *rationally* educated, as it is styled. They were marked by a microscopic acuteness, but when they looked at great things, all became a blank, and they saw nothing, and denied (very illogically) that anything could be seen, and uniformly put the negation of a power for the possession of a power, and called the want of imagination judgement, and the never being moved to rapture philosophy!'"[3]

Thus even as a boy Coleridge was emancipated from the bondage of the senses. By an inborn trait, by his peculiar genius, as well as by certain surrounding influences, he was prepared to believe, and did believe, that reality was not bounded by what the ear can hear, or the eye see, or the hand touch. And his early belief in immaterial or spiritual reality was nourished while he was still a boy in his 'teens by the study of Plato and the Neo-Platonists. Who that has read it can forget Lamb's picture of Coleridge when they were school-fellows at Christ's Hospital?—"Come back into memory, like as thou wert in the day-spring of thy fancies, with hope like

[3] *Letters,* ed. E. H. Coleridge, Vol. I, pp. 16-17.

a fiery column before thee—the dark pillar not yet turned —Samuel Taylor Coleridge—Logician, Metaphysician, Bard!—How have I seen the casual passer through the Cloisters stand still, intranced with admiration (while he weighed the disproportion between the *speech* and the *garb* of the young Mirandula), to hear thee unfold, in thy deep and sweet intonations, the mysteries of Jamblichus, or Plotinus (for even in those years thou waxedst not pale at such philosophic draughts), or reciting Homer in his Greek, or Pindar—while the walls of the old Grey Friars re-echoed to the accents of the *inspired charity-boy!*"[4]

Coleridge's biographer, J. Dykes Campbell, regards Lamb's words as substantially true, though he reminds us that there were probably Latin translations in the editions of the Neo-Platonists used by Coleridge, and that Thomas Taylor's translations appeared about this time; —"difficult Greek transmuted into incomprehensible English," Coleridge later remarked. It is not to be supposed, however, that, precocious though he was, he then had the capacity for any very serious reflexion upon his reading, or that he was led to it by any definite perception of its contrast with contemporary thought. Rather, one supposes, he found it congenial he knew not why, and it nourished seeds which had been imperceptibly growing since his boyhood, but which were not yet ready to mature.

This is the only supposition which makes it easy to account for the fact that a couple of years later, when Coleridge was at Cambridge, he was very ready to find Locke plausible and Hartley convincing. These writers, however, did not obtain the undivided sway over his mind that for a time they appeared to. Instead, they opened up a conflict, making him conscious that he was a born Pla-

[4] *Elia*, "Christ's Hospital Five and Thirty Years Ago."

tonist, and forcing him to the task of critical reflexion.
A mind less sensitive and acute than Coleridge's might
have rested not uncomfortably amidst contradictory beliefs. Such confusion was, as has already been said, encouraged by the condition of English thought in the
eighteenth century. And at all times, indeed, so common
is the mind divided against itself, the mind which is a
mere unconcerned lodging-house for ideas no matter
how heterogeneous or contradictory, that the phenomenon strikes many people as natural, and seems to call for
no special explanation. But Coleridge's mind was not of
this order, and he could not comfortably range his new
materialism beside the older Platonism of which it made
him definitely conscious. The two lodgers made each
other ill at ease; though materialism might seem irrefutable, still, the belief in spiritual reality would not away.
And the conflict thus originated is the source of all of
Coleridge's later thought.

It was apparently in the period immediately following
his final departure from Cambridge, in December, 1794,
that Coleridge took to reading some of the Christian
mystics, notably George Fox, Jacob Boehme, and William Law. How he came to take up their works is not
known. He was aware of their limitations, of the dangers
in their mode of apprehension. Of Boehme he says, in the
Biographia Literaria, "Many, indeed, and gross were
his delusions; and such as furnish frequent and ample
occasion for the triumph of the learned over the poor
ignorant shoe-maker who had dared think for himself."
Yet underneath all extravagance or credulity, underneath all mere 'enthusiasm,' Coleridge found in these
outcasts from the close guild of the philosophers a moving spirit, a living conviction of unmistakable and deep
sincerity, which he felt practically constituted a self-
authenticating assurance of the divine, of God's reality

and actual presence with his creatures of this world. And thus the writings of these mystics, as he says, "acted in no slight degree to prevent my mind from being imprisoned within the outline of any single dogmatic system. They contributed," he continues, "to keep alive the heart in the head; gave me an indistinct, yet stirring and working presentiment, that all the products of the mere reflective faculty partook of death, and were as the rattling twigs and sprays in winter, into which a sap was yet to be propelled from some root to which I had not penetrated, if they were to afford my soul either food or shelter. If they were too often a moving cloud of smoke to me by day, yet they were always a pillar of fire throughout the night, during my wanderings through the wilderness of doubt, and enabled me to skirt, without crossing, the sandy deserts of utter unbelief." Coleridge knew, as he says in a sentence immediately following this passage, that mysticism verged upon what he calls "an irreligious Pantheism," yet he also says: "At no time could I believe that *in itself* and *essentially* it is incompatible with religion, natural or revealed."

What does this come to? The mystics, Coleridge says, gave him a "presentiment that all the products of the mere reflective faculty partook of death." In other words, they suggested to him that the mind of man must after all be larger than Locke and Hume and Hartley had supposed. According to them the mind is entirely passive—the mere recipient of sensible impressions. On Hartley's basis it is strictly resolvable into mechanical vibrations which we are deluded in regarding as something different. But Coleridge came to feel that this was "a wilful resignation of intellect" against which "human nature itself fought." "How," he asked, "can we make bricks without straw? Or build without cement?" And he answered that we do "learn all things indeed by occasion of experience; but the very facts so learned force us inward on the antecedents that must be presupposed in order to render experience itself possible.'' Consequently he was led to reflect that what we actually and immediately know of our own experience, as soon as we proceed to examine it, shows us that an active power is there at work, an organizing centre which gives form and coherence to our sensible impressions.

Thus Coleridge was led into the beginnings, at any rate, of a critical attitude towards the intellect. And the same attitude suggested also another line of reflexion. With respect to religion he concluded that ''if the mere intellect could make no certain discovery of a holy and intelligent first cause, it might yet supply a demonstration that no legitimate argument could be drawn from the intellect against its truth. And what is this,'' he asked, ''more than St. Paul's assertion that by the powers of reasoning no man ever arrived at the knowledge of God?'' And he adds, ''I became convinced that religion . . . must have a moral origin; so far at least, that the evidence of its doctrines could not, like the truths of abstract science, be wholly independent of the will. It were, therefore, to be expected that its fundamental truth would be such as might be denied; though only by the fool, and even by the fool from the madness of the heart alone!''

So it was that Coleridge arrived for himself at a point of view which is closely similar to that which Immanuel Kant achieved after Hume had awakened him from his dogmatic slumber. The data of consciousness forced the conclusion upon both of them, at any rate, that the mind actually did something, that it worked, that it was a species of self-activity. And for both the moral responsibility of the individual, which meant the free, originative, in a sense creative, will of the individual, seemed an ultimate postulate, to deny which was equivalent to the denial of human nature itself—equivalent in short to suicide.

Kant, horridly arraying himself in a technical jargon, and advancing his positions with the utmost caution and thoroughness, proceeded from this starting-point to work a veritable revolution in philosophy—a revolution which was completed, or some would say perverted, by Fichte, Schelling, and other followers. Kant's most important works were published in the period from 1781 to 1794, but they remained for a considerable time, in common with German literature, practically unknown in England. As late as 1796 Coleridge only knew Kant as a metaphysician who had the reputation of being "most unintelligible." Of course, however, he and others more or less vaguely heard of stirrings of new life in thought and literature in Germany, and, at the same time, he apparently came to something of a stand in his efforts to think through and resolve the contradiction between his 'heart' and his 'head'—to use words which he himself chose on occasion to employ. Hence he naturally began to look towards Germany as a possible source of help. And in the fall of 1798, as soon as they had seen the *Lyrical Ballads* through the press, Coleridge and Wordsworth crossed the Channel and entered the unknown land. There Coleridge learned the language, talked to poets and read their poetry, began to write a life of Lessing, and gathered together a small library composed chiefly of philosophical works. He did not yet, however, undertake any real study of the new philosophy, and it was not until some time after the spring of 1801 that he began the serious reading of Kant.

He has told in the *Biographia Literaria* how Kant at once took possession of him "with a giant's hand," and it is easy to see why. Kant had been concerned with the same problem that he was, and had painfully and thoroughly worked out his own solution of it. By his analysis of the mind he had conclusively demonstrated the inadequacy alike of the dogmatic rationalism and of the sceptical materialism of earlier thought and, at the same time, he had vindicated the rationality of those convictions regarding man's spiritual nature which the mystics determinedly held but could not account for. Coleridge saw here the massive, systematic elaboration of the position at which he had already arrived for himself, and in particular he must have received with deep gratitude Kant's distinction between the understanding and the reason. In later years he repeatedly acknowledged his debt to the "sage of Königsberg," as he called him. The nature of this indebtedness, however, has often been misunderstood, for Coleridge has been regarded as the mere carrier of the philosophy of Kant, Fichte, and Schelling from Germany to England, and, not unnaturally, as an unsatisfactory, if not incompetent, interpreter. But it has already been shown that, as Coleridge's closest and ablest student of recent years says, his debt to Kant was on the whole "more formal than material," residing "rather in the scientific statement of convictions previously attained than in the acquisition of new truths."[5] Moreover, Coleridge could not accept Kant's limitation of knowledge to the phenomenal world. He was ready to agree that this is the sphere of the understanding, and that the understanding cannot transcend it; but through the reason, he insisted, we do actually obtain knowledge of spiritual reality "by occasion of experience." In other words, Coleridge maintained that Kant's ideas of the

[5] J. Shawcross, in Introduction to his edition of *Biographia Literaria*, p. xli. I am glad to acknowledge my indebtedness to Mr. Shawcross's edition, without which the earlier portion of this essay could hardly have been written in its present form.

pure reason are not merely regulative, but constitutive, and that his fundamental postulates arising from our moral nature—God, immortality, and freedom—are not merely hypotheses, however necessary, but are realities given in moral experience.

Thus, for all the help Kant gave him, Coleridge was still left with the task of constructing his own religious philosophy.[6] Furthermore, the better one understands what that religious construction was to be the more readily will one credit Coleridge's statement that "he had not gained any one great idea" from Fichte and Schelling.[7] I say what his religious construction was to be, rather than what it was, because unfortunately we have it only in the form of promises, forecasts, and fragments. Through the last twenty or more years of his life Coleridge considered that he was preparing himself for, or that he was making real progress with, his great book. This *magnum opus* was to gather together in systematic form the whole fabric of his thought and present to the world convincingly all he felt surging within him of assurance in the final truth of Christianity. But the *magnum opus* was never committed to paper, and remains perhaps the most famous unwritten book in English literature. Something, indeed, that purported to be just

6 And, as Mr. Shawcross is more particularly concerned to show, his own æsthetic theory.

7 Reported by Crabb Robinson, who also reports Coleridge as saying that "to Kant his obligations are infinite, not so much from what Kant has taught him in the form of doctrine, as from the discipline gained in studying the great German philosopher. Coleridge is indignant at the low estimation in which the post-Kantianers affect to hold their master." Later Coleridge also said to Robinson that "he adheres to Kant, notwithstanding all Schelling has written, and maintained that from the latter he has gained no new ideas. All Schelling has said, Coleridge has thought himself or found in Jacob Boehme." J. Dykes Campbell, who quotes these passages in his biography of Coleridge, questions Robinson's accuracy—needlessly, if the account given above is correct.

as good or almost as good was published in 1865 by Joseph Henry Green,[8] one of Coleridge's devoted followers. Coleridge had left the completion of his system to Green as a sort of legacy or trust—a trust which Green took with deep seriousness, devoting the last thirty years of his life to preliminary studies and to the writing of his *Spiritual Philosophy*. But this, it is no disparagement to say, is not Coleridge's *magnum opus*. The task, indeed, which Green piously and nobly undertook was an impossible one, and it is not his fault if we still have to go to Coleridge's own work, fragmentary as it is, in any attempt to learn what it was he wished to say.

II.

COLERIDGE was, in the first place, entirely at one with the empiricists in asserting that we learn all things by occasion of experience. He agreed also that the mere blind acquiescence in dogma imposed by authority, or, in other words, blind faith in the word of another human being, could lead to no good result whatever but, on the contrary, could lead only to superstition and the hopeless deadening of our real selves. "If the mere acquiescence in truth, uncomprehended and unfathomed, were sufficient, few indeed would be the vicious and the miserable,"[9] he thought, considering how the number of professed believers far outweighed that of professed infidels. And he felt that this was the mistake both of Roman Catholics and of the Evangelical members of the Anglican Church in his own day—that both in differing ways grounded themselves simply on external authority.

---

[8] Green died before his work was published, and it was brought out under the editorial care of John Simon. J. Dykes Campbell says: "In his Hunterian Orations of 1840 and 1847, Green probably accomplished more in the setting forth of Coleridge's philosophical views than in the *Spiritual Philosophy*."

[9] *Statesman's Manual*, in Bohn ed. of *Biographia Literaria*, p. 332.

But this was, in plain words, a perversion of their Christianity. If, he asked, "acquiescence without insight; if warmth without light; if an immunity from doubt, given and guaranteed by a resolute ignorance; if the habit of *taking for granted* the words of a catechism, remembered or forgotten; if a mere *sensation* of positiveness substituted—I will not say for the *sense* of *certainty;* but—for that calm assurance, the very means and conditions of which it supersedes; if a belief that seeks the darkness, and yet strikes no root, immovable as the limpet from the rock, and like the limpet, fixed there by mere force of adhesion; if these suffice to make men Christians, in what sense could the apostle affirm that believers receive, not indeed worldly wisdom, that comes to nought, but the wisdom of God, that we might *know* and *comprehend* the things that are freely given to us of God? On what grounds could he denounce sincerest *fervour* of spirit as *defective,* where it does not likewise bring forth fruits in the *understanding?*"[10] Coleridge wanted to strike down to the rock of knowledge for the foundation of his own religion, and this he was sure he could not do save by reliance upon his own personal experience, through which must be given anything that he could call knowledge. In this he was true to the English empirical tradition.

But he quarrelled with the empiricists—with the expounders of the 'mechanical philosophy,' as he called it —on the ground that they had not been true to their own principle. Both his own experience and the experiences of a host whom the world has agreed to count amongst its noblest characters assured him that the empiricists had arbitrarily denied some elements of experience for the sake of others. And thus they had opened themselves

10 *Aids to Reflexion,* Bohn ed., p. 7.

to that *reductio ad absurdum,* that total denial of the possibility of rational certitude, at which Hume had arrived. They had arbitrarily denied that we may have a clear conception of anything which cannot be represented by a distinct image, and thus they had reduced the conceivable to the bounds of the picturable. They had fallen subject to "that despotism of the eye" from which Pythagoras and Plato had vainly sought to free man.[11]

Yet actually as a matter of unmistakable experience, Coleridge contended, man does have a grasp of supersensible realities. If one of the simplest possible of cases be taken, we say that in all triangles the sum of any two sides must be greater than the third. But he points out that from experience alone we could not legitimately reach this conclusion. We could say only that all triangles we have hitherto measured have exhibited this characteristic, and consequently—if we have measured a great many of them—that there is a strong probability that all triangles always will do so. Whence then the certitude we do feel? Using the terms of a now antiquated psychology, Coleridge replies that the mind has more than one faculty, that it is the understanding only which generalizes from sensible impressions—whereas we are also equipped with reason. And reason supersedes the whole process of empirical observation. "On the first conception presented by the understanding in consequence of the first sight of a triangular figure, of whatever sort it might chance to be, it affirms with an assurance incapable of future increase, with a perfect *certainty,* that in all possible triangles any two of the enclosing lines *will* and *must* be greater than the third. In short, understanding in its highest form of experience remains commensurate with the experimental notices of the senses from which it

[11] *Biographia Literaria,* Bohn ed., pp. 135 and 52.

is generalized. Reason, on the other hand, either prede-
termines experience, or avails itself of a past experience
to supersede its necessity in all future time; and affirms
truths which no sense could perceive, nor experiment
verify, nor experience confirm.''[12]

Reason, then, ''is the power of universal and necessary
convictions, the source and substance of truths above
sense, and having their evidence in themselves.'' In its
mode of apprehension reason ''is much nearer to sense
than to understanding; for reason is a direct aspect of
truth, an inward beholding, having a similar relation to
the intelligible or spiritual as sense has to the material
or phenomenal.'' Reason is an ''intuition or immediate
beholding, accompanied by a conviction of the necessity
and universality of the truth so beholden not derived
from the senses, which intuition, when it is construed by
pure sense gives birth to the science of mathematics, and
when applied to objects supersensuous or spiritual is the
organ of theology and philosophy.''[13]

But Coleridge quarrelled further with the expounders
of the mechanical philosophy because, in obedience to the
inexorable demands of their theory, they denied the freedom of the will. Dr. Johnson's familiar words concerning
this famous controversy are that all theory is against the
will's freedom, while all experience is for it. Coleridge
of course was in full agreement with the latter half of
this statement, but was far from agreeing with the
former half. For he considered that any theory which
denied the will's freedom denied human nature itself,
and was in reality completely unintelligible when confronted with the testimony of actual experience. In other
words, whatever difficulties were solved by necessitarianism, they were far fewer and less important than the diffi-

[12] *Aids to Reflexion*, p. 154.
[13] *Ibid.*, pp. 143, 148, and 155.

culties which necessitarianism raised. Coleridge did not suppose that he could prove or demonstrate the existence of a free will, or of an originative, creative power in man, any more than one can prove the axioms of geometry or the premises of the materialist and necessitarian. All sciences begin in postulates or assumptions or axioms— in truths taken to be self-evident. Coleridge simply took the free will to be the basic axiom of personality. If man has no free will he is no longer a person, but a thing. And this is just what the necessitarian asks one to take for granted, to take as *his* axiom. He of course does not prove the non-existence of a free will—for this is one of the things that can neither be proved nor be disproved— but, as Coleridge puts it, ''he desires you only to take for granted that all reality is included in nature, and he may then safely defy you to ward off his conclusion— that nothing is excluded!'' Coleridge puts it in this way because he recognizes that ''whatever is comprised in the chain and mechanism of cause and effect'' is of course necessitated, has ''its necessity in some other thing, antecedent or concurrent,'' and ''this is said to be *natural;* and the aggregate and system of all such things is Nature. It is, therefore, a contradiction in terms to include in this the free will, of which the verbal definition is—that which *originates* an act or state of being. In this sense, therefore,'' he concluded, ''spiritual and supernatural are synonymous.''[14]

Coleridge declares that in this the only difference between his procedure and that of the geometricians is that, while ''the postulates of geometry no man *can* deny, those of moral science are such as no good man *will* deny. For it is not in our power to disclaim our nature as sentient beings; but it is in our power to disclaim our prerogative as moral beings.'' And this difference is bound

[14] *Aids to Reflexion*, pp. 91 and 42.

up with our very conception of duty. Thus he assumes, he
says, ''a something the proof of which no man can give
to another, yet every man may find for himself. If any
man assert that he cannot find it, I am bound to disbelieve him. I cannot do otherwise without unsettling the
very foundations of my own moral nature. For I either
find it as an essential of the humanity common to him and
me, or I have not found it at all, except as an hypochon-
driast finds glass legs.'' Coleridge also regards as a self-
evident fact of consciousness the reality of the law of
conscience, and as a self-evident fact of history the existence of evil—''of evil essentially such, not by accident of
outward circumstances, not derived from its physical
consequences, nor from any cause out of itself.''[15]

These, I should say, are the bases of Coleridge's religious thought, about which we must be clear if it is to be
understood. He then went on, after distinguishing the
reason from the understanding, to distinguish two aspects of the reason, ''derived from the different modes of
applying it and from the objects to which it is directed.''
This is hinted at in a passage which I have already
quoted. Coleridge's terms are those used by Kant, but
the meaning he attaches to them is his own. He terms
the reason speculative in relation to formal principles
or abstract truth, ''but in reference to actual, or moral,
truth,'' he says, ''as the fountain of ideas and the light
of conscience, we name it the practical reason.'' And the
latter, the practical reason, alone is reason, he contends,
''in the full and substantive sense. It is reason in its own
sphere of perfect freedom, as the source of ideas, which
ideas in their conversion to the responsible will become
ultimate ends.'' While the theoretic or speculative reason,
he thinks, ''is rather the light of reason in the under-

15 *Aids to Reflexion*, pp. 89 and 90.

standing.'"[16] According to this it is only by responsible
acts in obedience to the law of conscience that we can
realize absolute truth in its fulness and reality—but in
such acts we do realize it, in such acts we really are in
living communion with God.

This bars the speculative reason from any positive
office in theology, though not from a negative one. "Do
I," Coleridge asks, "utterly exclude the speculative
reason from theology? No! It is its office and rightful
privilege to determine on the negative truth of whatever
we are required to believe. The doctrine must not contradict any universal principle; for this would be a doctrine that contradicted itself. Or philosophy? No. It may
be and has been the servant and pioneer of faith by convincing the mind that a doctrine is cogitable, that the soul
can present the Idea to itself, and that if we determine
to contemplate, or think of, the subject at all, so and in
no other form can this be effected. So far are both logic
and philosophy to be received and trusted. But the duty,
and in some cases and for some persons even the right,
of thinking on subjects beyond the bounds of sensible
experience; the grounds of the real truth; the life, the
substance, the hope, the love, in one word the faith—
these are derivatives from the practical, moral, and
Spiritual nature and being of man.'"[17]

By responsible acts, then, and by these alone in obedience to the law of conscience do we come into communion
with God, and so realize the divine nature in our present
selves. But, as has been said, Coleridge also postulates
as a fact of historic experience the existence of evil—"of
a law in the nature of man resisting the law of God."
This he holds to be a mystery—a problem, that is, 'of
which any other solution than the statement of the fact

[16] *Aids to Reflexion,* pp. 143 and 277.
[17] *Ibid.,* pp. 122-123.

itself is demonstrably impossible.' And that it is so follows from the fact, if it be granted as such, that we are
responsible beings. "For this is the essential attribute
of a will, and contained in the very idea, that whatever
determines the will acquires this power from a previous
determination of the will itself. The will is ultimately
self-determined, or it is no longer a will under the law of
perfect freedom, but a nature under the mechanism of
cause and effect. And if by an act to which it had determined itself, it has subjected itself to the determination
of nature (in the language of St. Paul, to the law of the
flesh), it receives a nature into itself and so far it becomes a nature; and this is a corruption of the will and a
corrupt nature. It is also a *fall* of man, inasmuch as his
will is the condition of his personality—the ground and
condition of the attribute which constitutes him man."
And further: "A moral evil is an evil that has its origin
in a will. An evil common to all must have a ground
common to all. But the actual existence of moral evil we
are bound in conscience to admit; and that there is an
evil common to all is a fact; and this evil must therefore
have a common ground. Now this evil cannot originate
in the divine will; it must therefore be referred to the
will of man. And this evil ground we call original sin.'"[18]
Coleridge regards this term as really a pleonasm, for if
sin be not original, that is, originated within the will, it
would not *be* sin;—"a state or act that has not its origin
in the will may be a calamity, deformity, disease, or mischief; but a *sin* it cannot be.'"[19]

Coleridge's treatment of original sin, which I have
outlined as far as possible in his own words, may be taken
as a fair example of his method of treating the whole
body of Christian dogma, or of the way in which he felt

[18] *Aids to Reflexion*, pp. 189, 190, 192.
[19] *Ibid.*, p. 178.

confident it could be treated. The method consists in the resolution of a given dogma into those terms of personal experience from which in the beginning, as he supposes, it took its rise. It has been believed by very many, perhaps by most, that original sin means hereditary guilt. But this Coleridge terms a "monstrous fiction," and he agrees with all the professed infidels who have regarded it as a revolting and essentially immoral conception. For him the dogma simply expresses a fact of individual experience, undeniably common to all human beings. It is not, then, the bald statement of a mystery beyond reason which we are directed blindly to accept, nor is it an historic fact external to ourselves transmitted to us only by heredity, though in the Biblical story of the fall of our first parents it is symbolically expressed in the garb of history. On the contrary, it is a present fact in the lives of all human beings, with a meaning which can be realized through the practical reason. And so it is with the Redemption, with the Trinity, with the whole body of doctrines which make up the sum of Christian belief. All have their rational meaning, according to Coleridge, in relation to the facts of personal experience. And in order that any one may realize that meaning in his own life he has only to exercise his will in moral action so as to discover the saving truth through his practical reason.

Thus, as he regards it, Christianity is the *rationale* of life; it is, he says, "the perfection of human intelligence." He does not deny, of course, that there may be speculative difficulties in the tenets peculiar to Christianity. He imagines some one saying, How can I comprehend them? How are they to be proved? And he answers, to the first question, "Christianity is not a theory, or a speculation, but a Life;—not a philosophy of life, but a life and a living process. To the second: *Try it.*"[20]

[20] *Aids to Reflexion*, pp. xvi, 134.

By this he means simply that Christian doctrine, if given an opportunity in the only possible way, will prove itself true. In other words, Christian doctrine is merely a formal statement of what is in reality the deliverance of man's practical reason, or of the responsible will acting in obedience to the law of conscience. And in the concluding paragraph of the *Biographia Literaria* he says that his desire has been to show "that the scheme of Christianity, as taught in the liturgy and homilies of our Church, though not discoverable by human reason [*i.e.,* speculative reason], is yet in accordance with it; that link follows link by necessary consequence; that religion passes out of the ken of reason only where the eye of reason has reached its own horizon; and that faith is then but its continuation: even as the day softens away into the sweet twilight, and twilight, hushed and breathless, steals into the darkness."

Coleridge sought to rest his exposition of Christianity from beginning to end on experience—not on some other person's experience, but for himself on his own experience, and for others on theirs. This is what religion was for him: an inner experience of the individual, expressed outwardly in a way of life, in action. Its only test, he thought, was the individual's actual and adequate trial of it. "Believe, and if thy belief be right, that insight which gradually transmutes faith into knowledge will be the reward of that belief."[21] And of course for him religion meant Christianity; it meant, as he sometimes said, all the beliefs held in common by the leaders of the Protestant Reformation, or, as he said at other times, the doctrines embodied in the homilies and liturgy of the Anglican Church. He objected against the deists that they substituted a colourless abstraction, a mere speculative concept, for the one true and living God—"as if the

21 *Table Talk and Omniana,* Oxford ed., p. 404.

main object of religion were to solve difficulties for the satisfaction of the intellect." "In religion," he added, "there is no abstraction."[22] To his mind it was at once the glory and the substantiating testimony of Christianity that it did express completely the insight into the nature of life gained from moral action originated by the free will. Tried, it was not found wanting; it did unlock the meaning of life; its peculiar doctrines did sum up as far as words could that "total act of the soul," that absorption of the whole man in the being of God, which was religion true and undefiled.

Coleridge maintained the same attitude towards the Bible as towards the articles of Christian belief. Several years after his death was published his *Confessions of an Inquiring Spirit,* in which he endeavoured to distinguish between "the right and the superstitious use" of the Bible. He declared that he could accept all of the articles of belief elaborated by the Protestant reformers except one. This exceptionable doctrine was that of "the divine origin and authority of all and every part of the Canonical Books" of the Bible—a doctrine which required the belief that every word of the sacred volume "was—not alone inspired by, that is, composed by men under the actuating influence of the Holy Spirit, but likewise—dictated by an Infallible Intelligence;—that the writers, each and all, were divinely informed as well as inspired."[23]

This doctrine, he said, planted the vineyard of the Word with thorns for him and placed snares in its pathways. He admitted that in this he might be suffering from the delusions of an evil spirit, but added that before he harshly questioned the seeming angel of light—that is,

[22] *Statesman's Manual,* Bohn ed. of *Biographia Literaria,* pp. 353, 354.
[23] *Confessions of an Inquiring Spirit,* Bohn ed. of *Aids to Reflexion,* p. 296.

his reason and his moral sense conjoined with all his
clearest knowledge—which bade him reject the doctrine
of the verbal inspiration of the Bible, he would inquire
into the authority on which this doctrine rested. And his
inquiry resulted in his condemnation of the doctrine as
both superstitious and unscriptural. Whether for his
reasons or for others, to-day so many accept his conclusion that we need hardly follow with him through his
treatment of the question. Nowadays an overwhelming
number would echo him when he asks: "How can absolute infallibility be blended with fallibility? Where is the
infallible criterion? How can infallible truth be infallibly
conveyed in defective and fallible expressions?" And
similar agreement will be felt with his assertion that he
condemns the doctrine of the plenary inspiration of the
Scriptures just because he does prize and revere them
for the truth they do contain. Why should I disbelieve
this doctrine? he says. Because it "petrifies at once the
whole body of Holy Writ with all its harmonies and
symmetrical gradations—the flexile and the rigid—the
supporting hard and the clothing soft—the blood *which
is the life*—the intelligencing nerves, and the rudely
woven, but soft and springy, cellular substance in which
all are embedded and lightly bound together. This breathing organism, this glorious panharmonicon, which I had
seen stand on its feet as a man, and with a man's voice
given to it, the Doctrine in question turns at once into
a colossal Memnon's head, a hollow passage for a voice,
a voice that mocks the voices of many men, and speaks
in their names, and yet is but one voice, and the same;—
and no man uttered it and never in a human heart was
it conceived."[24] In short, he felt that the doctrine of
plenary inspiration removed the Bible at one blow from
the circle of humanity and robbed it of all significant con-

[24] *Confessions, u.s.*, pp. 299, 305.

nexion with us and our concerns. The doctrine externalized the Bible and made of it in effect a cheat and a delusion, for this doctrine declared the Bible to be something
the nature of which no man could possibly understand.

But, said Coleridge, when I read the Bible as far as
possible in the same way that I read any other book,
when I contemplate it as a record of the reflexions and
experiences of men like myself, striving like myself for
the truth which giveth life, *then* I discover that there is in
it "more that *finds* me than I have experienced in all
other books put together; that the words of the Bible
find me at greater depths of my being; and that whatever
finds me brings with it an irresistible evidence of its
having proceeded from the Holy Spirit."[25]

Thus he consistently asked of the Bible what he asked
of the articles of Christian belief, that it should prove
itself. The Bible commanded his assent just so far as it
did this by arousing an answering voice within him, and
no further. He of course recognized that where the Bible
spoke to him in vain the fault might lie within himself,
and he accordingly concluded that, if at any time he
should find a discord between the living spirit within
him and the written letter, he should not straightway
decide that the Bible was in the wrong of it. But on the
other hand neither, he said, "will I fall under the condemnation of them that would *lie for God,* but seek as I
may, be thankful for what I have—and wait."[26]

He regarded the Bible, then, as much as possible in the
same way that he regarded any other book. He regarded
it as literature;—but it is of some importance that what
this meant to him should be made clear. A piece of literature may be either a history or a fiction, and if the latter
it may or may not be an allegory, but it was something

25 *Confessions, u.s.,* p. 296.
26 *Ibid.,* p. 294.

still different that Coleridge saw in the Bible. It was, he thought, amongst the miseries of his age that it recognized no medium between literal and metaphorical, whereas such a medium the Bible really was. "Faith," he says, "is either to be buried in the dead letter or its name and honours usurped by a counterfeit product of the mechanical understanding, which in the blindness of self-complacency confounds symbols with allegories. Now an allegory is but a translation of abstract notions into a picture-language, which is itself nothing but an abstraction from objects of the senses; the principal being more worthless even than its phantom proxy, both alike unsubstantial, and the former shapeless to boot. On the other hand a symbol is characterized by a translucence of the special in the individual, or of the general in the special, or of the universal in the general;—above all by the translucence of the eternal through and in the temporal. It always partakes of the reality which it renders intelligible; and while it enunciates the whole, abides itself as a living part in that unity of which it is the representative."[27]

Coleridge had a definite object in view in attempting to make this distinction, the essential point in which is that the symbol "always partakes of the reality which it renders intelligible." Thus the life of Christ came to him as a revelation, indeed, in just the sense in which we often say that some poem or picture is a revelation to us, meaning that there is some magic in it which touches our inmost being and suddenly commands an assent from us which is an act of our whole personality—feeling and thought united or fused for the moment into an unexplainable yet unmistakable, profound certitude. Such a revelation the life of Christ was to him, but the symbol "always partakes of the reality which it renders intelli-

[27] *Statesman's Manual*, Bohn ed. of *Biographia Literaria*, p. 322.

gible," and hence he also asserted the life of Christ to be an historic revelation which conscience bids us accept as such, and gave his assent to Christianity as an historic religion in the orthodox sense of those words.

It was thus by means of his definition of a symbol that he was enabled to use the word revelation in two senses of the same object, and so was enabled in the end to embrace the same Christianity as did those who received it simply as an external, historic revelation. He defines this double aspect of religion in a concluding paragraph of the *Confessions of an Inquiring Spirit:* "I comprise and conclude the sum of my conviction in this one sentence. Revealed religion (and I know of no religion not revealed) is in its highest contemplation the unity, that is, the identity or co-inherence, of Subjective and Objective. It is in itself, and irrelatively, at once inward life and truth, and outward fact and luminary. But as all power manifests itself in the harmony of correspondent opposites, each supposing and supporting the other—so has religion its objective, or historic and ecclesiastical pole, and its subjective, or spiritual and individual pole. In the miracles, and miraculous parts of religion—both in the first communication of divine truths, and in the promulgation of the truths thus communicated—we have the union of the two, that is, the subjective and supernatural displayed objectively—outwardly and phenomenally—*as* subjective and supernatural."

III.

SUCH was Coleridge's progression from the period when he "sported infidelity" after reading Voltaire, and when he was a materialist and necessitarian after the manner of Hartley, to a complete acceptance of Christianity as set forth in the liturgy and homilies of the Anglican

Church and as an historic revealed religion. This last stage in his progression is significant in showing the completeness of his repudiation of eighteenth-century rationalism and scepticism, but it is overshadowed in importance by his method of reaching full acceptance of historic Christianity. He did so not in obedience to any external authority, whether of a book or of a church, but by exercising the 'right and duty of private judgement.' He saw glimmering through moral experience 'phantoms of sublimity,' lessons which could be stated only in terms of Christian doctrine. Such experience was a real, indeed a central, fact of life, yet it was unintelligible unless so explained—while the materialists and necessitarians for the sake of their doctrine perforce had to deny this whole tract of experience.

Coleridge was deeply read in English divinity of the seventeenth century, and he was also impressed by the evidences of sensibility or pietism which followed in the wake of the narrow rationalism of the eighteenth century. Thus he was nourished by both branches of Protestant individualism. The mystics encouraged him to trust his religious feelings, while the Cambridge Platonists and other Protestant writers of the seventeenth century encouraged him to believe that these were susceptible of rational interpretation. It was this which he strove for through the later years of his life—the convincing demonstration of the objective validity of his beliefs. H. D. Traill, in the life of Coleridge in the series of "English Men of Letters," quotes a sentence which sums up what he calls "the great Coleridgean position": "Christianity, rightly understood, is identical with the highest philosophy, and apart from all question of historical evidence, the essential doctrines of Christianity are necessary and eternal truths of reason—truths which man, by the vouchsafed light of Nature and without aid from documents or tradition, may always and anywhere discover from himself."

This might almost have been written by Toland or by Tindal, yet Coleridge was in no danger of reverting to deism in his attempt to revive Christianity. He was not seeking an argument which should demonstrate the propriety of religious belief, but an explanation of his own undeniable experience. That experience was the highest and fullest reality of his own life. His effort was not to discover some objective ground for belief, but to vindicate philosophically what, for himself, he already knew unmistakably.[28]

Yet he failed in his effort. One reason for his failure was personal. The reading of his prose is generally regarded as no light task, but there is also a certain real painfulness in it. For the trouble is not only that Coleridge's thought is abstruse, but that he was never in complete control of his faculties. He was an inveterate fumbler, reaching uncertainly for the truth he wished to express, and helpless in the face of every by-path suggested by his exposition. What he found in those by-paths nearly always has its interest, sometimes its absorbing interest, but it did not help him to reach his goal. And

[28] I have not attempted to reproduce Mr. Shawcross's luminous exposition of the dependence of poetic creation upon moral experience as this was first clearly revealed to Coleridge through one of Wordsworth's poems. This started Coleridge in his attempt to distinguish the imagination from the fancy—a distinction corresponding to that between the reason and the understanding. The experience aided him to see natural objects as the creation of God, which could speak to us symbolically of spiritual realities when we brought to their contemplation that joyful disposition which is the fruit of moral activity. But the same natural objects, he found, remained mute unless we were in a state of harmony with their meaning. In the light of Mr. Shawcross's comment *Dejection* becomes, to the student of his thought, the most significant of Coleridge's poems. And his experience of the influence of natural objects upon the reason, while to the understanding they remained merely a mass of little things, seemed to give additional ground for seeing an objectively valid meaning in moral activity.

his repeated, vain struggles to get forward to what is really central are pitiable, and painful merely to watch.

Carlyle says in his *Life of Sterling* that Coleridge's path on a garden walk was that of a cork-screw; he could never make up his mind which side of the walk to stay on, and so perpetually seesawed, back and forth. It was much the same with his talk. Carlyle has remarkably described that talk as he heard it at Highgate, where Coleridge in his old age was accustomed to discourse almost as an oracle to a group of younger men, of whom John Sterling was for a time one. "No talk," says Carlyle, "in his century or in any other, could be more surprising. . . . It was talk not flowing anywhither like a river, but spreading everywhither in inextricable currents and regurgitations like a lake or sea; terribly deficient in definite goal or aim, nay often in logical intelligibility; *what* you were to believe or do, on any earthly or heavenly thing, obstinately refusing to appear from it. So that, most times, you felt logically lost; swamped near to drowning in this tide of ingenious vocables, spreading out boundless as if to submerge the world. . . . He began anywhere: you put some question to him, made some suggestive observation: instead of answering this, or decidedly setting out towards answer of it, he would accumulate formidable apparatus, logical swim-bladders, transcendental life-preservers and other precautionary and vehiculatory gear, for setting out; perhaps did at last get under way—but was swiftly solicited, turned aside by the glance of some radiant new game on this hand or that, into new courses; and ever into new; and before long into all the Universe, where it was uncertain what game you would catch, or whether any. . . . Glorious islets, too, I have seen rise out of the haze; but they were few, and soon swallowed in the general element again. Balmy sunny islets, islets of the blest and the intelligible. . . . Eloquent artistically expressive words you always had; piercing radiances of a most subtle insight came at intervals; tones of noble pious sympathy, recognizable as pious though strangely coloured, were never wanting long: but in general you could not call this aimless, cloudcapt, cloud-based, lawlessly meandering human discourse of reason by the name of 'excellent talk,' but only of 'surprising'; and were reminded bitterly of Hazlitt's account of it: 'Excellent talker, very— if you let him start from no premises and come to no conclusion.' "

Carlyle evidently indulged his love of humorous exaggeration when he wrote these words, and for that allowance must be made. It has been suggested also that one reason for the unkindness in his tone was the fact that he too was a talker, whereas Coleridge suffered no interruptions. Unfortunately no one who knows Carlyle can dismiss this suggestion lightly; and there is additional ground for concluding that it was not altogether Coleridge's fault that his auditor could not grasp his meaning. But, despite these abatements, no reader of Coleridge's prose can fail to recognize the picture, and there is a pathos in it which even Carlyle's hardness cannot obscure. Coleridge would hardly have succeeded had his task been an easier one. His strength lay not in rigorous, systematic thought pursued without deviation to its furthest reach; it lay rather in moments of sudden insight, in fugitive glimpses of the 'phantoms of sublimity.' And circumstances not only of temperament, but of misfortune, of ill-health, of unhappiness prolonged and irremediable, all conspired to place a burden upon him which might well have been too great for a more phlegmatic person and which inevitably sapped his powers as it weakened his character.

Moreover, Coleridge's task was not only difficult, it

was in its fulness impossible. He was dazzled, as many still are and are long likely to be, by the immemorial pretensions of both philosophers and religious apologists to symmetry, completeness, and finality in their systems. He was confident of the wrongness of the system he opposed, but he felt its strength and had himself been captured for a time by its superficial plausibility; he wanted to confront it with a system equally symmetrical, complete, and final. He saw as clearly as any one all the dangers of making mere uncontrolled feeling or inarticulate stubborn conviction the guide of life, and he had ever before him the confidence of seventeenth-century English theologians in the rational nature of Christianity when they were confronted with anarchic wild 'enthusiasm.' In addition, nineteenth-century criticism of the Bible and historical research into the origins of Christianity and into the general development of the religions of the earth had scarcely begun at the time when he was forming what came to be his life-long intention or hope. It was thus natural, perhaps inevitable, that he should have conceived his task as he did, but it was nevertheless in its fulness an impossible undertaking. It would have required irrefutable proof that miraculous revelations recorded in the Bible and the essential dogmas of Christianity are necessary elements in any intelligible account of human nature; and it would also have required irrefutable proof that these historic revelations and their formulation into dogmas are direct communications, in human terms, from a Spiritual Being who is the creator of the universe in the likeness of his own nature. It is hardly needful to add to these major requirements others which follow from them. Apart from the questions they raise on the side of history, they demand, unfortunately, a vast extension of certitude from its basis in experience —an extension, indeed, which that basis cannot support, since we are raised into regions of absolute spirituality where, at the most, as long as we remain human we can only say that one man's guess or another's must be something like the truth.

Yet Coleridge's failure to accomplish his task, his failure even to visualize that task consistently and definitely, ought not to obscure the significance and value of what he did do. John Stuart Mill, descendant and representative of the 'mechanical' philosophers though he was, still saw in Coleridge one of "the two great seminal minds of England" in the opening years of the nineteenth century; and he did so because he recognized that Coleridge spoke, imperfectly, yes, but imperatively and truly for a side of human nature and a corresponding aspect of reality for which his own philosophy could find no room. Mill saw in Coleridge's 'attempt to arrive at theology by way of philosophy much straining, and most frequently total failure.' Yet, none the less, he valued Coleridge just because he did seek to revive and re-establish that estimate of life which Christianity has managed by one means or another to conserve and hand down through the generations of men. Mill perceived that there was truth in Coleridge's distinction between the understanding and the reason; that, in other words, through moral activity we may really rise to a direct apprehension of an organizing and connecting spiritual principle which gives unity and meaning to life and experience, and which cannot be apprehended through the work of the understanding, through the observation and classification of phenomena.

Mill's estimate is certainly of high significance; yet it may be remembered that Carlyle, who should have sympathized with Coleridge's aims even if he could not fully understand them, said mockingly that the sage of Highgate had discovered "the sublime secret of believing by the reason what the understanding had been obliged to

fling out as incredible.'' Moreover, it is undeniable that
Coleridge's great and perhaps still active influence upon
English theology has practically tended in this direction.
But Coleridge cannot be blamed for the well-meant eva-
sions and sophistries of men who have followed after
him, and who have attempted, not to spread abroad and
strengthen his high achievement, but rather to carry forward and uphold his chimerical aspirations. And in Coleridge's own case it is safe to say that the better one
knows him the less can one doubt his complete sincerity
and honesty of intention. He may be taken, moreover,
alike in what he accomplished and in what he failed to
accomplish as a true index of what it was possible at the
beginning of the nineteenth century to do in the direction
of reviving Christianity on Protestant lines.

In proportion as we rightly understand him we are
bound, it seems to me, to think of him with feelings approaching veneration. He is a painful figure to contemplate, but the truer emblem of humanity for that—humanity with all its deep confusion of grandeur and
misery bared relentlessly to sight. He was a good man
of noble genius, yet helplessly irresolute. In his writing
and in his talk exactly as in his life he wandered vaguely,
caught in the net of his own images and words, unable
to beat himself clear. In belief as in action he went widely
astray in the world's labyrinth; yet never did he give
up, but always returned again and again to the attack
with a sort of bewildered yet undaunted courage. He saw
deeply, he felt intensely, he had a profound, immediate
assurance of certitude; and he is still able to move his
readers strangely, making them too feel on occasion his
own assurance that the truth is with him, making them
feel also that they are in contact with a high and serious
nature whose words they will take lightly at their own
peril. And we see in him, at the last, one who, amidst

powerful and determined opposition around him and even within him, did yet remain faithful to the highest experience of humankind, holding fast to the conviction that human life *is* significant, that it does have a spiritual meaning beyond and above the activity of the senses, and a meaning which the processes of the exact sciences cannot fathom.

III.

CARDINAL NEWMAN

BETWEEN Newman and Coleridge there are many resemblances, many contrasts. Strikingly alike in certain inborn qualities of temperament, they both dedicated themselves to the renewal of a living Christianity. And their efforts to establish the validity of Christian belief followed, up to a certain point, so much the same line that at least one contemporary in the spring of 1834 supposed that Newman was a disciple of Coleridge. In this he was wrong, as Newman never even read any of Coleridge's works until the spring of 1835, but he was then at once struck with the resemblance, and wrote: "I am surprised how much I thought mine, is to be found there." Accordingly when, in 1839, he was writing about the origins and progress of the Oxford Movement he credited Coleridge with a share in the preparation of the public mind for the reception of "Catholic truth."

It is consequently not surprising that Carlyle was as contemptuous of Newman as he was of Coleridge—Newman, he said, had not the intellect of a moderate-sized rabbit.[1] Yet it is a fact that those faults for which Carlyle castigated Coleridge, his mistiness or cloudiness, his unintelligibility, his vague purposelessness, his rambling expansiveness, Newman did not share with him. This contrast, indeed, is the first thing that strikes any reader who turns from the one to the other. No praise can be too high for Newman's unmatched style, for the noble,

[1] *Carlyle's Life in London*, J. A. Froude, II, 247.

severely controlled fire of his utterance, for his clarity, his definiteness, and his purposiveness. His primacy amongst English prose-writers of the nineteenth century is, of course, merely the outer mark of a deeper-lying difference between the two men, a difference ultimately of character. While Coleridge's high-mindedness and insight were perpetually and often vainly struggling against irreconcilable foes within him, Newman's character was straight and sound and resolute. It was more. He is now recognized as the greatest figure in English religious life of the nineteenth century not alone because he exerted a profound and abiding influence upon both the Anglican Church and the Catholic, but also because his character was at once manly and saintly, while it had as its ready instruments a rich imagination and a powerful intellect.

Newman was almost thirty years younger than Coleridge. He was born in 1801, the son of a London banker. Like Coleridge, he was apparently born with an unusual sense, or conviction, of immaterial reality. As a child he lived naïvely in a world of real or fancied spiritual influences. He says: "I used to wish the Arabian Tales were true; my imagination ran on unknown influences, on magical powers, and talismans. . . . I thought life might be a dream, or I an Angel, and all this world a deception, my fellow-angels by a playful device concealing themselves from me, and deceiving me with the semblance of a material world."[2] He was, as he says, a superstitious youngster. He used to cross himself on going into the dark. In later years he could not recollect how he had come by this practice, nor what meaning it had had for him; but it seems evident that, however it is to be accounted for, even at this early time he felt a connatural

---

[2] *Apologia pro Vita Sua*, Oxford ed., pp. 105-106. Succeeding quotations are from this volume unless another is mentioned in the text or in a note.

sympathy for certain religious symbols. And all his reminiscences of his childhood go together to testify that from his earliest days he lived in the consciousness of a world beyond the world of sensible experiences to which he felt himself linked by the most real chains.

On the other hand, it would be a mistake to think of him as escaping the influences which had made Coleridge for a time a materialist and necessitarian. As a youth he read Thomas Paine, Hume, Voltaire; and during his undergraduate days he carefully studied the works of Gibbon and of Locke. It has sometimes been said that Newman's career can be very simply explained in terms of his ignorance, but this is itself a hasty and ignorant verdict. On the contrary, he was thoroughly familiar with the development of English thought, with its consequences in relation to the problem of knowledge, and with the encouragement it gave to an exclusive worldliness and to merely practical and historical studies. The better one knows him the more remarkable seems his prescience of the course of nineteenth-century thought, his appreciation of the added force which naturalistic views were presently to acquire through the progress of science, and his realization that religion was on the point of suffering at least a temporary banishment from educated minds.

An illustration of this is his description of the agnostic man of science, written in the eighteen-fifties, before the term agnosticism had been invented: "He will begin, as many so far have done before him, by laying it down as if a position which approves itself to the reason, immediately that it is fairly examined—which is of so axiomatic a character as to have a claim to be treated as a first principle, and is firm and steady enough to bear a large superstructure upon it—that Religion is not the subject-matter of a science. 'You may have opinions in religion, you may have theories, you may have argu-

ments, you may have probabilities; you may have anything but demonstration, and therefore you cannot have
science. In mechanics you advance from sure premises to
sure conclusions; in optics you form your undeniable
facts into system, arrive at general principles, and then
again infallibly apply them: here you have Science. On
the other hand, there is at present no real science of the
weather, because you cannot get hold of facts and truths
on which it depends; there is no science of the coming
and going of epidemics; no science of the breaking out
and the cessation of wars; no science of popular likings
and dislikings, or of the fashions. It is not that these
subject-matters are themselves incapable of science, but
that, under existing circumstances, *we* are incapable of
subjecting them to it. . . . And, as it would be absurd
to dogmatize about the weather, and say that 1860 will
be a wet season or a dry season, a time of peace or war,
so it is absurd for men in our present state to teach anything positively about the next world, that there is a
heaven, or a hell, or a last judgement, or that the soul is
immortal, or that there is a God. . . . Well, then, if Religion is just one of those subjects about which we can
know nothing, what can be so absurd as to spend time
upon it? what so absurd as to quarrel with others about
it? Let us all keep to our own religious opinions respec-
tively, and be content; but so far from it, upon no subject
whatever has the intellect of man been fastened so intensely as upon Religion. And the misery is, that, if once
we allow it to engage our attention, we are in a circle
from which we never shall be able to extricate ourselves.
Our mistake reproduces and corroborates itself. A small
insect, a wasp or a fly, is unable to make his way through
the pane of glass; and his very failure is the occasion of
greater violence in his struggle than before. . . . Such
is the state in which the world has lain ever since the

introduction of Christianity. Christianity has been the
bane of true knowledge, for it has turned the intellect
away from what it can know, and occupied it in what it
cannot. . . . Truth has been sought in the wrong direction, and the attainable has been put aside for the visionary.' "[3]

The truth is that Newman did clearly perceive and
understand the forces which were opposed to religion in
the nineteenth century, and that his career and his writings, both as an Anglican and as a Catholic, can simply
not be comprehended except in the light of this fact. To
many, now as in the past, the fact is almost unbelievable,
and for many it is far easier to deny it than to digest its
consequences. It deeply bewildered Huxley, so far as he
grasped it, and caused him to write to Knowles, the
editor of the *Nineteenth Century:* "I have been reading
some of his works lately, and I understand now why
Kingsley accused him of growing dishonesty. After an
hour or two of him I began to lose sight of the distinction
between truth and falsehood." This, I need hardly observe, is a statement which may have a very different
meaning from that which its writer intended. And to
another correspondent Huxley wrote of Newman: "That
man is the slipperiest sophist I have ever met with.
Kingsley was entirely right about him."[4] By universal
consent since the publication of the *Apologia* Kingsley
was *not* right about Newman, and Huxley's words are a
tacit confession that the latter more nearly met him on
his own ground than any other Christian writer he had

[3] *Idea of a University,* Pt. II, pp. 387-389. For a much earlier illustration of Newman's sense of impending danger to religion see his letter to
his mother of 13 March, 1829, printed in *Letters and Correspondence* (edited
by A. Mozley), I, 204.

[4] *Life and Letters of T. H. Huxley,* by Leonard Huxley, II, 239. In an
article in the *Nineteenth Century* (June, 1889) Huxley stated that he could
easily compile a primer of infidelity from Newman's works.

encountered and, at least, gave him questions which he could not answer.

Newman fully understood, then, all the difficulties of his faith, yet he never gave up his early conviction of a world of immaterial reality in which we share and in which our earthly lives may be fulfilled. On the contrary, this conviction strengthened as he grew older, and it took on a definitely religious form when he was only in his sixteenth year. At that time he experienced what is known as 'conversion,' and from this event he dated his distinct religious convictions. The influences to which he was subjected were Calvinistic on the whole, and through them and through the reading of William Law's *Serious Call* he was led to range himself, as a young man, with the Evangelical party of the Anglican Church. Distinctively Calvinistic doctrines he held for no very long time, but he considered that his experiences and reading at fifteen and in several following years strengthened in him those childish imaginings already mentioned. They aided, he says, "in isolating me from the objects which surrounded me, in confirming me in my mistrust of the reality of material phenomena, and making me rest in the thought of two and two only supreme and luminously self-evident beings, myself and my Creator."

From this time Newman never wavered in his faith. The form of his belief and the manner of its expression— these were to change tremendously; but through all he held to his certainty of the spiritual nature and destiny of man, to his belief in a personal God, to his conviction that there had been a revelation committed to men and handed down from one generation to another. He wrote in a notebook in 1817: "The reality of conversion, as cutting at the root of doubt, providing a chain between God and the Soul, that is with every link complete; I

know I am right. How do you know it? I know I know.'"[5]
In this he remained always unshaken. Was it to prejudge
the whole matter? He was as anxious as any man to know
the truth at any cost to himself, and we shall see that he
was later much occupied with this question and did his
best to answer it faithfully.

The course of Newman's development is to a peculiar
extent bound up with certain outward facts of his life
which must now be briefly noticed. It is recorded that
even until the moment of his son's first journey to a university Newman's father remained undecided between
Oxford and Cambridge for the boy. The final decision,
however, was for Oxford, and Newman was entered there
in Trinity College. His career as an undergraduate was
not without distinction, though marred at the end by a
break-down which contributed to his failure in the
schools, so that he came out with a Second Class instead
of a First. Despite this handicap he was in 1822 elected
a Fellow of Oriel College, which set him on his feet, opening up what he supposed would be a lifelong career at
Oxford. In 1824 he took holy orders. In 1826 he became
one of the tutors of his college, and was beginning to be
known. About this time he also preached his first university sermon, and in 1827 he was one of the public exam-
iners for the B.A. degree. In 1828 he became Vicar of
St. Mary's Church at Oxford. Fellow of Oriel College
and Vicar of St. Mary's—that remained Newman's outward position for a number of years; until in fact the
close of the Oxford Movement when, in 1843, he resigned
St. Mary's and in 1845 resigned his Oriel fellowship and
entered the Roman Catholic Church.

These, then, were the momentous years of his life, the
years of his change from the Evangelical to the Catholic

[5] *Letters and Correspondence*, I, 25.

point of view, the years of that great ecclesiastical campaign known as the Oxford or the Tractarian Movement,
the years of that long struggle of the spirit which threw
Newman finally into the arms of the Church of Rome.
These were the years when Newman became a national
figure whose every movement was anxiously watched by
thousands, whose every word was subjected to the closest, and often the bitterest, criticism, and whose decisions
were believed almost to mark the fate of the English
Church.

In order to understand these years it is necessary in
the first place to realize that, though some aspects of
Oxford life were godless enough in the early nineteenth
century, still, Oxford was an active centre of Christianity. It was so to an extent not easy now to imagine. From
immemorial days religion had been a part of the atmosphere of the place, and one could scarcely breathe without taking it in. All members of the university were much
and constantly concerned with the outward observances
of religion; college dignitaries were almost universally
clergymen; and religious discussion was everywhere.
Much that passed for religion had little enough of reality
in it, but nevertheless the shell, so to say, of a community
formed in the interest of religion remained. For this is
one fact which accounts for the apparently overwhelming
place of religion in the university. It occupied that place
because of the inertia of human institutions. Oxford had
been since the mediæval age a vital part of the material
establishment of the visible church in England; many of
its colleges were in their origin, and in their still persisting rules, religious houses or memorials; they were the
training schools of the higher clergy; religious professions were necessary for entrance into them as well as
for university degrees; religious instruction stood promi-
nent in their courses of study; and religion was, as it

were, the one common professional topic and concern of all college officers.

Of course, since the Renaissance learning had been pursued less and less for the sake of religion, more and more for other ends if not for its own sake. But this change had not yet produced any corresponding alteration in the structure of the university or in its relation to the established church. Scholarship still had practically no recognition in its own right. Intellectual excellence was one recognized claim, indeed, to preferment within the church, but, of course, within the church, so that in the England of the early nineteenth century the clerical was still the distinctively learned class, really much as it had been in the mediæval age. Men who were in their primary interests logicians, metaphysicians, historians, classical or oriental scholars, men who in their primary interests were even mathematicians or scientists of one kind or another—all were gathered together under the shelter of the church.

This, as things were, operated together with the rationalistic development of Protestantism in the eighteenth century to make Christianity in the case of many individuals more a matter of form than a living reality. But, on the other hand, the form remained, visibly and pervasively present, for those who might at any time want to breathe fresh life into it. Moreover, the belief in a visible church, not as something added to religion nor as a mere means to its continuance, but as an integral part of religion itself, had continued with many Anglicans ever since the separation from Rome in the sixteenth century. There it stood, the continuing divine society instituted by the Apostles of Christ, embodying in its churches, in its creeds, and in its liturgy a tradition extending far behind the Protestant Reformation and seeming to form a visible connecting link between the believer of the present day and the miraculous revelation in the person of Jesus.

And this was the atmosphere into which Newman was plunged when yet a mere youth, and in which he remained for many years, until he was past middle age. His Oriel fellowship, in addition, made him one of a group where religious interests and discussion were particularly active, and it was at Oriel that he came into personal contact with most of those who were to be closely associated with him in the beginnings or the progress of the Oxford Movement, especially with Richard Hurrell Froude, a brother of the historian James Anthony Froude, and with John Keble, the author of *The Christian Year*. Both of these were conservative by temperament. Perhaps one of Newman's references to Keble may stand for the kind of influence which they exerted: "Keble was a man who guided himself and formed his judgements, not by processes of reason, by inquiry or by argument, but, to use the word in a broad sense, by authority. Conscience is an authority; the Bible is an authority; such is the Church; such is Antiquity; such are the words of the wise; such are hereditary lessons; such are ethical truths; such are historical memories; such are legal saws and state maxims; such are proverbs; such are sentiments, presages, and prepossessions. It seemed to me as if he ever felt happier, when he could speak or act under some such primary or external sanction; and could use argument mainly as a means of recommending or explaining what had claims on his reception prior to proof. . . . What he hated instinctively was heresy, insubordination, resistance to things established, claims of independence, disloyalty, innovation, a critical, censorious spirit."

Clearly the circumstances both of Newman's youth and of his manhood made it inevitable that with him the conviction of man's spiritual nature and destiny should take the form of whole-hearted adherence to Christianity. As has been seen, it did so before he went to Oxford, and through the remainder of his life Newman 'knew that he knew' the truth of Christianity, but all questions were not thereby disposed of once and for all. A new question, indeed, was immediately opened up—which of the existing forms of Christianity was the true one? But beyond this question there was also another, and one more fundamental. Newman laid claim to no miraculous inner light, to no occult power beyond the reach or the criticism of other human beings, and consequently he wished to give a rational account of the certitude he had reached, and he believed he could do so. His certitude did not render him insensible of the intellectual difficulties of Christian faith, nor did it close his mind to questions concerning historical evidence, and he honestly attacked both of these problems.

As regards the former he says in the *Apologia:* "I am far of course from denying that every article of the Christian Creed, whether as held by Catholics or by Protestants, is beset with intellectual difficulties; and it is simple fact that, for myself, I cannot answer those difficulties. Many persons are very sensitive of the difficulties of religion; I am as sensitive of them as any one; but I have never been able to see a connexion between apprehending those difficulties, however keenly, and multiplying them to any extent, and on the other hand doubting the doctrines to which they are attached. Ten thousand difficulties do not make one doubt, as I understand the subject; difficulty and doubt are incommensurate. There of course may be difficulties in the evidence; but I am speaking of difficulties intrinsic to the doctrines themselves, or to their compatibility with each other. A man may be annoyed that he cannot work out a mathematical problem, of which the answer is or is not given to him, without doubting that it admits of an answer, or that a certain particular answer is the true one. Of all points of faith, the being of a God is, to my own apprehension, encompassed with most difficulty, and yet borne in upon our minds with most power.''

He goes on to speak of what most would regard as a crucial instance: ''People say that the doctrine of Transubstantiation is difficult to believe; I did not believe the doctrine till I was a Catholic. I had no difficulty in believing it, as soon as I believed that the Catholic Roman Church was the oracle of God, and that she had declared this doctrine to be part of the original revelation. It is difficult, impossible, to imagine, I grant;—but how is it difficult to believe? . . . For myself, I cannot indeed prove it, I cannot tell *how* it is; but I say, 'Why should not it be? What's to hinder it? What do I know of substance or matter? Just as much as the greatest philosophers, and that is nothing at all';—so much is this the case, that there is a rising school of philosophy now, which considers phenomena to constitute the whole of our knowledge in physics. The Catholic doctrine leaves phenomena alone. It does not say that the phenomena go; on the contrary, it says that they remain: nor does it say that the same phenomena are in several places at once. It deals with what no one on earth knows anything about, the material substances themselves.''

This, of course, is perfectly true, and it brings out the crux of the problem. Religion deals with matters beyond the range of verifiable experience, and so necessarily makes pronouncements which are mysterious to the human intellect. What is to hinder belief, however, if one is satisfied that the doctrine promulgated, mysterious though it be, does have a divine origin? On the contrary, belief then becomes not only a possibility, but a fundamental moral duty.

Here is the real question—how is one to reach certainty of the being of a God? Newman did not endeavour to revive any of the so-called proofs of God's existence which had been examined and discredited by Kant. On the contrary, he tacitly recognized that a formal demonstration is impossible; yet he nevertheless considered that a valid certitude is attainable. It could be attained, he thought, on grounds of probability. He saw an accumulation of probabilities pointing towards the existence of God which so far outweighed the probabilities pointing in the opposite direction as to afford an adequate ground for the certitude which, as a matter of experience, some men actually feel. It was possible, he knew, for the doctrine of probability to lead to the attitude embodied in the famous saying, "O God, if there be a God, save my soul, if I have a soul!" But the study of Bishop Butler's *Analogy* and *Sermons,* which taught him the argument from probability, taught him also to base it primarily on the conscience. "If I am asked," he said, "why I believe in a God, I answer that it is because I believe in myself, for I feel it impossible to believe in my own existence (and of that I am quite sure) without believing also in the existence of Him, who lives as a Personal, All-seeing, All-judging Being in my conscience."[6] The conscience he regarded as the voice of God speaking to the individual as an ultimate authority which he will disobey at his peril, behind which he cannot go. This was his basic principle, and the only one he required for his purpose. The proposition he took to be self-evident to all those who actually listen to the voice of conscience and who, by

[6] For a fuller treatment see *Grammar of Assent,* especially pp. 101-121.

unquestioning obedience, make its commands living and
central realities in their lives. ''The religious mind,'' he
wrote to Wilfrid Ward, ''sees much which is invisible to
the irreligious mind. They have not the same evidence
before them.'' And to another correspondent he wrote
of the *Grammar of Assent:* ''My book is to show that
a right moral state of mind germinates or even generates
good intellectual principles.''[7]

The argument is from the data of experience, and Newman's contention was that there is a sufficient empirical
basis to justify our feeling the same certainty of God's
existence that we feel concerning the uniformity of nature. The data of conscience are given to us, arbitrarily
if we like, but in exactly the same way as the data of the
senses, and no more arbitrarily in the one case than in the
other. There is even in both cases a dependence on the
will for the reception of the data, though there is a difference in degree. One may easily close one's ears to the
voice of conscience—not so easily to the roar of a tiger.
And yet, as Newman truly says, ''None are so deaf as
those who won't hear.''[8] Moreover, in both cases the data
given us fall short of logical demonstration—they suggest but do not formally prove the conclusions we draw.
But the grounds of probability from which we draw our
generalizations in the sphere of sensible phenomena are
so strong that we should be fools to doubt those generalizations, and in fact we do feel about them a certitude
which is none the less genuine for the recognition that in
some ways they must fall short of the reality they represent. We realize that our experience is conditioned by
our senses and limited in extent, and hence we say, 'This
or something like this is true,' or we say, 'This is the

[7] *Life of Newman,* by Wilfrid Ward, II, 247, 270.

[8] Letter to Henry Wilberforce, Ward's *Life of Newman,* II, 249. The
whole letter should be read.

human expression of a reality which in its own nature or in an absolute sense we cannot know.' But that a man should refuse to have faith in or believe in the uniformity of nature, and should refuse to act on it, we would regard as a wanton neglect of his duty to himself and to those dependent on him. Newman considered the case to be the same in the sphere of religion, with these differences: that the commands of conscience are not forced on us as are sensible experiences, and that, since conscience speaks to us as one person to another, it is a wanton neglect of our duty to God as well as to ourselves to refuse to believe in the existence of Him who thus speaks.

"We need a *Novum Organum* in theology," he wrote in one of his letters,[9] and it was to provide this or, at least, suggestions towards it that much of his work was done. About this initial question of God's existence he so clearly summarized his position in another letter that parts of it must be quoted. He asked his correspondent "whether our nature does not tell us that there is something which has more intimate relations with the question of religion than intellectual exercises have"—that is, the conscience. And he continued: "We have the idea of duty —duty suggests something or some one to which it is to be referred, to which we are responsible. That something that has dues upon us is to us God. I will not assume it is a personal God, or that it is more than a law (though of course I hold that it is the Living Seeing God), but still the idea of duty, and the terrible anguish of conscience, and the irrepressible distress and confusion of face which the transgression of what we believe to be our duty, causes us, all this is an intimation, a clear evidence, that there is something nearer to religion than

9 Ward's *Life*, I, 436.

intellect; and that, if there is a way of finding religious truth, it lies, not in exercises of the intellect, but close on the side of duty, of conscience, in the observance of the moral law. . . . You must not suppose that I am denying the intellect its real place in the discovery of truth—but it must ever be borne in mind that its exercise mainly consists in reasoning—that is, in comparing things, classifying them, and inferring. It ever needs points to start from, first principles, and these it does not provide—but it can no more move one step without these starting points, than a stick, which supports a man, can move without the man's action. In physical matters, it is the senses which give us the first start—and what the senses give is physical fact—and physical facts do not lie on the surface of things, but are gained with pains and by genius, through experiment. Thus Newton, or Davy, or Franklin ascertained those physical facts which have made their names famous. After these primary facts are gained, intellect can act; it acts too of course in gaining them; but they must be gained; it is the senses which *enable* the intellect to act, by giving it something to act upon. In like manner we have to ascertain the starting points for arriving at religious truth. The intellect will be useful in gaining them and after gaining them—but to attempt to *see* them by means of the intellect is like attempting by the intellect to see the physical facts which are the basis of physical exercises of the intellect, a method of proceeding which was the very mistake of the Aristotelians of the middle age, who, instead of what Bacon calls 'interrogating nature' for facts, reasoned out everything by syllogisms. To gain religious starting points, we must in a parallel way, interrogate our hearts, and (since it is a personal individual matter) our *own* hearts—interrogate our consciences, interrogate, I will say, the God who dwells there.''[10]

In this way Newman reached certitude concerning the being of a God, but he had further to deal with the question whether any doctrines promulgated in His name actually came from Him. ''Starting then with the being of a God,'' he wrote in the *Apologia,* ''I look out of myself into the world of men, and there I see a sight which fills me with unspeakable distress. The world seems simply to give the lie to that great truth, of which my whole being is so full; and the effect upon me is, in consequence, as a matter of necessity, as confusing as if it denied that I am in existence myself. If I looked into a mirror, and did not see my face, I should have the sort of feeling which actually comes upon me, when I look into this living busy world, and see no reflexion of its Creator. . . . To consider the world in its length and breadth, its various history, the many races of man, their starts, their fortunes, their mutual alienation, their conflicts; and then their ways, habits, governments, forms of worship; their enterprises, their aimless courses, their random achievements and acquirements, the impotent conclusion of long-standing facts, the tokens so faint and broken of a superintending design, the blind evolution of what turn out to be great powers or truths, the progress of things, as if from unreasoning elements, not towards final causes, the greatness and littleness of man, his far-reaching aims, his short duration, the curtain hung over his futurity, the disappointments of life, the defeat of good, the success of evil, physical pain, mental anguish, the prevalence and intensity of sin, the prevailing idolatries, the corruptions, the dreary hopeless irreligion, that condition of the whole race, so fearfully yet exactly de-

[10] Ward's *Life,* II, 330-331.

scribed in the Apostle's words, 'having no hope and without God in the world,'—all this is a vision to dizzy and appal; and inflicts upon the mind the sense of a profound mystery, which is absolutely beyond human solution.''

We can only say in the face of ''this heart-piercing, reason-bewildering fact,'' that either there is no God or we are at present cast off from Him. ''*If* there be a God, *since* there is a God, the human race is implicated in some terrible aboriginal calamity. It is out of joint with the purposes of its Creator. This is a fact, a fact as true as the fact of its existence; and thus the doctrine of what is theologically called original sin becomes to me almost as certain as that the world exists, and as the existence of God. And now, supposing it were the blessed and loving will of the Creator to interfere in this anarchical condition of things, what are we to suppose would be the methods which might be necessarily or naturally involved in His object of mercy? Since the world is in so abnormal a state, surely it would be no surprise to me, if the interposition were of necessity equally extraordinary—or what is called miraculous.''

He goes on to remind us that, not right reason, but reason as it acts ''in fact and concretely in fallen man,'' has ever had a tendency ''towards a simple unbelief in matters of religion.'' It was so in the ancient world, it is so in the modern world, and Protestantism has shown itself incapable of combating the tendency. Protestants had in the beginning been forced into rationalism against their will, because there is in fact no half-way house between rationalism and the principle of authority. This, however, they did not realize, nor did they foresee the consequences of an untrammelled rationalism. Protestant doctrine was of necessity an assertion of private judgement, and this basis of individual self-reliance, though it could be obscured, could not be escaped. The doctrine of justification by faith made the religious starting-point subjective, and "in proportion as the Lutheran leaven spread, it became fashionable to say that Faith was, not an acceptance of revealed doctrine, not an act of the intellect, but a feeling, an emotion, an affection, an appetency; and, as this view of Faith obtained, so was the connexion of Faith with Truth and Knowledge more and more either forgotten or denied." So-called spirituality of heart and the virtue of faith came to be regarded as identical, and religion was considered to be based, not on argument, but on taste and sentiment, and everything in doctrine was subjective. Men came to think "that Religion, as such, consisted in something short of intellectual exercises, *viz.*, in the affections, in the imagination, in inward persuasions and consolations, in pleasurable sensations, sudden changes, and sublime fancies. They learned to believe and to take it for granted, that Religion was nothing beyond a *supply* of the wants of human nature, not an external fact and a work of God. . . . Thus Religion was useful, venerable, beautiful, the sanction of order, the stay of government, the curb of self-will and self-indulgence, which the laws cannot reach: but, after all, on what was it based? Why, that was a question delicate to ask, and imprudent to answer; but, if the truth must be spoken, however reluctantly, the long and the short of the matter was this, that Religion was based on custom, on prejudice, on law, on education, on habit, on loyalty, on feudalism, on enlightened expedience, on many, many things, but not at all on reason; reason was neither its warrant, nor its instrument, and science had as little connexion with it as with the fashions of the season, or the state of the weather."[11]

[11] *Idea of a University*, pp. 28-29.

Thus Protestantism degenerated into a subjective sentimentalism, into a form of irrational self-indulgence; it could not properly claim an objective validity; it was kept in existence by the state and by considerations of social expediency, but it had no strength of its own and no inner principle of coherence. It could not restrain human nature or correct the free march of mind. Indeed, the principle of private judgement encouraged the free march of mind and, by a parallel development with sentimental pietism, so encouraged what Newman called Liberalism or Latitudinarianism. "By Liberalism," he said, "I mean false liberty of thought, or the exercise of thought upon matters, in which, from the constitution of the human mind, thought cannot be brought to any successful issue, and therefore is out of place. Among such matters are first principles of whatever kind; and of these the most sacred and momentous are especially to be reckoned the truths of Revelation. Liberalism then is the mistake of subjecting to human judgement those revealed doctrines which are in their nature beyond and independent of it, and of claiming to determine on intrinsic grounds the truth and value of propositions which rest for their reception simply on the external authority of the Divine Word."

So it was that Protestantism gave birth to developments which the earliest reformers would have been the first to denounce, and not only proved itself unable to make a stand against the "deep, plausible scepticism" of the natural man but actually encouraged it. And if experience has conclusively shown that Protestantism has been a pathway to atheism, it has also shown that the Bible taken by itself is not a sufficient "means of maintaining religious truth in this anarchical world." Though the Bible be divine, its contents had in the first place to

They are but me

be determined by an authority outside of itself, by a
council of the one Catholic Church. And, after it was thus
constituted, it never answered a purpose for which it
was never intended. "It may be accidentally the means
of the conversion of individuals; but a book, after all,
cannot make a stand against the wild living intellect of
man, and in this day it begins to testify, as regards its
own structure and contents, to the power of that universal solvent, which is so successfully acting upon religious
establishments."

What we need is a "concrete representative of things
invisible" which has "the force and the toughness necessary to be a breakwater" against the "deep, plausible
scepticism" of the natural man. Protestantism, natural
religion, the Bible by itself—none of these, history itself
conclusively shows, will suffice. "Supposing then," Newman says, "it to be the will of the Creator to interfere
in human affairs, and to make provisions for retaining in
the world a knowledge of Himself, so definite and distinct
as to be proof against the energy of human scepticism,
in such a case—I am far from saying that there was no
other way—but there is nothing to surprise the mind, if
He should think fit to introduce a power into the world,
invested with the prerogative of infallibility in religious
matters. Such a provision would be a direct, immediate,
active, and prompt means of withstanding the difficulty;
it would be an instrument suited to the need; and, when
I find that this is the very claim of the Catholic Church,
not only do I feel no difficulty in admitting the idea, but
there is a fitness in it which recommends it to my mind."

The certainty of God's existence, then, and the certainty that for some reason the human race is cast off
from His presence created in Newman's mind a strong
antecedent probability in favour of a miraculous revela-

tion and of an infallible church placed in the world to guard through the generations the *depositum fidei*. He gave his unconditional assent to the Christian revelation because, *some* revelation being strongly probable, there were also other probabilities indicating that the Christian revelation alone, amongst many making the same claim, came from God. Christianity is the only one of the world's religions which strikes the mind as the inevitable, perfect fulfilment of the anticipations raised by natural religion. Moreover, the history of the Hebrew nation and of the Mosaic religion present to us a foreshadowing of Christianity which so clearly shows the hand of divine providence as to constitute powerful evidence in favour of Christianity. And likewise the early history of the Christian religion exhibits features which are utterly inexplicable unless the religion did have in fact the divine origin which it claimed to have.[12]

Similarly Newman concluded that the Roman Catholic Church rightly claimed to be the infallible guardian of the revealed word of God. There is an overwhelming probability that, since a revelation did take place, means were provided to maintain it perpetually in its purity. The one Catholic and Apostolic Church was, indeed, constituted to this end. Had it been broken into pieces with the passage of centuries, or, if it still existed, where was it to be found? The Anglican communion could claim Apostolic succession, but other notes of the true church it lacked. The Roman Church, however, had consistently and continuously asserted itself to be the one infallible custodian of the *depositum fidei*. The foundation of that

[12] These grounds for the acceptance of the Christian revelation are treated at length in the *Grammar of Assent*, Chap. X, Pt. 2. In connexion with the last-mentioned, Newman examines Gibbon's five causes for the early spread and success of Christianity (see above, p. 26 *et seq.*) and condemns them as inadequate.

claim was a revelation for which there was such evidence as to make it a duty to believe it *ex animo;*—was it not equally a duty to believe the Roman Church the one true Christian communion? Separation from Rome in the sixteenth century could be justified only on the ground that Rome had become so corrupt as to be the incarnation of Antichrist, and that those who separated composed the one Catholic and Apostolic Church restored to its ancient purity. But the Anglican communion was the only one which could take this ground, and it was local and national; it could not claim catholicity.

For some years Newman thought that the Anglican Church could successfully stand on the Apostolic succession and on Roman corruption, but in the end the study of church history made him see that this position was untenable. The study of the Monophysite controversy in the fifth century brought before him a picture which unmistakably reproduced the Anglican conflict with Rome in the sixteenth. But the Church had solemnly judged the Monophysites to be heretics and the judgement had been accepted as final and absolute, *i.e.*, as infallible. "It was difficult to make out how the Eutychians or Monophysites were heretics, unless Protestants and Anglicans were heretics also; difficult to find arguments against the Tridentine Fathers, which did not tell against the Fathers of Chalcedon; difficult to condemn the Popes of the sixteenth century, without condemning the Popes of the fifth. The drama of religion, and the combat of truth and error, were ever one and the same. The principles and proceedings of the Church now, were those of the Church then; the principles and proceedings of heretics then, were those of Protestants now. I found it so—almost fearfully; there was an awful similitude, more awful, because so silent and unimpassioned, between the dead records of the past and the feverish chronicle of the present. The shadow of the fifth century was on the sixteenth. It was like a spirit rising from the troubled waters of the old world, with the shape and lineaments of the new. The Church then, as now, might be called peremptory and stern, resolute, overbearing, and relentless; and heretics were shifting, changeable, reserved, and deceitful, ever courting civil power, and never agreeing together, except by its aid; and the civil power was ever aiming at comprehensions, trying to put the invisible out of view, and substituting expediency for faith.''

It was shortly after he had made this discovery that a friend pointed out to him the words of St. Augustine written against the Donatists, *Securus judicat orbis terrarum.* The case of the Donatists was not parallel with that of the Anglicans but, nevertheless, Augustine's words did apply as well to the Monophysites as to the Donatists, and did define the position the Church had taken equally against them, against the Arians, and against the Anglicans. The words rang in Newman's ears. He had seen a ghost. ''Who can account for the impressions which are made on him? For a mere sentence, the words of St. Augustine struck me with a power which I never had felt from any words before. . . . They were like the *Tolle, lege—Tolle, lege,* of the child, which converted St. Augustine himself.'' The thought had distinctly crossed his mind, ''The Church of Rome will be found right after all.'' Nor could he ever afterwards get away from that, though at times he thought he might and though he resolved to be guided, not by his imagination, but by his reason and to do nothing hastily.

Moreover, St. Augustine's words did not change the fact, clear and unescapable, that the Roman Church of the sixteenth century and the nineteenth differed vastly from the Catholic Church of the first Christian centuries. What did the difference mean? Was it a proof of the corruption and decay of the Roman communion, or was it, on the contrary, simply the measure of the necessary, logical development of the living Church, comparable to the development of a living organism? Newman set himself to study this question. He proceeded to distinguish seven tests of legitimate development, or notes of the true Church, by the application of which he sought to determine the significance of the changes within the Roman Church brought about during the passage of the Christian centuries. First, a true development preserves, while a corruption destroys, the central idea or typical character of a religion. Second is the continuity of principles. Doctrines vary in appearance with the minds receiving them, but in a genuine development one can always discern a continuity of principle underneath their different expressions and their successive expansions. Thirdly, life means growth, and so the power of assimilation, the power of a doctrine to gather up truth from the outer world and incorporate it within itself, is another test of a faithful development. Logical sequence is a fourth test. Ideas grow silently and spontaneously, without conscious system, but, when they form part of a true development, subsequent analysis shows them to have a logical character and connexion. Fifthly, in a real development one can discover in its earlier stages anticipations of its future. Instances, though perhaps vague and isolated, of what is later to be elaborated, may occur from the first, while only after the passage of time are they brought to perfection. Sixthly, a true development is conservative of the course of earlier developments. It illustrates and corroborates, instead of obscuring and contradicting, the body of thought from which it pro-

ceeds. And permanence, or chronic vigour, is a seventh
test of a faithful development. Heresy is an unstable
compound of truth and falsehood and consequently, being
divided against itself, it soon dies or disappears, while
doctrine having within it a genuine vitality lives on un-
impaired.

Newman applied these tests to the Roman Church in
his *Essay on the Development of Christian Doctrine.* Life
as we know it is a process of constant change. It is so
with institutions as it is with organisms. Christianity he
had come to see as an incarnation of the spiritual world
accommodated to earthly conditions. Circumstances were
always altering themselves, and with them the expression
of doctrine. But in a living church, carrying through the
generations a revelation made once and for all, successive changes of circumstance would but give constantly
fresh opportunities for the appearance of new aspects
of the transcendent truth which is in its reality one and
eternal. And a communion which attempted not to change
at all, or which attempted chimerically, with antiquarian
zeal, to return to Apostolic conditions, or which admitted
development up to a certain period in history and then
attempted arbitrarily to arrest it as did the Anglican—
such communions had lost the principle of life. "In a
higher world it is otherwise, but here below to live is to
change and to be perfect is to have changed often." The
application of the seven tests to the Church of Rome
showed, as far as they went, that through all changes
Rome had maintained continuously her distinctive character. With "gravity, distinctness, precision, and ma-
jesty" she had advanced through the ages in a true
development, so that she remained always the same in
her still continuing growth towards the full and perfect
expression of the Christian faith.

So it was that he reached the end of his long pilgrimage of the spirit in the full conviction that the Roman was the one infallible Church of God upon earth. Yet this conviction by itself would perhaps never have caused him to leave the Anglican for the Roman communion. He felt an indescribably deep love for Oxford and for the English Church. He had consecrated his life wholeheartedly to their service, nor was he one to forget his solemn responsibility as an Anglican priest. He was bound in his position, too, by personal ties whose severance was a cruel pain. It is difficult to grasp, and impossible to relate, the anguish he certainly felt as he contemplated this final step. Moreover, the course of the Oxford Movement itself gave him a powerful reason for remaining an Anglican, though, on the other hand, it was also a development of the Oxford Movement which finally turned him out of the English Church and so brought him to consider it his duty to himself to go over to Rome.

The story of the Oxford Movement has often been told, and I shall say of it only what is needful to explain Newman's final conversion. I have already indicated the circumstances, inner and outer, which made Newman as a young man a sincere, unconditional believer in dogmatic Christianity. And two men have been mentioned, Keble and R. H. Froude, who were largely instrumental in bringing Newman to the Catholic view of Christianity. It has been said, probably with much truth, that the publication of Keble's *Christian Year* was the real beginning of the Oxford Movement. In those poems Keble quietly and serenely assumed that the English Church was 'catholic and reformed.' He was not polemical; but he presented Anglican doctrine as a consistent whole which had existed as such from the beginning of Christianity. Religion was to be accepted on authority; it had come down by Apostolic succession; the presence of our Lord was renewed in the sacraments; those in communion with Him composed one Holy Catholic Church;—such propositions as these Keble tacitly opposed to the Protestant and rationalistic doctrines then current, and he made them seem the natural or even inevitable counterparts of his own sincere piety and high otherworldliness. The effect of the book was deep and widespread, and showed that there was a large public ready for a strong re-assertion of 'Catholic truth.'

It exhibits, moreover, in concrete form the kind of influence which was exerted on Newman by several of his friends, and which he was ready to receive. By the late 1820's he saw Christianity in grave danger from forces which, so far as he understood them, he could neither approve nor respect. Private judgement and rationalism he estimated from their fruits—a suicidal anarchy in religion, in morals, and in social affairs. The horrors and excesses of the French Revolution were still too close to be forgotten—its spirit of hot-headed violence, its repudiation of divine authority in the name of reason, which suddenly and fearfully released all that is malign in human nature and gave the lie to all plausible talk about man's natural goodness. He saw, in short, only destruction and the release of evil resulting from the use of reason as it acts "in fact and concretely in fallen man." He saw some philosophers denying man's power to know reality as it is in itself, and others straightway assuming that there is nothing to know save phenomenal appearances, and proceeding to erect a new philosophy, purporting to be based on the solid foundation of experience, in which human nature was submerged in mechanism and the senses. This was a denial of human nature as he knew it existing in himself, and he not unnaturally concluded that men were still pursuing, as of old, a vain wisdom and a false philosophy. Liberalism and rationalism were of the devil, whatever seemingly good things they offered to catch the unwary, and he would neither accept them nor compromise with them. The spirit of worldliness had always shown itself, under the mask of common sense, to be the spirit of madness and base folly. Given time, it would do so again; meanwhile, whatever came of it, he would not be taken in with the common run of men.

His resultant temper can be seen in a number of the poems which he composed for the *Lyra Apostolica*. England he called the 'Tyre of the West' and bade her shun the pride of earthly power—

> Dread thine own power! Since haughty Babel's prime,
>   High towers have been man's crime.
> Since her hoar age, when the huge moat lay bare,
>   Strongholds have been man's snare.

When he sought to utter the truth that burned within him,

> A hundred reasoners cried—"Hast thou to learn
>   Those dreams are scattered now, those fires are spent?" . . .
> Perplexed, I hoped my heart was pure of guile,
>   But judged me weak in wit, to disagree;
> But now, I see that men are mad awhile,
>   And joy the Age to come will think with me:—
> 'Tis the old history—Truth without a home,
> Despised and slain, then rising from the tomb.

To the rationalizers in religion he said:

> Ye cannot halve the Gospel of God's grace;
>   Men of presumptuous heart! I know you well.
>   Ye are of those who plan that we should dwell,
> Each in his tranquil home and holy place;
> Seeing the Word refines all natures rude,
> And tames the stirrings of the multitude.

And ye have caught some echoes of its lore,
  As heralded amid the joyous choirs;
  Ye marked it spoke of peace, chastised desires,
Good-will and mercy—and ye heard no more;
But, as for zeal and quick-eyed sanctity,
And the dread depths of grace, ye passed them by.

And so ye halve the Truth; for ye in heart,
  At best, are doubters whether it be true,
  The theme discarding, as unmeet for you,
Statesmen or Sages. O new-encompassed art
Of the ancient Foe!—but what, if it extends
O'er our own camp, and rules amid our friends?

When these lines were written he had taken his stand,
and knew that he had a work to do. Already he was asking himself about the possibility of re-uniting the Anglican and Roman Churches, though he did not think it could
be hoped for. "Oh that Rome were not Rome," he wrote
to his sister in 1833, "but I seem to see as clear as day
that a union with her is *impossible*. She is the cruel
Church asking of us impossibilities, excommunicating us
for disobedience, and now watching and exulting over
our approaching overthrow.''[13] But, if Rome was cruel
and corrupt, it followed that the Church of England was
the one Catholic and Apostolic Church; and it was his
duty to try to purge it of its taint of Protestantism and
rationalism. He expected to be called a Papist when his
aims became known, but he was confident of his rightness
and did not fear opposition.[14]
England at this time was beginning to recover from
the fright administered by the French Revolution and
the Napoleonic wars, and the spirit of liberalism was beginning more or less cautiously to show itself in politics

[13] *Letters and Correspondence*, I, 385.
[14] *Ibid.*, I, 490.

as well as in religion. Long-agitated demands for governmental reform at length forced the passage of the so-called Great Reform Bill in 1832. In the following year the forces of liberalism succeeded in abolishing certain bishoprics of the Established Church in Ireland. Their abolition was really no more than a recognition of the fact that for the most part the Established Church in Ireland was only an empty shell. At the same time this step saved a considerable amount of money. It was, however, opposed by the Church, and was finally passed against the suffrage of the bishops of England and Ireland. Thus it became an overt assertion of that secular sovereignty which in theory the British government had been able to claim since the sixteenth century, but which in practice it had not frequently asserted. Churchmen who took the high ground of a divine authority vested in them through Apostolical succession directly by our Lord could scarcely stand quiet under so direct an affront. The government's action taken by itself might be unimportant, but the principle it illustrated was fundamental, for it exhibited the English Church under the absolute control of a political party which did not hesitate to 'rob' and affront the Church for its own ends. The act showed the liberalism of England to be one in spirit with the liberalism of the Continent, and opened it to the charge of being anti-clerical in its sympathies and intentions. From a small beginning to what lengths might it not go? The Irish bill probably aroused stronger feeling in Oxford than anywhere else, and on 14th July, 1833, Keble preached in St. Mary's Church a sermon against it, in which he termed its passage an act of national apostasy.

The political situation gave Newman and his friends a concrete, unmistakable case against liberalism. It gave Newman, young, comparatively unknown, and without influence though he was, a definite opportunity to undertake the large task which he had conceived to be his duty. He regarded Keble's sermon as the actual beginning of a concerted movement towards the renewing and strengthening of the Apostolic Church in England, and he immediately took steps to follow it up effectively. An informal organization was created, the publication of the *Tracts for the Times* was begun, and other measures were undertaken incident to a thorough campaign. Newman was the real centre and soul of the movement, though for a time one of his friends, E. B. Pusey, was popularly regarded as its avowed leader. When Pusey joined the movement he at once gave it, Newman said, a position and a name;—"he had a vast influence in consequence of his deep religious seriousness, the munificence of his charities, his Professorship, his family connexions, and his easy relations with University authorities." In addition, Pusey was the only contributor to the *Tracts* who published his contributions over his own initials. Thus Puseyism came to be the colloquial term of the day for tractarian doctrine, while Archbishop Whately's remark that a Newmania had appeared in Oxford, which showed a truer appreciation of the facts, never gained a wide currency.

The tractarian position was that the English Church properly occupied, or should occupy, a middle ground between the two extremes of Popery and Protestantism —it was Catholic and Reformed. Great efforts were made to work out this position and to give it a solid foundation, for which recourse was had both to the early fathers of the Church and to many Anglican divines of the seventeenth century. How Newman's historical studies finally convinced him that this position was untenable and that the Anglican Church was in schism I have already told. But, as I have said, this crushing discovery did not at once carry him to Rome. For better or worse he was *in* the English Church and there his duty lay, to do what good he could. He continued to feel grave difficulties in some points of Roman doctrine and grave objections to certain devotional practices which, if they were not commanded, were tolerated or even encouraged by the Roman Church. And he continued to feel that as long as the acceptance of 'Catholic truth' was not expressly condemned by Anglican bishops he could not only remain safely within the English communion, but should do so in the hope of purging his own Church of its errors. He desired a reunion with Rome, but one to be effected under conditions, not by individuals, but by Church with Church.

It is perhaps the very simplicity of his position which in his own day and since has caused it to be misunderstood. He could not conceive that a sincere Christian would not whole-heartedly desire an united church. Reunion with Rome might be as vain a hope in 1841 as he had considered it in 1833, yet to hope for it and work for it was the one right thing he saw. It might not come in his day, yet come it could if ever Rome should give up its idolatry and England should give up its Protestantism. It was not his business to preach to Rome, nor to conduct diplomatic negotiations looking towards any such hollow reunion as would alone be possible save on the basis of a general, sincere desire and conviction on both sides. Romanists must cleanse themselves of their idolatry if they were ever to be cleansed, and on the same principle his business was with his own Church. "Our business is with ourselves," he wrote, "to make ourselves more holy, more self-denying, more primitive, more worthy of our high calling." He aimed to continue, then, in his effort to purge England of its Protestantism, trusting that, however distant the end he desired, he was doing his clear duty in trying to bring it nearer.

Meanwhile, however, despite strong and unremitting opposition, the tractarian movement had flourished, and its very success was now a source of embarrassment to Newman. He had gained a large following by the advocacy of Catholic doctrine, accompanied by what R. H. Froude called dreadful cursing and swearing against Rome. He could no longer continue to curse and swear against Rome, and was not this tacitly to invite the conclusion that if he were logical he would go over to that communion? He had long held, with Bishop Bull and other seventeenth-century divines, that nothing could justify the separation of the sixteenth century short of the contention that Rome was Antichrist, and that this was accordingly an essential article of Anglican theology.[15] Some of his followers began to be seriously uneasy, and they were, in addition, troubled about remaining longer in the Anglican communion when the Thirty-Nine Articles contained, in the opinion of many, a condemnation of Catholic doctrine. Newman held that the Articles could be so interpreted as to show that they condemned the abuse, but not the use, of the essential doctrines of the Apostolic Church. He now considered it a matter of life and death to bring this out explicitly, as a final measure towards holding his unruly followers within their own Church. To this end he wrote *Tract Ninety,* the last of the *Tracts for the Times.*

It has been said that he was not prepared for the outbreak of hostile demonstrations and abuse called forth by the tract, though he afterwards wrote in the *Apologia* that he had recognized at the time that he was engaged in an *experimentum crucis.* "I have no doubt," he says, "that then I acknowledged to myself that it would be a trial of the Anglican Church which it had never under-

[15] Coleridge had held the same opinion (*On the Constitution of the Church and State,* 1830, pp. 157-158).

gone before—not that the Catholic sense of the Articles had not been held or at least suffered by their framers and promulgators, and was not implied in the teaching of Andrewes or Beveridge, but that it had never been publicly recognized, while the interpretation of the day was Protestant and exclusive.'' Those who were responsible for the Protestant and exclusive interpretation of the day at once proceeded to condemn Newman's tract, publicly, officially, and as thoroughly as they could. For some years they had been growing more and more alarmed at both the aims and the success of the tractarian leaders. They had cried out against the 'Popery' of the 'Oxford malignants,' as Thomas Arnold with Christian love and charity had dubbed them, but they had not seen their way to put the movement down. Now Newman himself had given them their chance, and they promptly attempted to make the most of it.

It is generally agreed that Newman's interpretation of the Articles was more adroit than just, that, in fact, he went against their obvious sense. But it is undeniable that the Articles are intentionally ambiguous and, in addition, Newman's real attitude and the difficulty he faced are not always remembered. He had concluded it to be his duty to remain in the English Church and to attempt to purge it of its taint of Protestantism; but, then, he was confronted with the danger that his aim would be discredited and defeated by individual secessions to Rome on the part of some of his followers, and he was forced to an open and premature test of Anglican toleration of Catholic doctrine in order to meet this danger. It might be—he himself admitted that it was— difficult to interpret the Articles as he attempted to interpret them; nevertheless the experiment had to be made whether or not the English Church was Catholic, for if it expressly denied his contention he could no longer in conscience remain within it or ask his followers so to do.

The test was decisive, *Tract Ninety* was unmistakably condemned, and the English Church deliberately resolved to continue in its traditional ambiguous position. In the spring of 1839 Newman had published an article in which he said that at any rate the tractarian agitation must have the good result of rousing men to think earnestly about their religion, so that, whether they came to true or false conclusions, at least the ideas of the coming age upon religion would be real, whereas "in the present day mistiness is the mother of wisdom. A man who can set down half-a-dozen general propositions, which escape from destroying one another only by being diluted into truisms, who can hold the balance between opposites so skilfully as to do without fulcrum or beam, who never enunciates a truth without guarding himself against being supposed to exclude the contradictory—who holds that Scripture is the only authority, yet that the Church is to be deferred to, that faith only justifies, yet that it does not justify without works, that grace does not depend on the sacraments, yet is not given without them, that bishops are a divine ordinance, yet those who have them not are in the same religious condition as those who have—this is your safe man and the hope of the Church; this is what the Church is said to want, not party men, but sensible, temperate, sober, well-judging persons, to guide it through the channel of no-meaning between the Scylla and Charybdis of Aye and No."

Without doubt the Oxford Movement had the effect Newman claimed for it upon hundreds, probably thousands, of individuals. Time also was to show that its effect upon the English Church was permanent and far-reaching, but for the moment the 'safe' men had a complete triumph, and the Church, in repudiating Newman,

forced him into his final repudiation of Anglicanism. He
was forced to see, as he says of Charles Reding in *Loss
and Gain,* "that the profession of faith contained in the
Articles was but a patchwork of bits of orthodoxy, Lu-
theranism, Calvinism, and Zuinglism; and this too on
no principle; that it was but the work of accident, if there
be such a thing as accident; that it had come down in the
particular shape in which the English Church now receives it, when it might have come down in any other
shape; that it was but a toss-up that Anglicans at this
day were not Calvinists, or Presbyterians, or Lutherans,
equally well as Episcopalians. This historical fact did
but clench the difficulty, or rather impossibility, of saying what the faith of the English Church was. On almost
every point of dispute the authoritative standard of doctrine was vague or inconsistent, and there was an imposing weight of external testimony in favour of opposite
interpretations."

This was what Anglicanism was, and Newman felt that
churchmen were determined to keep it so because, as it
stood, it was established and safe. It led to no unknown
risks but, on the contrary, conduced to a mild and very
pleasant worldliness. Reding says of Oxford in *Loss and
Gain,* that "there is a worldly air about everything, as
unlike as possible the spirit of the Gospel. I don't impute
to the dons ambition or avarice; but still, what Heads of
houses, Fellows, and all of them evidently put before
them as an end is, to enjoy the world in the first place,
and to serve God in the second. Not that they don't make
it their final object to get to Heaven; but their immediate
object is to be comfortable, to marry, to have a fair income, station, and respectability, a convenient house, a
pleasant country, a sociable neighbourhood. . . . The
notion of evangelical poverty, the danger of riches, the
giving up all for Christ—all those ideas which are first

principles in Scripture, as I read it, don't seem to enter into their idea of religion.''

The same character is made to say elsewhere in the book that English churchmen commonly did not even exercise the 'right and duty of private judgement.' They exhorted each other to seek the truth and bade each other to rely on private judgement, but all the while they pointed to a predetermined conclusion. They asserted that this had been 'providentially' reached, and so in effect sought to impose it by authority, though in words they disclaimed any such intention. ''Tell me,'' Reding asks, ''supposing that we ought all to seek the truth, do you think that members of the English Church do seek it in that way which Scripture enjoins upon all seekers? Think how very seriously Scripture speaks of the arduousness of finding, the labour of seeking, the duty of thirsting after the truth. I don't believe the bulk of the English clergy, the bulk of Oxford residents, Heads of houses, Fellows of Colleges (with all their good points, which I am not the man to deny), have ever sought the truth. They have taken what they found, and have used no private judgement at all. Or if they have judged, it has been in the vaguest, most cursory way possible; or they have looked into Scripture only to find proofs for what they were bound to subscribe, as undergraduates getting up the Articles. . . . No, they may talk of seeking the truth, of private judgement, as a duty, but they have never sought, they have never judged; they are where they are, not because it is true, but because they find themselves there, because it is their 'providential position,' and a pleasant one into the bargain.''

Loss and Gain is a work of fiction, but the passages quoted obviously represent Newman's opinion of the English Church at the time when he left it. And it is indeed difficult to see how any earnest and sincere Christian, who put his religion before all else in life, and who took the one Catholic and Apostolic Church to be something other than a mere empty form of words, could have come to any different conclusion. But there was another element of great weight which entered into the Anglican opposition to Newman, and which also entered at least to some extent into his final secession to Rome. R. H. Hutton, in commenting upon the pamphlet by Charles Kingsley which led Newman to write his *Apologia,* said that Kingsley permitted himself a perfect licence of insinuation against Newman 'so long as these insinuations were suggested by the vague sort of animal scent by which he chose to judge of other men's drift and meaning.'[16] The same gross instrument had long been used by Englishmen in the detection of Romanism and the same licence of insinuation in the denunciation of supposed signs of it. Despite his 'cursing and swearing against Rome,' Newman, from almost the beginning of the Oxford Movement, had been accused of Papistical tendencies. Later it was openly asserted that he was a secret emissary from the Pope, with a special licence to assume the disguise of an Anglican priest, with the object of making converts 'from the inside.' Such assertions were too wildly absurd to have any effect by themselves; but close friends also misunderstood him and increasingly made him feel himself a stranger in their midst. In the course of time this told on him. He came to feel that not only was *Tract Ninety* formally condemned by the Church but he was personally repudiated by its members. In 1842 he wrote, concerning a young friend whom he was at the time holding back from conversion to Rome: "If all the world agree in telling a man he has no business in our Church, he will at length begin to think he

16 Quoted in Ward's *Life of Newman*, II, 12.

has none. How easy it is to persuade a man of any thing, when numbers affirm it! so great is the force of imagination. Did every one who met you in the streets look hard at you, you would think you were somehow in fault. I do not know any thing so irritating, so unsettling, especially in the case of young persons, as, when they are going on calmly and unconsciously, obeying their Church and following its divines (I am speaking from facts), as suddenly to their surprise to be conjured not to make a leap, of which they have not a dream and from which they are far removed." A few months earlier he had written to R. W. Church, "I speak most sincerely when I say that there are things which I neither contemplate, nor wish to contemplate; but, when I am asked about them ten times, at length I begin to contemplate them."[17]

It was the English Church's decisive repudiation of "the ancient Catholic doctrine" which, Newman felt, forced him out of that communion and so absolved him from further public responsibilities. It was then, when he could act as a private individual, or rather, as he felt, he was forced so to act, that he could consider primarily his own soul's safety; and it was then that he did begin to contemplate going over to Rome. Of course, with the conclusions he had already reached, to contemplate that step for himself was to make it in effect only a question of time when he would move. And so it proved.

Many have wondered if Newman found at length in the Roman Church the peace he had looked for. I can see no reason to doubt it. He had not been seeking rest or learned leisure, or stimulating or cultured companionship, or popular reputation or high public position; nor had he expected to find human nature miraculously dif-

[17] In this connexion the note on pp. 340-341 of *Sermons Bearing on Subjects of the Day* should be read.

ferent amongst Catholics from what it was amongst Protestants. Wilfrid Ward's account of Newman's life within the Roman Church is a book full of pathos. Newman was misunderstood, calumniated, conspired against by his co-religionists; his ideas were met with opposition, his aims were frustrated, his pen all but silenced. Through many years he was so uniformly defeated that he almost concluded he had only to support a project in order to insure its failure. He could not remain blind to the fact that his enemies were often unscrupulous and did not hesitate to use underhand tactics against him, nor could he fail to see that he forfeited influential connexions by disdaining the arts of the flatterer and courtier. He found other men ready and anxious to use him for their purposes, but cold, suspicious, or hostile when he did not prove a docile instrument or when he announced purposes of his own. Yet, through all, one can detect no sign that Newman ever doubted the Roman Church to be the divine society invested with plenary authority in the days of the Apostles and infallibly proclaiming through the generations the religion of Christ. It was from this belief that he became a Roman Catholic, and in this belief he remained steadfast until his death, and so retained through all his troubled years the peace he had sought. It has to be remembered, of course, that to Newman throughout his life the invisible kingdom, the spiritual world, was almost literally the one real world and the end of all his aspirations and endeavours, and that the peace he sought was the certainty that he was doing all that could lie with a human being to make the invisible kingdom eternally his own. And if it was, as it seems to me and as I have tried to show, inevitable that his eager and intense spirituality should have taken the mould of historic Christianity, I do not see how he could have done otherwise than seek the one Catholic Church.

Nor is it at all likely that such faith as his would have been undermined by the crosses and disappointments he had to bear during his life as a Roman Catholic, and indeed he has himself sufficiently answered this question in certain passages of *Loss and Gain,* in his *Apologia,* and in a number of the letters printed by Wilfrid Ward.

Whether or not he was in the right of it is a different question, but one to which there can be no simple answer. No more convincing testimony could be desired than that in Ward's *Life of Newman* to show that the Roman Church is no divine, infallible authority, but a merely human institution. To most this is no longer an open question but, if it were, the testimony in this book should be conclusive. I need hardly draw out the notes of worldliness, of a low ethical level, of blindness to fact, of superstition, of pride, and the like which are sounded in this unadorned and candid narrative of Newman's years of conflict with Roman ecclesiasticism, because, as I say, to most the question is already a closed one. But, though closed, it is not disposed of. The Roman Church not only has shown, but continues to show, a stubborn vitality which cannot be cavalierly disregarded. Though not equally nor at all times, nevertheless on the whole it does have, besides those other and contradictory ones just mentioned, the notes of a living church which Newman distinguished. What can we make of this? It is preposterous simply to reiterate the shallow charge of eighteenth-century rationalism that the Church subsists through chicanery and fraud. Chicanery and fraud are perennial, inside and outside of the Church, but these have not enabled that body to keep long a-dying through nineteen centuries and more while heresies and philosophies and sciences and Protestant innovations have had their little day and then have languished or perished. No, if we are candid and unbiassed we must concede that the

Roman Church stands for something which is valuable
and true. It does so in a grossly imperfect way, yet less
imperfectly, less doubtfully, than any other religious
body claiming the same ultimate origin. It is impossible
to deny that on the whole Protestantism has been anti-
Christian in its development and influence, that on the
whole it has been, as Newman said, a pathway to atheism.
Here the voice of history is unambiguous, and its verdict
is wholly on Newman's side. If, then, there is truth in a
spiritual interpretation of life, and if this truth makes
a difference in men's lives, it is something to have it
enshrined in an abiding institution which through the
generations presents it concretely and unswervingly regardless of all passing fashions in thought and conduct
which men turn up from year to year in their restless
hunger for novelty. And this the Roman Church has
somehow done, despite great stupidities, monstrous corruptions, and almost unnumbered superstitions. And it is
the only institution the western world has known which
has had, and has still, the strength and toughness to keep
on doing this, permanently. It is easy to say that the work
should have been done better, but the obvious fact is that
it has been done just as well as we ourselves and our like
have permitted.

Even so, however, to deny the Roman Church's infallibility is to deny that thus far Newman's belief was well
founded. And it is to question much more. Newman saw
no stopping-point between atheism and Catholicism; and
at any rate it is clear that, if the miraculous revelation
of Christianity is not infallibly conveyed to us by the
Church, we do not and cannot ever have complete evidence that it took place. Further, we do not and cannot
ever have a perfect witness to the truth of the creeds or,
in other words, of the body of Christian dogma. The 'ten
thousand difficulties which do not make a doubt' if they

are propped by adequate authority may run to something more than a doubt if they have to support themselves. Yet here again there is the same real or apparent contradiction in the evidence and the same impossibility of an absolute or unqualified decision. For Newman had a knowledge of human nature and of life, of its real problems and issues, which for subtlety and depth few men in any age have rivalled. Where did he get it? From wide and varied experience of the world? No, he lived secluded from the world all his life, and many of his great sermons were written when he was young. He anticipated experience, and from a full mind and heart he beautifully gave out sober and wise counsel to the weary, the oppressed, the wayward, the worldly-wise, the forward-looking, the self-reliant, the 'useful-knowledge' people, the mean-spirited rich. He knew them all; he knew their discouragements, their self-deceptions, their inordinate desires, their feebleness and blindness and coarseness, their bubble-like theories and hopes, their hardness and emptiness; he knew the thousand ills to which they were subject and the inward workings and infinite abysses of the heart; he knew too the smothered good that lay within them and the calls to which it might respond. And all that he knew he learned from the Christian religion, and some of it from dogmas now most widely discredited even within Christian churches—original sin, eternal punishment, baptismal regeneration. Through his words men could see life itself, in all its variety and apparent incoherence, scrutinized, criticized, sifted finely, until its essential character came out, intelligibly expressed. And this they could see because this was what had been done for Newman, and for them, by Christianity.

In his hands, then, the Christian conception of the world proved itself true to the abiding facts of individual experience, and gave life an intelligible meaning and an intrinsic worth which men could learn for themselves by trial. It gave them a work to do, which was sufficiently its own reward, which tested all their powers, and which was the full expression of all that was distinctively human in their nature. And if despite this evidence we still cannot believe with Newman the traditional account of the origin of Christianity, nor accept fully its development in the Roman Church, we may at least be forced, so far as we are not blinded by sheer prejudice, to accord the life of Jesus and the essential Christian beliefs an unique symbolic value. But, then, it is the fact, surprising as it may be to many, that this is precisely the value which Newman accorded to them.

He tells in the *Apologia* how as a young man he was carried away by a philosophy which he found expressed in the writings of Clement and Origen. "Some portions of their teaching, magnificent in themselves, came like music to my inward ear, as if the response to ideas which, with little external to encourage them, I had cherished so long. These were based on the mystical or sacramental principle, and spoke of the various Economies or Dispensations of the Eternal. I understood them to mean that the exterior world, physical and historical, was but the manifestation to our senses of realities greater than itself. Nature was a parable: Scripture was an allegory: pagan literature, philosophy, and mythology, properly understood, were but a preparation for the Gospel. The Greek poets and sages were in a certain sense prophets; for 'thoughts beyond their thought to those high bards were given.' There had been a directly divine dispensation granted to the Jews; but there had been in some sense a dispensation carried on in favour of the Gentiles. He who had taken the seed of Jacob for His elect people had not therefore cast the rest of mankind out of His sight. In the fulness of time both Judaism and Paganism had come to nought; the outward framework, which concealed yet suggested the Living Truth, had never been intended to last, and it was dissolving under the beams of the Sun of Justice which shone behind it and through it. The process of change had been slow; it had been done not rashly, but by rule and measure, 'at sundry times and in divers manners,' first one disclosure and then another, till the whole evangelical doctrine was brought into full manifestation. And thus room was made for the anticipation of further and deeper disclosures, of truths still under the veil of the letter, and in their season to be revealed. The visible world still remains without its divine interpretation; Holy Church in her sacraments and her hierarchical appointments will remain, even to the end of the world, only a symbol of those heavenly facts which fill eternity. Her mysteries are but the expressions in human language of truths to which the human mind is unequal."

Elsewhere Newman developed this conception more fully and explicitly, in his treatise on the Arians and in the last of his *Oxford University Sermons,* and it is bound up indissolubly with his acceptance of Christianity. In the sermon just mentioned he says that strictly all that we know of the physical world "is the existence of the impressions our senses make on us." We do not have, then, "any true idea of matter, but only an idea commensurate with sensible impressions." We find that our generalizations from sense-data are trustworthy for practical purposes within certain limits. We take them for true, as far as they go, but we are not so foolish as to think them commensurate with reality, even with physical reality alone, because the moment we attempt to do so we find ourselves landed amidst fundamental contradictions, intolerable absurdities—in short amidst what in religion are called mysteries. Our calculation "has run its length; and by its failure shows that all along it has been but an expedient for practical purposes, not a true analysis or adequate image of those recondite laws which are investigated by means of it. It has never fathomed their depth, because it now fails to measure their course. At the same time, no one, because it cannot do every thing, would refuse to use it within the range in which it will act; no one would say that it was a system of empty symbols, though it be but a shadow of the unseen. Though we use it with caution, still we use it, as being the nearest approximation to the truth which our condition admits.''

In other words, our scientific generalizations are what in theological language are called economies or accommodations—they are approximations, adapted to our human condition, of truths which transcend these formulæ. Such are fables or myths. ''Mythical representations, at least in their better form, may be considered facts or narratives, untrue, but like the truth, intended to bring out the action of some principle, point of character, and the like. For instance, the tradition that St. Ignatius was the child whom our Lord took in His arms may be unfounded; but it realizes to us his special relation to Christ and His Apostles with a keenness peculiar to itself.'' The myth brings home to us concretely the human meaning of our generalizations in the sphere of moral experience and generally in the realm of spiritual values. And so, Newman ends, ''not even the Catholic reasonings and conclusions, as contained in Confessions, and most thoroughly received by us, are worthy of the Divine Verities which they represent, but are the truth only in as full a measure as our minds can admit it; the truth as far as they go, and under the conditions of thought which human feebleness imposes.'' They ''are, after all, but symbols of a Divine fact, which, far from being compassed by those very propositions, would not

be exhausted, nor fathomed, by a thousand.'' And it follows, he points out, that the business of the reason is
but to act as an instrument or servant, drawing out as
best it may into intelligible form the transcendent truths
which are told us, as he believed, by direct Divine revelation, or are suggested to us by our experience.

Like Coleridge, Newman considered that a symbol
must partake of the reality which it represents, though,
unlike him, he did not attempt to fortify in this way the
evidence for the historic basis of Christianity. He merely
contended that religious truth is and must be imperfectly
symbolized when reduced to human terms, but he did, as
far as they go, accept in the orthodox or literal sense,
simply on the authority of the Church, the supernatural
character and mission of Jesus and the body of dogma
developed therefrom. Yet there remains this significant
consequence of his view: that, since Christian dogma
and its systematic exposition in a theology are but approximations to the truth, adaptations conforming it to
those who receive it, as age succeeds age not only changes
in expression, but developments, are to be looked for.
''Here below to live is to change and to be perfect is to
have changed often.'' As a Roman Catholic Newman constantly lamented the centralization within the Church
which had followed upon the Reformation, and the decline or disappearance of the great theological schools.
In them in earlier days theology had developed by free
debate and controversy into a form suitable to the age
and the condition of knowledge. But in his day he found
nothing like the same opportunity for further development which was equally necessary. It was one of his vain
efforts to found an institution of this kind in Dublin.
There, had he had his way, men in all departments of
learning and science would have had complete freedom

to develop their own work on its own lines. This may sound like a dream, and, as things were, a dream it proved. But it was actually Newman's aim for the Catholic University of Dublin, and he was completely confident of the result.

Truth issues, slowly and by degrees, but still does issue, he thought, from many minds working freely together. In the midst of the great modern age of discovery he remained sceptical of much that passes amongst us for 'science' because he saw it constantly changing and saw men nevertheless hastily and madly building vast and solemn philosophies on these shifting foundations. He preferred to build more surely if more slowly, and he distrusted daily proclamations of revolutionary change which had to be modified or withdrawn in the light of the next day's news. In the university he planned he considered that theologians and scientists working together would hold each other in check, and that knowledge would come slowly out of their joint endeavours. Scientific hypothesis and theology would be subjected to mutual criticism, objection, argument, and a gradual sifting. And of no truth which came in such an orderly, responsible fashion would he have been afraid. "How dreadful it is to have to act on great matters so much in the dark," he wrote to a friend in 1845. He was ready to welcome new light, so it *was* light, not with fear and misgiving but with profound gratitude.

I say this with confidence, despite the popular impression as to what it must mean to be a Roman Catholic. And I do so because I think it clear that Newman's fundamental concern was with certain factors of individual experience which no changes in our knowledge of the physical world and no changes in our conclusions from human history can in any wise alter. Howsoever it might be that conscious life depends for its manifestation on a physical organism, that it is temporary, the sport of chance, and the victim of sin, still, he knew that he was essentially, centrally, a spiritual being. He knew by direct experience that there is an invisible, timeless world which is the fulfilment of life, that even 'here below' he could maintain a precarious connexion with this world which was strengthened by the very ills he had to endure, and that he was led in so doing by a light which came not from himself and which was beyond his deserts. This ultimately was what he knew that he knew, and he sought its meaning. He was certain that this search, and unswerving faithfulness to the best answer he could get, were necessary steps towards the fulfilment of his life, but he was certain also that new knowledge, if it *was* knowledge, could give him one thing only—a still better answer, which he knew was possible, and which he knew he needed, if it could be had.

He may have gone wrong, with such light as was vouchsafed him. Nevertheless with single-hearted and life-long devotion he bore witness, in a way whose significance may not even yet be fully apparent, to what is central and abiding in human nature. It may or may not be right or possible to follow the whole way in the path which he took, but this cannot impair, and should not obscure, the importance and significance of his life and work. We at least cannot disregard the fact that a brilliantly-gifted and keen-minded man of the nineteenth century, a man whose character was at once saintly and manly in the full sense of both words, did utterly revolt from the materialism of his day and stand uncompromisingly for the reality and primacy of man's spiritual nature and destiny. His words and acts may tell his real story brokenly and faultily, as human words and acts do, yet they tell the story of one who lived, not amongst shadows and dreams, but in the real world of moral experience and spiritual values, and who did what he could to fathom the meaning of that experience and so to live a consciously and distinctively human life.

IV.

HUXLEY

MARK PATTISON has told in his *Memoirs* how the exact
sciences entered Oxford with amazing rapidity and began
to exercise a momentous influence as soon as the 'night-
mare' of Newman's ascendancy was ended by his conversion to Rome. But, indeed, the current of naturalistic
thought in England had not been interrupted in the
eighteenth century by the rise of Methodism and Evan-
gelicalism, and it was scarcely disturbed in the first half
of the nineteenth century by the Romantic Movement in
literature or the Oxford Movement in religion. The scientific activities which it fostered were kept out of Oxford
or discouraged there longer than they would otherwise
have been; but elsewhere Utilitarianism flourished, despite the efforts of Keble and Newman, the protests of
Coleridge, and the heated outcries of Carlyle and others.
Applied science steadily went on achieving its triumphs
and working its vast changes in the constitution and outlook of society. And scientific investigations were being
carried on fruitfully by an increasing number of men,
one notable result being the publication of Lyell's *Principles of Geology* in 1830. As the century advanced, fresh
discoveries combined with their striking industrial application to give, year by year, firmer ground for the independence of science and for its authority. The industrial
revolution had given science a firm hold on the daily lives
of men; the steam railroad, the electric telegraph, and the
like developments soon began to exercise a similar sway
over their imaginations. And in 1859 the climax of the

rise of science came with the publication of Darwin's *Origin of Species.*

Evolution, or development, of course, was not an entirely new concept. Though modern and recent, it had been in the air for half a century or longer and had begun perceptibly to influence thought. It is fair, however, to say that before Darwin it had been only a more or less interesting speculation, whereas, rightly or wrongly, it became invested very quickly after 1859 with all the authority of actual fact, which only the ignorant man or the fool would attempt to deny. As a fact, its crucial importance was unescapable. It gave to the sciences of organic life the centre of the intellectual stage, while to science as a whole it gave an unifying concept of apparently unlimited application. Evolution became a magic word, a talisman which was to explain everything in terms of a common process, from the tailless condition of guinea-pigs and men to the configuration of the starry firmament above us. This crowning achievement of the secular development of modern thought was, in fact, exactly what was needed in order to convince men that a new dispensation was at hand. Naturalistic thinkers were now prepared to step forth as the accredited interpreters of life, bringers of a new gospel which was to displace the outworn creeds and accumulated superstitions of the past, giving us instead the truth itself.[1]

In endeavouring to learn the new truth we may begin

[1] Professor A. K. Rogers, in his *English and American Philosophy Since 1800* (p. 129), quotes a passage from Robert Owen which illustrates the assured temper already present in naturalistic thinkers in the first half of the century and widespread after 1859. Owen, after referring to the "various phases of insanity called religion," says: "Rejoice, all ye who have so long desired to see the period arrive when all the human race shall become wise and good in habits: for this weapon of mighty power has been discovered! Its name is TRUTH. Its sharpness and brilliancy, now that it is, *for the first time,* unsheathed to open view, no mortal can withstand."

with Huxley, the devoted friend and champion of Darwin and, as Leslie Stephen has called him, "the best wrestler in the intellectual ring." Thomas Henry Huxley was born in 1825. His father, a man of indifferent abilities, was at this time senior assistant-master of the semi-public school at Ealing, the school at which Newman studied until he went to Oxford. Huxley's early training was of a haphazard character, and it was apparently as much from accident as from inclination that he was thrown into the study of natural science and medicine. As it turned out, fortune was kind, for nothing could easily have been happier for him. He obtained his medical degree from the University of London in 1845. The next year he entered the naval medical service and was appointed assistant-surgeon of the surveying-ship *Rattlesnake,* which was on the point of going to sea. The ship's major business was to chart a passage through reefs off the coast of Australia, but the admiralty recognized the opportunities to natural science offered by its voyage, and not only did the ship carry an official naturalist, but Huxley's own appointment was the result of his known scientific interests. He was on the *Rattlesnake* for approximately four years, and during that time wrote several papers and accumulated material for others which laid the foundation of his career as a man of science.

The year after Huxley's return to England he was elected a Fellow of the Royal Society in acknowledgement of his work, and in 1852 he received the Society's Gold Medal. This was satisfactory. His work was being published; despite the active jealousy of fellow-scientists he was gaining the recognition at which he aimed, and he was thinking of science as a vocation. He was thinking of it, he wrote to a friend, because it was clear to him that he could not get through life contentedly without full

scope for the development of his faculties, and science
alone offered this possibility. Other callings—law, divinity, medicine, politics—were "in a state of chaotic vibra-
tion between utter humbug and utter scepticism." Even
so, however, for a time he hesitated, because, as he wrote
to his future wife, to whom he had become engaged in
Australia, "To attempt to live by any scientific pursuit
is a farce. Nothing but what is absolutely practical will
go down in England. A man of science may earn great
distinction, but not bread. He will get invitations to all
sorts of dinners and conversaziones, but not enough income to pay his cab fare." [2] Nevertheless he had fully
determined that he was to make a name for himself, [3] and
so science, bread or no bread, won the day.

His discouragement, moreover, soon faded in the light
of better prospects. In 1854 he was appointed Professor
of Natural History and Palæontology in the Royal School
of Mines and Curator of Fossils in the Museum of Practical Geology. Three years later he was appointed Exam-
iner in Physiology and Comparative Anatomy in the
University of London and in the same year was also appointed Fullerian Professor of Comparative Anatomy
at the Royal Institution. This may suffice to show that
he was, on the whole very rapidly, achieving substantial
recognition of his ability and his scientific accomplish-
ments; and so true is this that when Darwin published
the *Origin of Species* he named Huxley as one of two or
three men who in his opinion composed his critical audi-

[2] *Life and Letters of T. H. Huxley*, by Leonard Huxley, I, 101, 72.

[3] He had written to his sister in the fall of 1850: "I don't know and
I don't care whether I shall ever be what is called a great man. I will leave
my mark somewhere, and it shall be clear and distinct [T. H. H., his mark]
and free from the abominable blur of cant, humbug, and self-seeking which
surrounds everything in this present world—that is to say, supposing that
I am not already unconsciously tainted myself, a result of which I have a
morbid dread." (*Life*, I, 69.)

ence. If these accepted his theory, he intimated, he would rest satisfied with his work and would feel assured that it must attain general acceptance in the course of time. The above list of posts held by Huxley may also indicate that he was entering upon an extremely busy life. He was. One is tempted to say that he could always see good reason why his aid was essential in any scientific or educational enterprise, but it is also the fact that his remarkable abilities caused unusual and pressing demands to be made upon him and that many of them he welcomed because, through the greater part of his life, he continued to be badly in need of money for the support of his large family. Thus, until his health finally broke under the burden, he continued to do a certain amount of strictly scientific work and a large amount of academic lecturing, he sat on ten royal commissions, he held various other government posts, and he administered the affairs of several scientific societies. And, in addition to all this, Huxley found another kind of work to do, arising in the first instance out of the fact that in 1859 he did accept evolution as practically proved by the *Origin of Species.* He was led into active championship of the theory by the controversies which it immediately aroused, and from this time on, through popular lectures and essays, he increasingly took the rôle of chief propagandist for the cause of evolution and, also, for the cause of science in general.

For this he was admirably fitted, and indeed it is because of this activity that Huxley is still remembered outside of the laboratory or the museum. He was a clear and vigorous writer, an accomplished master of controversial attack and defence, and he was emphatically a party-man. It was with very good reason that at one time he was urged to enter English political life. All of this is so well illustrated by his rejoinder to Bishop Wilber-

force at Oxford in 1860 that it must be quoted here,
though it has become famous and has been many times
repeated. The British Association for the Advancement
of Science met in Oxford in 1860, and the theory of evolution had already raised that inevitable clerical storm
which it still raises wherever people are at once sufficiently ignorant and sufficiently religious. The Bishop of
Oxford accordingly took the opportunity to deliver an
address in which he assured his audience that evolution
was an empty as well as an impious conjecture. In its
course he turned to Huxley, who was sitting near him on
the stage, and inquired ''was it through his grandfather
or his grandmother that he claimed his descent from a
monkey?'' Perhaps the Bishop's question was not quite
so directly insulting, as later accounts of his words
vary, but there is agreement that Huxley exclaimed to
Sir Benjamin Brodie, who sat next to him, ''The Lord
hath delivered him into mine hands.'' And when the
Bishop had finished Huxley arose, ''a slight tall figure,
stern and pale, very quiet and very grave,'' and ''spoke
those tremendous words'': ''I asserted—and I repeat—
that a man has no reason to be ashamed of having an ape
for his grandfather. If there were an ancestor whom I
should feel shame in recalling it would rather be a *man*,
a man of restless and versatile intellect, who, not content
with success[4] in his own sphere of activity, plunges into
scientific questions with which he has no real acquaintance, only to obscure them by an aimless rhetoric, and
distract the attention of his hearers from the real point
at issue by eloquent digressions and skilled appeals to
religious prejudice.''

Those are memorable words. They are almost irresist-

---

[4] I have omitted the word 'equivocal,' which precedes 'success' in the
account written by J. R. Green, in obedience to Huxley's statement that
he was sure he had not used it.

ible. They have a simplicity and downright force which
only the fewest men attain. I do not say they are the
words of a seeker after truth, I do not inquire about the
legitimacy of the claim that religion and science occupy
distinct and separate spheres, I do not ask if this is
really a rhetorical appeal to scientific prejudice, nor do I
ask if there was actually more than one point at issue. It
is enough to say that Huxley was conscious of an imme- ⟨0⟩
diate, practical need of the moment. The cause he represented was being opposed by a powerful guild, and it
would be a shrewd blow to discredit one of its foremost
members in the very centre and home of 'religious prejudice.' He was delighted at the gift of so excellent an
opportunity, and he rose to make the best of it in a manner which required, and showed, full conviction, unusual
courage, and the height of controversial skill. We should
hardly need contemporary testimony, were it lacking, to
prove that he succeeded in his object; but, on the other
hand, we do not need to ponder his words long in order
to the discovery that he considered only the immediate
need before his eyes.

This famous episode marks the beginning of a conflict
with the representatives of religion in which Huxley was
engaged through the remainder of his life. He says in the
Preface to *Science and Hebrew Tradition* that for over a
thousand years the greater number of the most highly
civilized and instructed nations of the world "have confidently believed and passionately maintained that certain writings, which they entitle sacred, occupy an unique
position in literature, in that they possess an authority,
different in kind and immeasurably superior in weight,
to that of all other books." Throughout this period they
have held it to be indisputable that, "whoever may be the
ostensible writers of the Jewish, Christian, and Mahometan scriptures, God himself is their real author; and,

since their conception of the attributes of the Deity excludes the possibility of error and—at least in relation to this particular matter—of wilful deception, they have drawn the logical conclusion that the denier of the accuracy of any statement, the questioner of the binding force of any command, to be found in these documents is not merely a fool, but a blasphemer. From the point of view of mere reason he grossly blunders; from that of religion he grievously sins.'' But fidelity to their discoveries forced Huxley and his fellow-scientists to commit this grievous sin of blasphemy, and so forced them to question the authority of the Bible.

The quarrel between Christianity and the 'carnal reason' of man is, of course, as old as Christianity itself, but it has taken different forms in different ages. It is one thing to point out intellectual difficulties in a doctrine; it is a different thing to prove that it rests on or embodies mistakes in matters of fact. The Christian position was successfully maintained so long as it was merely a question of human opinion or human argument pitted against supposedly divine authority. But with the Renaissance the quarrel assumed a new aspect. The Copernican hypothesis, confirmed by the observations of Galileo, was the first great modern instance of natural knowledge in open conflict with the plain statements or implications of the Bible. This was not a matter for argument; it was a verifiable fact which demonstrated that the astronomy hitherto received as in accordance with the Bible was simply wrong. Strictly, it need scarcely be said, a single important instance of this kind should be sufficient to upset the whole doctrine of the plenary inspiration or infallibility of the Bible, but practically it was not so. It would seem that the dawn of modern astronomy had more effect in finally killing the pseudo-science of astrology than in unsettling religion. In various ways this con-

tradiction between knowledge and the infallible Book
was glossed over, so that the belief in the plenary inspiration of the Bible was still in Huxley's younger days
widely prevalent; and indeed as late as 1893 he thought
that "many persons of unimpeachable piety, a few of
learning, and even some of intelligence" yet continued
to share it.

But the theory of evolution was not only palpably in
contradiction with the Bible, but in contradiction with it
at a point which brought the full force of the difficulty
home to men and made inevitable a renewal of active,
probably bitter conflict between science and religion. If
evolution was a fact, verifiable by any one who chose to
study the available data, no one could longer pretend that
the Biblical version of the creation was anything other
than a mistaken guess such as was possible to men like
ourselves at a time when nothing was really known about
the origin of the earth and of life. But to admit this was
not only to abandon the claim that the Bible was itself
the inspired Word of God—or at least that certain portions of it were—but also to abandon, or at least radically
to change the character of, certain developments of
Christian theology. And this men were not prepared to
do in 1859. On the contrary, they were roused to attack
the evolutionists and to hinder their work. Huxley was
undoubtedly right in insisting that his controversial battles were forced on him, though it is also evident that he
welcomed with enthusiasm the necessity of bearding the
lions.

He tells of the situation as he saw it in *Science and
Christian Tradition*. "I had set out," he says, "on a
journey, with no other purpose than that of exploring
a certain province of natural knowledge; I strayed no
hair's breadth from the course which it was my right and
my duty to pursue; and yet I found that, whatever route

I took, before long I came to a tall and formidable-looking fence. Confident as I might be in the existence of an ancient and indefeasible right of way, before me stood the thorny barrier with its comminatory notice-board— 'No thoroughfare. By order. Moses.' There seemed no way over; nor did the prospect of creeping round, as I saw some do, attract me. True there was no longer any cause to fear the spring guns and man-traps set by former lords of the manor; but one is apt to get very dirty going on all-fours. The only alternatives were either to give up my journey—which I was not minded to do—or to break the fence down and go through it.''

As Huxley implies, this was not a real alternative to him, and without hesitation he resolutely set about breaking down the fence. He used for his purpose both the instruments furnished by natural science and those which were being fashioned, then chiefly in Germany and France, by the application of the principles of historical criticism to the Bible. And he did his work with such thoroughness and zest that one wonders now how the result could ever have seemed doubtful.

Moreover, he did not—as one might suppose both from his own words which I have quoted and from the fact that the conflict was begun because of the theory of evolution—confine his attack on the Bible to Genesis and its stories of the creation, temptation, and flood. Taking Saul's visit to the witch of Endor as a text, he showed that the religious conceptions of Saul and his contemporaries were strictly comparable with those of other peoples of the same level of civilization, and that there could be no better reason for giving credence to them than to the notions concerning the supernatural of other half-barbarous races. Likewise he extended his criticism to the New Testament, seizing on the story of the Gadarene swine as an illustration not only of grave injustice done to the innocent owners of the swine, which Christians cannot square with even elementary ethical principles, but also of heathen demonology, to a belief in which Christians are, if they are logical, committed.

Briefly, Huxley undertook to show that the application of the principles of historical criticism to the Biblical documents tended strikingly to weaken the value of many of them as first-hand evidence for the truth of their contents, and that, besides, the definitely ascertained facts or the overwhelming probabilities established by the modern increase of natural knowledge plainly contradicted much that the Bible contains. The general result was to deprive the Bible of all unique or peculiar authority, and so to place it on a level with other merely human documents which have come to us out of the past. In other words, so far as the Bible contained verifiable truth it was to be accepted, not because it was in the Bible but because it was verifiable. Extraordinary stories were to be believed no more because they are in the Bible than similar stories are to be believed because they are found in, for example, the *Iliad*, or *Beowulf*. This was quite to cut away Christianity's basis in authority. And it was more, it was also to see the Gospels as legendary narratives in which evident falsehood was so confounded with merely possible fact as to cast doubt upon the whole. It was in effect to discredit the claim that at least Jesus was to be regarded as a great moral teacher, if indeed such a person had really lived at all. This was what Huxley himself saw as the result of his criticism.

His quarrel with Christianity had begun with the trouble over Genesis, but it could not stop there. He encountered much the same thing as what had happened when the Church had managed to digest modern astronomy. It was one of the exasperations of his later years to see Churchmen swallowing defeat when compelled, to see them giving up Genesis to the realm of myth and adopting naturalistic explanations of the miracles of Jesus, and yet go on unchangeably asserting their old claims to the infallible truth of the Christian religion, as if nothing really had occurred to disturb their position. And thus he came to see the issue as one between two fundamental principles, between authority and freedom of thought, as he sometimes said, or between two kinds of authority, legitimate and illegitimate. No one has made loftier claims for the supreme authority of science than Huxley, but he has based those claims on the position that the scientist can produce just warrant for his authority, whereas the priest's claim to authority rests on fraud and humbug. Consequently he saw his object as the demolition of Christianity. Being an excellent tactician, he did not say this directly; on the contrary, he habitually protested that he had no hostile feeling towards Christianity, but was simply contending for freedom to follow the path of truth wherever it might lead. Of course, too, this is what he was doing. But he was also aiming at something more than tolerance, so that his protests were, at the least, disingenuous.

In 1888 he wrote a letter to Lady Welby in which, as he told her, he went to the root of the matter.

Christian beliefs [he wrote] profess to be based upon historical facts. If there was no such person as Jesus of Nazareth, and if his biography given in the Gospels is a fiction, Christianity vanishes.

Now the inquiry into the truth or falsehood of a matter of history is just as much a question of pure science as the inquiry into the truth or falsehood of a matter of geology, and the value of evidence in the two cases must be tested in the same way. If any one tells me that the evidence of the existence of man in the Miocene epoch is as good as that upon which I frequently act every day of my life, I reply that this is quite true, but that it is no sort of reason for believing in the existence of Miocene man.

Surely no one but a born fool can fail to be aware that we constantly, and in very grave conjunctions, are obliged to act upon extremely bad evidence, and that very often we suffer all sorts of penalties in consequence. And surely one must be something worse than a born fool to pretend that such decision under the pressure of the enigmas of life ought to have the smallest influence in those judgements which are made with due and sufficient deliberation.[5]

The root of the matter is, I suppose, twofold. Huxley had an interest in making Christianity vanish if he could because it hindered the free development of science. But he also had an interest in making even a tolerant Christianity vanish because he considered it to be a fundamentally immoral institution. He wanted what all of us want and somehow or other have to attain—certitude. He had a deep conviction that it made a real difference whether or not one accepted falsehood for truth, and, much more, whether or not one rested lazily content with unexamined beliefs. He had an unqualified hatred of all hypocritical professions, whether made for the sake of appearances, or for the sake of peace, or with some supposedly good intent. This had been brought to life in him by his early reading of Carlyle, particularly of *Sartor Resartus,* from which, however, he learned only what it suited him to learn. He could not merely drift, he could not take the meaning of life on trust. He could not found himself on anything that was even partially doubtful, much less on anything evidently false, but wanted to conduct his life on a basis of unassailable truth. In this he was wholly at one with Newman, or with Coleridge, yet for this reason he sought to demolish Christianity. He regarded the Church as a fundamentally immoral

fault

[5] *Life and Letters,* II, 226-227.

institution because it exercised an illegitimate authority and pretended to a certitude it could not properly claim. It deluded men with falsehoods in the name of truth. It depended on history for its basis; but history was a matter of science, and science showed that the Church's so-called history was a tissue of fables and lies. Moreover, the Church pretended to communicate knowledge about matters beyond the bounds of human experience, and this was deception, because knowledge about such matters is impossible.

But knowledge of matters within the bounds of human experience is possible—exact, verifiable knowledge, for which we reserve the name science. Here, then, Huxley found his rock of unassailable truth. He would believe only what science bade him believe, and would conduct his life on this basis of legitimate certitude. Yet it is not altogether easy to state what, as a consequence, he did believe, because, if he was not loose or confused in his thought, he was at any rate chiefly a controversial writer. It is, indeed, astonishing how completely his reply to Bishop Wilberforce exhibits within its small compass his qualities as an essayist and lecturer. Practically all of his essays are occasional in character, and a part of their apparent effectiveness, when taken singly, lies in the extent to which he succeeded in adapting his words to the immediate needs of the moment. But his preoccupation with momentary needs and his success in meeting them operated to make his expression of his views not only fragmentary but incoherent. It is probable that he himself never realized how singularly unfortunate for his cause in the long run was the heady stimulant of controversial success, as it is also probable that he never realized how difficult his position really was, because he never attempted to draw it out connectedly as a whole. As a result his readers, seeking the guidance which he professed to give, find themselves confronted with several Huxleys, quite different from each other, perhaps irreconcilable. In particular two Huxleys stand out prominently: one, the man who urged the cause of science on all occasions, the other, the man who shrewdly defended himself from attack. The difference between them will presently show itself.

In the letter to Lady Welby from which I have quoted, Huxley admits that frequently we have to make practical decisions, or to act, on a basis of imperfect knowledge, and he adds that frequently we have to pay extreme penalties as a consequence. If we are wise we act from knowledge as much as possible, subjecting ourselves to chance no more than we can help. Hence our first step in wisdom is to realize that knowledge is a word to be used carefully, and that its boundaries are of the utmost importance to us.

In seeking to define knowledge and its boundaries Huxley bids us recollect that we are born ignorant, that we have no inner sense or faculty which furnishes us with certainties concerning ourselves or our relations to this world or to any other. For all we know to the contrary, anything is possible at any time. We cannot say that because human beings always have died they always will; we cannot say that because hitherto we have not been able to float in the clouds at our will we shall not find ourselves able to do so to-morrow. There can be, in short, no *a priori* objections to any doctrine whatsoever. Hence such certitude as we can obtain depends wholly on concrete evidence which the mind of man can clearly comprehend and test. Facts, then—actual, concrete, individual facts—are the only certainties of life. All else may be more or less probable, or may be merely guesswork, pertaining to that limbo of speculation where nothing can be adduced in the way of proof or disproof. Facts alone are certain. Consequently knowledge is bounded by the range of verifiable human experience;—beyond that there may be an indefinite amount that we should like to know, but all is darkness.

Concerning immortality Huxley wrote to Charles Kingsley: "I neither deny nor affirm the immortality of man. I see no reason for believing in it, but, on the other hand, I have no means of disproving it. Pray understand that I have no *a priori* objections to the doctrine. No man who has to deal daily and hourly with nature can trouble himself about *a priori* difficulties. Give me such evidence as would justify me in believing anything else, and I will believe that. Why should I not? It is not half as wonderful as the conservation of force, or the indestructibility of matter. . . . But the longer I live, the more obvious it is to me that the most sacred act of a man's life is to say and to feel, 'I believe such and such to be true.' All the greatest rewards and all the heaviest penalties of existence cling about that act. The universe is one and the same throughout; and if the condition of my success in unravelling some little difficulty of anatomy or physiology is that I shall rigorously refuse to put faith in that which does not rest on sufficient evidence, I cannot believe that the great mysteries of existence will be laid open to me on other terms. It is no use to talk to me of analogies and probabilities. I know what I mean when I say I believe in the law of the inverse squares, and I will not rest my life and my hopes upon weaker convictions. I dare not if I would. Measured by this standard, what becomes of the doctrine of immortality?"[6]

What indeed? What is the difference between not believing something and disbelieving it? Is the difference much more than verbal? At any rate it can scarcely be pretended that it is the same thing as the simple confes-

[6] *Life and Letters*, I, 234.

sion of ignorance which Huxley's principles demanded, and it points to a difficulty in those principles which appears more or less clearly in most of his illustrations of their working. To take another instance, Huxley contended that belief in demonology is inseparably bound up with the view-point of the writers of the Gospels, and that acceptance of the revelation of a spiritual world made in them involves belief in the existence of evil spirits. But, he said, the actual existence of this spiritual world—the value of the evidence both for this and for its influence upon the stream of things—are matters "which lie as much within the province of science as any other question about the existence and powers of the varied forms of living and conscious activity." And he added: "It really is my strong conviction that a man has no more right to say he believes this world is haunted by swarms of evil spirits, without being able to produce satisfactory evidence of the fact, than he has a right to say, without adducing adequate proof, that the circumpolar antarctic ice swarms with sea-serpents. I should not like to assert positively that it does not. I imagine that no cautious biologist would say as much; but while quite open to conviction, he might properly decline to waste time upon the consideration of talk, no better accredited than forecastle 'yarns,' about such monsters of the deep. And if the interests of ordinary veracity dictate this course, in relation to a matter of so little consequence as this, what must be our obligations in respect of the treatment of a question which is fundamental alike for science and for ethics? For not only does our general theory of the universe and of the nature of the order which pervades it, hang upon the answer; but the rules of practical life must be deeply affected by it.'"[7]

Here Huxley on the whole more cautiously follows his

[7] *Science and Christian Tradition*, pp. xiii-xiv.

principles than in the first illustration I quoted, yet here too it is difficult to see much reality in the distinction between not believing and disbelieving the proposition in question. And in fact this instance, more plainly than the former one, shows that the attempted distinction opened the way at any rate, for those who might care to take advantage of it, to a very disingenuous attitude. The refusal to deny the possible existence of those sea-serpents strikes me, try how I may to look at it generously, as simply uncandid. Yet this very difficult feat of suspending the mind somewhere short of disbelief Huxley made much of, and called it agnosticism. In *Science and Christian Tradition* he tells how he came to coin the word. He was a member of the Metaphysical Society, a somewhat odd organization which Newman was invited to join and which included W. G. Ward and Cardinal Manning. Men of every shade of philosophical and theological opinion were gathered together in it for the free expression of their views, in the entirely futile hope that they might discover that they had more in common than they had supposed, and so might make a start towards the formulation of a comprehensive philosophy. Huxley found that most of the other members were *-ists* of some kind, while he had no name for his position. Despite the friendliness with which he was welcomed, this gave him some of the uneasy feelings "which must have beset the historical fox when, after leaving the trap in which his tail remained, he presented himself to his normally elongated companions." Consequently he took thought, and invented for himself the title 'agnostic,' which occurred to him as "suggestively antithetic to the 'gnostic' of Church history, who professed to know so much about the very things" of which he was ignorant. He seized the earliest opportunity of parading his new term at a meeting of the Metaphysical Society, 'to show

that he, too, had a tail, like the other foxes,' and he was
highly pleased when the word took and gave promise of
coming into general use.

Agnosticism, then, as Huxley used it, was a confession
of doubt or ignorance. Positively it meant, 'Hold fast to
definitely ascertained fact'; negatively it was equivalent
to philosophical scepticism. And such scepticism was the
defensive armour which Huxley constructed for himself
after his early study of Hamilton's essay on the uncondi-
tioned and his later acquaintance with the writings of
David Hume. But Hume had discovered that his scepticism vanished away the moment he quit his study and its
atmosphere of severe reflexion, so that when he mingled
with men, after three or four hours' amusement he found
it impossible to return to his speculations, so cold, and
strained, and ridiculous did they appear. Huxley's defensive scepticism had the like peculiarity; it too vanished
when he went forth amongst men to teach.

In 1890 he wrote to Sir J. G. T. Sinclair: "Only one
absolute certainty is possible to man—namely, that at
any given moment the feeling which he has exists. . . .
We poor mortals have to be content with hope and belief
in all matters past and present—our sole certainty is
momentary."[8] To this point he was ready enough to
carry his scepticism whenever need arose; yet in practice
he was no more able to rest in it than are other men—
perhaps less able than many, because in his championship of science he felt himself to be a leader in a new
crusade, and he never missed any opportunity to make
large claims for his cause.

He came to America in 1876, journeyed west to see his
sister, delivered an address at the opening of the Johns

---

[8] *Life and Letters*, II, 278. It may be worth recalling that this is identical with Walter Pater's view, as expressed in the Conclusion of the *Renaissance* and in *Marius the Epicurean*.

Development of the Agnostic in Huxley

Hopkins University in Baltimore, and lectured on evolution in New York. His reception in this country was, we are told, compared to a royal progress—with such veneration or curiosity did our countrymen regard him. And his son writes significantly in the *Life and Letters* of his father that the events of the American visit were "a signal testimony to the wide extent of his influence, hardly suspected, indeed, by himself; an influence due above all to the fact that he did not allow his studies to stand apart from the moving problems of existence, but brought the new and regenerating ideas into contact with life at every point, and that his championship of the new doctrines had at the same time been a championship of freedom and sincerity in thought and word against shams and self-deceptions of every kind. It was not so much the preacher of new doctrines who was welcomed, as the apostle of veracity—not so much the student of science as the teacher of men."

"The teacher of men"—certainly, one feels, Huxley had a very strong inclination to assume that rôle, and unquestionably he was so regarded. "The teacher of men"—the words bring before the mind's eye a strong, positive figure, preaching with absolute conviction no mere chilling and sceptical negations, but a new gospel filled with regenerating ideas about the actual problems of life. What were these regenerating ideas resting on adequate evidence? What conception of life was to replace the shams and self-deceptions of men? Strictly he could assure men of only one certainty, of which they scarcely needed to be told—the certainty that at any given moment the feelings they had existed. But beyond this he could and did, with wonderful impressiveness and complete personal conviction, go on to build up, on inadequate evidence, an interpretation of life suggested partly by science, partly by qualities of his own temperament,

as in consonance with this single initial certainty. And
this interpretation he used all his great powers to impress upon his readers and hearers as indisputably true.

The universe, he taught, consists of phenomena stretch-
ing backward one knows not how far, yet never the same,
always changing, constant only in change, phenomena
succeeding each other in invariable trains of succession.
For convenience we distinguish the phenomena as organic and inorganic, but in reality there is no fast line
between inorganic matter and vegetable life, no fast line
between vegetable and animal life, and no essential difference between the two most general classes. All organic
life from the human being to the rock-lichen is fundamentally one and has for its essential constituent protoplasm, which is resolvable into its inorganic elements.
All organic life in its present variety and complexity has
developed through vast reaches of time from one simple
ultimate form, and at no stage whatsoever of this development has there been any violent break in or shadow
of interference with the chain of necessary, regular,
natural causation. "The universe is one and the same
throughout." Hence we are as much as the rocks we walk
on, the air we breathe, or the vermin we kill, parts of the
same natural order.

Further, while human consciousness is real, it is something we share with the animals. We can trace it as one
and the same thing from almost imperceptible beginnings
in very simple organisms through an ascending scale,
where we see it gradually extending in scope until it
culminates in ourselves. And, though real, consciousness
is merely an epiphenomenon, which is to say that it is
merely an accompaniment of molecular changes and has
no slightest influence on our movements or actions, and
no slightest influence on the course of our lives, which
for all we can see might—and in some cases of physical

injury to the brain apparently do—go on as well without it as with it. Concerning this I must quote some sentences from the volume of essays entitled *Method and Results*. "We have," Huxley says, "no knowledge of any thinking substance, apart from extended substance; and . . . thought is as much a function of matter as motion is. . . . I hold, with the Materialist, that the human body, like all living bodies, is a machine, all the operations of which will, sooner or later, be explained on physical principles. I believe that we shall, sooner or later, arrive at a mechanical equivalent of consciousness, just as we have arrived at a mechanical equivalent of heat. If a pound weight falling through a distance of a foot gives rise to a definite amount of heat, which may properly be said to be its equivalent; the same pound weight falling through a foot on a man's hand gives rise to a definite amount of feeling, which might with equal propriety be said to be its equivalent in consciousness."

Later in the same volume we are told that "the consciousness of brutes would appear to be related to the mechanism of their body simply as a collateral product of its working, and to be as completely without any power of modifying that working as the steam-whistle which accompanies the work of a locomotive engine is without influence upon its machinery. Their volition, if they have any, is an emotion indicative of physical changes, not a cause of such changes. . . . To the best of my judgement, the argumentation which applies to brutes holds equally good of men; and, therefore, . . . all states of consciousness in us, as in them, are immediately caused by molecular changes of the brain-substance. It seems to me that in men, as in brutes, there is no proof that any state of consciousness is the cause of change in the motion of the matter of the organism. If these positions are well based, it follows that our mental conditions are simply the symbols in consciousness of the changes which take place automatically in the organism; and that, to take an extreme illustration, the feeling we call volition is not the cause of a voluntary act, but the symbol of that state of the brain which is the immediate cause of that act. We are conscious automata, endowed with free will in the only intelligible sense of that much-abused term—inasmuch as in many respects we are able to do as we like— but none the less parts of the great series of causes and effects which, in unbroken continuity, compose that which is, and has been, and shall be—the sum of existence.''

In what sense automata can be said to do as they like I am unable to see. It makes no difference that they can do so only in some respects. To do so at all implies a genuine choice, which in turn implies a true volitional agent. Either the admission is a fundamental contradiction or it is meaningless. Moreover, Huxley goes on to discuss human life in terms which everywhere imply that we are in fact capable of genuine choices; and thus he unwittingly emphasizes, beyond possibility of mistake, his own sense of the falsity of his assertion that there has never been, and can never be, any violent or unaccountable break in the chain of necessary, regular, natural causation. The existence of a single volitional agent is an unaccountable anomaly in Huxley's unitary natural order.

He tells us, as I have already said, that we are born ignorant. Brutes are born in a state of satisfactory harmony with their environment, but with us it is not so. We are, however, fortunately able by the application of scientific method to learn something about the workings of surrounding phenomena, which makes it possible for us, the more we learn, the better to conform ourselves to the nature of things. And life itself, not to speak of material well-being and peace of mind, depends upon our success in getting adequate guidance and in following it when we do get it. "My business," Huxley wrote to Kingsley, "is to teach my aspirations to conform themselves to fact, not to try and make facts harmonize with my aspirations. . . . Sit down before fact as a little child, be prepared to give up every preconceived notion, follow humbly wherever and to whatever abysses nature leads, or you shall learn nothing. I have only begun to learn content and peace of mind since I have resolved at all risks to do this."[9]

And material well-being, as well as content and peace of mind, follows upon entire surrender to the guidance of nature. For thus we acquire much practically useful knowledge. In his famous lecture on *The Advisableness of Improving Natural Knowledge* Huxley recalls the Plague and Great Fire of London which occurred in the 1660's, and points out that the practically complete absence of any danger of the recurrence of those calamities is due simply to our increased knowledge of nature, which has also put at our command instruments of wealth and convenience of untold number and value. Accordingly he concludes that the improvement of natural knowledge is "a something fraught with a wealth of beneficence to mankind, in comparison with which the damage" done by fire and famine and plague shrinks "into insignificance."

But not only does nature become for us, in proportion as we learn and conform to her ways, "a sort of comfort-grinding machine"; she is in the fullest sense "the bountiful mother of humanity," "bringing them up with kindness, and, if need be, with sternness, in the way they should go, and instructing them in all things needful for their welfare." For the improvement of natural knowledge has done far more than confer practical benefits

[9] *Life and Letters*, I, 235.

on men. While they intelligently sought comfort and
wealth, they unawares turned up knowledge which also
brought about a revolution in their conception of the
universe and of themselves, and which has wonderfully
changed their ways of thinking and their notions of right
and wrong. "I say," Huxley adds, "that natural knowledge, seeking to satisfy natural wants, has found the
ideas which can alone still spiritual cravings. I say that
natural knowledge, in desiring to ascertain the laws of
comfort, has been driven to discover those of conduct,
and to lay the foundations of a new morality."

The doctrine of automatism, so far as it found acceptance, should effectually still spiritual cravings, though
this, I suppose, is not what Huxley consciously meant.
He meant rather that preoccupation with natural knowledge tends to turn men's minds from what he would have
called the blunder or crime of other-worldly speculations
and aspirations and to subdue their spirits to the physical realities that now are, to the work of bettering earthly
life;—"intelligent work is the only acceptable worship."[10]

As for the new morality, he had in mind lessons taught
both by the methods and by the discoveries of science.
The "moral convictions most fondly held by barbarous
and semi-barbarous people" are, that "authority is the
soundest basis of belief; that merit attaches to a readi-
ness to believe; that the doubting disposition is a bad
one, and scepticism a sin; that when good authority has
pronounced what is to be believed, and faith has accepted
it, reason has no further duty." But the fact is that the
increase of natural knowledge is brought about only by
"methods which directly give the lie to all these convictions, and assume the exact reverse of each to be true."

[10] *Science and Christian Tradition*, p. 38.

The scientist "absolutely refuses to acknowledge authority, as such. For him, scepticism is the highest of duties; blind faith the one unpardonable sin."[11]

Further, science gives a new solidity to moral precepts by exhibiting to men concretely the real grounds for prudential conduct. Huxley speaks of this in a letter about some lectures to working-men which he delivered in 1855: "I want the working classes to understand that Science and her ways are great facts for them—that physical virtue is the basis of all other, and that they are to be clean and temperate and all the rest—not because fellows in black with white ties tell them so, but because these are plain and patent laws of nature which they must obey 'under penalties.' "[12] Science, moreover, exhibits not only the character of these penalties, but the rightness or justice of the whole eternal plan of which they form a part. We read, in a letter to Kingsley from which I have already quoted, "I am no optimist, but I have the firmest belief that the Divine Government (if we may use such a phrase to express the sum of the 'customs of matter') is wholly just. The more I know intimately of the lives of other men (to say nothing of my own), the more obvious it is to me that the wicked does *not* flourish nor is the righteous punished. But for this to be clear we must bear in mind what almost all forget, that the rewards of life are contingent upon obedience to the *whole* law—physical as well as moral—and that moral obedience will not atone for physical sin, or *vice versa*. . . . Life cannot exist without a certain conformity to the surrounding universe—that conformity involves a certain amount of happiness in excess of pain. In short, as we live we are paid for living. . . . The

11 *Method and Results*, p. 40.
12 *Life and Letters*, I, 149.

absolute justice of the system of things is as clear to me as any scientific fact.''[13]

Finally, science brings to light and emphasizes as it has never been emphasized before the fundamental basis of morality. The student of science learns in his heart of hearts, as it cannot be learned in any other way, that ''the foundation of morality is to have done, once and for all, with lying; to give up pretending to believe that for which there is no evidence, and repeating unintelligible propositions about things beyond the possibilities of knowledge.'' The student of science knows, as does no one else, what the real sanction of morality is. He knows that the safety of morality does not depend on the adoption of any philosophical speculation or any theological creed, but on ''a real and living belief in that fixed order of nature which sends social disorganization upon the track of immorality, as surely as it sends physical disease after physical trespasses.''[14]

On the other hand, Huxley did not believe that the course of evolution was bringing ever nearer an earthly paradise, to be inhabited by physically, mentally, and morally perfect men, such as was prophesied by Herbert Spencer; nor did he think, with the positivists and eugenists, that the indefinite further improvement of humanity could be effected by the deliberate application to society of the methods of the 'cosmic process' as these were revealed by science. Natural selection was wasteful and cruel, and civilized man had done well in practically nullifying it; nor could it be replaced by artificial selection, because the knowledge needed for determining and applying selective standards was unobtainable. Here and in other connexions Huxley showed that it was not so much a new morality as a revision of existing morality

---

13 *Life and Letters*, I, 236.
14 *Evolution and Ethics, etc.*, p. 146.

and a change in its sanctions that he thought science was bringing about. His utterances on the subject cannot in any way be reconciled with each other, but it would appear that he followed an inner guidance, similar to Coleridge's method of detecting the inspired portions of the Bible. He assumed that the moral compulsions and admirations which he found actually operative within himself, and hence presumably within other equally good men, were a satisfactory product of evolution. In some cases, as for instance in the case of the sceptical attitude, science gave him clear ground for regarding as virtuous what for one reason or another others had regarded, or still did regard, as vicious. Again, certain virtues, such as temperance, cleanliness, and the like, science gave him good reasons for, whereas previously they had been preached on merely fantastic grounds. But, in addition, there were other ethical ideals about which science, he thought, was simply silent. He contemptuously repudiated the 'religion of humanity';—he would, he said, just as soon bow down and worship a "wilderness of apes." Yet he considered that humanitarian sympathy, stoical strength, patience, 'ethical purity and nobility,' devotion to the service of society, carried if need be to the point of martyrdom—that these made up an ethical ideal of duty with an absolute sanction. If religion were properly understood it would consist simply of reverence and love for this ethical ideal, and of the desire to realize it in life "which every man ought to feel." Why ought men to feel it? Huxley does not say. He cannot tell. He merely asserts that his words are "surely indisputable."

This is sufficiently curious, though it can be explained. Science could not help Huxley to account for his 'pure intuition' of the ethical ideal of duty, yet he had no other source of information. Consequently, since he had within him indubitable witness to its existence, he could only say that it was self-evident. He could not take a single step towards motivating this characteristic of humanity or towards relating it to other human characteristics. But, however mysterious, its existence was "surely indisputable."[15] And this enables us to see why Huxley in his later years was irritated both by those who were on evolutionary grounds prophesying the near approach of the millennium and by others who were utilizing the methods of the 'cosmic process' to justify a "fanatical individualism." In his Romanes lecture on *Evolution and Ethics* he turned on these false prophets and advocates of "reasoned savagery" and told them that no ethical principles can be learned from the natural universe. On the contrary, he said, it is the self-evident fact that the ethical ideal of duty has to be pursued even though in this world, as all men know and agree, the wicked and the unjust flourish while righteous men are punished.[16] And he asserted that there is one law for things and another law for men. But it is not merely that man's ways are different from nature's ways, for man's moral character not only finds no analogy in the order of nature but is radically opposed to that order. 'The cosmic process has no sort of relation to moral ends; the imitation of it by

[15] Huxley says that *Sartor Resartus* led him "to know that a deep sense of religion was compatible with the entire absence of theology." (*Life and Letters*, I, 237.) It was a lesson for which he had small reason to feel grateful, as otherwise he might not have been so easily tempted to uphold by sheer force an ideal of duty which was meaningless on his own view of life.

[16] "If there is a generalization from the facts of human life which has the assent of thoughtful men in every age and country, it is that the violator of ethical rules constantly escapes the punishment which he deserves; that the wicked flourishes like a green bay tree, while the righteous begs his bread; that the sins of the fathers are visited upon the children; that, in the realm of nature, ignorance is punished just as severely as wilful wrong; and that thousands upon thousands of innocent beings suffer for the crime, or the unintentional trespass, of one." (*Evolution and Ethics, etc.*, p. 58.)

man is inconsistent with the first principles of ethics.' Consequently "the ethical progress of society depends, not on imitating the cosmic process, still less in running away from it, but in combating it."[17]

What are we to make of this, when we remember that "the universe is one and the same throughout"? In the face of this uncompromising dualism what has become of that unitary natural order, "the sum of existence," of which men ineluctably form a part? The Romanes lecture at once caused a great outcry, and Huxley's friends and enemies united to ask him these and similar difficult questions. He himself, obedient as always to the immediate needs of the moment, had not realized just what he was doing. In the preface to the second edition of the lecture he admitted as much, though he characteristically covered the admission by accusing all of his readers collectively of 'invincible ignorance.' However, in the same edition he set about repairing the damage as well as he could in a "Prolegomena" longer than the lecture itself. In effect he pointed out that it was not the task of science to explain or reconcile facts, but to describe them. It was not his business to answer insoluble questions, or to penetrate the mystery which surrounds existence, but simply to be faithful to the facts as they actually are. The facts are that although "man, physical, intellectual, and moral, is as much a part of nature, as purely a product of the cosmic process, as the humblest weed," nevertheless his ethical character is in complete antagonism with its parent. If this is an inconceivable proposition, so much the worse for reason, because the facts are so.[18] He also

---

[17] *Evolution and Ethics, etc.*, p. 83. On pp. 81-82 Huxley says: "The practice of that which is ethically best—what we call goodness or virtue—involves a course of conduct which, *in all respects,* is opposed to that which leads to success in the cosmic struggle for existence." (Italics mine.)

[18] *Ibid.*, pp. 11-12.

drew out an analogy, using the case of the gardener who
combats the 'cosmic process' in order to grow fruits and
flowers. The analogy doubtless helps, if help is needed,
to show that 'the facts are so,' but that is all. For it begs
the question at issue, and it leaves all the other contradictions between Huxley's latest position and his earlier
utterances exactly where they were.

Clearly the "apostle of veracity" and "teacher of
men" had a more difficult task than he realized. He set
out to clear away the shadows cast by ancient and respectable shams, to let the light of truth shine upon men without obstruction. Nothing could be better, as all would
agree. And success was to be his because he had a new
method unparalleled for simplicity and efficiency. He
would simply use common sense. He would give the name
of truth only to that which could be fully tested and verified, and about all else he would frankly confess his ignorance. Knowledge was a sacred word; he would reverence
it properly by safeguarding its use. He would show men
that by following his simple rule of taking nothing on
trust, of demanding adequate, concrete, objective evidence, of building only on results so confirmed, they
would arrive at a sure and genuine understanding of life.
It is amazing enough, this all too simple plan, yet it
should be remembered that even the best of men might
easily have been dazzled by the triumphs of science in the
middle years of the nineteenth century when Huxley was
entering into his career. And to a young man with a one-
sided training in science, innocent alike of religion and of
philosophy, full of headlong self-confidence, not seriously
or deeply reflective, and eager to leave his mark on the
world, it was probably inevitable that the 'improvement
of natural knowledge' should seem the royal road, for-

tunately just opened up, to the one final, true interpretation of life.

Huxley accepted it as such. It was a great, enthusiastic act of faith, and of blind faith, too. For while he supposed he was taking the path to knowledge, with entirely open and unprejudiced mind, he was in reality swearing allegiance to a particular, specialized kind of knowledge. He was undertaking to accept only one kind of evidence, to take a sectarian view of reality, to see life in terms of its external, sensible forms. He was committing himself to the view that "the universe is one and the same throughout." And concurrently 'the absolute justice of the system of things became as clear to him as any scientific fact.' These were the prejudices in which he tied himself. This was the self-deception lurking unconsciously within his heart. For he already knew that he had the truth within him, although he enrolled himself as an ignorant and humble inquirer. This was the dogmatism with which he armed himself—to take the field against all dogmatists. An unconscious, unexamined, uncriticized dogmatism could blind Huxley to evidence and to the meaning of evidence as surely as it ever blinded any victim of vulgar superstition—and it did. His scepticism, had it ever been honest and thorough, would here have served him well. But he used it only as a tool, as a fighting weapon, as a retreat when difficulties threatened, as a means of escape from rigorous thought—he used it, in short, when it suited him and carefully shielded from it his sacred verities.

Those verities and his own purposes in life were above examination and criticism. The former bade him look outside of himself for the truth, and find it in the appearances of things. The roar of the tiger, his body springing at one through the air, his teeth buried in one's writhing flesh—*there* was something unmistakable, indubitable, real. There could be no question of self-deception, of subjective imaginary vapourings in that. It has ever been the inevitable starting-point of common sense. Yet where did it lead? It led to dust and ashes, to the doctrine of automatism, to the doctrine of the absolute rightness of all things as they are, to a dehumanized world of *things,* from which people had vanished as surely as their illusions. This was the further end of objectivity—as violent a contradiction of common sense as ever brain-sick fool propounded. Huxley dutifully preached it; as far as words could go he said it was the truth and the whole truth; and it is the only coherent form of naturalism to be found in his writings. Yet, as we have seen, even while he preached it and did what he could to help impress it upon his generation, he himself recoiled from his own picture and rendered it, in reality, only an equivocal lip-service. It made life meaningless; it opened up a hideous abyss, without bottom, infinite, which swallowed all human purposes, duties, activities, loves, hates, the whole human content of existence, and left us nothing;—nothing save, indeed, that with which we had started, the regular necessary sequences of matter in endless motion. But it was in obedience to the command of duty, and with the purpose of serving the cause of truth and so liberating men from unworthy bondage, that Huxley had begun the journey which carried him into the bottomless abyss. And this obedience and this purpose too were real; he had direct 'indisputable' testimony to them from within himself. Hence he incontinently turned about and proclaimed that 'iron necessity' was a mere figment of the mind, and happily proceeded to drive home those moral lessons—selfish counsels of prudence for the most part— to be learned from science, which were always so close to his heart. Yet he continued nevertheless to uphold naturalism; the universe was still one and the same throughout.

Such wilful inconsequence it is which makes it a vain attempt to give any coherent outline of what Huxley stood for. He stood, indeed, for 'truths' which exclude or destroy each other, for propositions meaningless in the form in which he held them, for impossibilities. So far as his inconsistencies did not spring from his obvious limitations as a thinker, they came, it would appear, from the fact that he chiefly wrote as a propagandist and controversialist fighting for a cause to which he had unconditionally committed himself. It was not his own views which required examination and sifting, but those of his opponents; what his own views required was wholehearted advocacy, or justification of the 'crushing' variety. This was a situation which promoted dexterity and adroitness in thinking rather than care and thoroughness. In addition, he wrote for immediate needs, and for special audiences and causes; he wrote hurriedly; he felt at times, apparently, that any stick would do with which to beat the dog; and at other times he seems to have felt that, for the sake of appearing to overreach his opponent in his own virtues, a little in the way of consistency might well be temporarily sacrificed. Doubtless, too, his success in controversy encouraged in him his astonishing self-confidence. It was his life-long conviction that all who differed from him must be hypocrites, humbugs, or liars. This was a great source of strength, of course, in beating down opponents, but it caused R. H. Hutton to suspect that Huxley must have been inoculated with papal infallibility, and it certainly implies a temper very different from that of the seeker after truth. At times it seems, indeed, as if he felt so confident that the truth was already within him that he could venture boldly to play fast and loose with it.

This is to end on a harsh note. Yet I have no wish to
minimize Huxley's unusual gifts as a writer or to belittle
his honest purpose in attacking superstition and prejudice. In many of his battles he stood, at a time when it
required great courage and promised no reward save
his own consciousness of integrity, for what we all now
take to be the truth. No one now doubts the fact of evolution, even though many perplexing questions surround
it and its meaning, and this momentous change of opinion
is in large part Huxley's work. Every one now agrees
that the stories of the creation, temptation, and flood in
Genesis are myths, and for this too Huxley is largely
responsible. And these are two only out of a not incon-
siderable number of cases where he accomplished his aim
in such fashion as to set his mark indelibly on the history
of popular thought. But besides pricking certain bubbles
of delusion and popularizing certain discoveries of science Huxley undertook the larger and graver task of
formulating a theory of knowledge and an interpretation
of life in naturalistic terms. It is his success in this endeavour which I have sought to determine, as much as
possible by letting him speak for himself. And it is a
matter of very great importance that, if his unmistakable
though unwilling testimony is to be trusted, a purely
naturalistic interpretation of human life is an impossibility.

MATTHEW ARNOLD

ARNOLD began his literary career as a poet. Had he not been without money, or had he been as patient in poverty and singleness of life as was Tennyson, he might have brought to fruition the full measure of his high poetical aims. About that it is useless to speculate. The facts are that he did have to depend for his livelihood upon what he could earn, and that a few years after he had secured his Oxford degree he was anxious to take the shortest course to marriage with Miss Lucy Wightman. He desired a diplomatic post, but the future in that direction was uncertain, and in 1851 he obtained through Lord Lansdowne an inspectorship of schools, a position which he filled until within two years of his death. The work was exacting and uncongenial. In time he became more or less reconciled to it, realizing its importance. It gave him, too, opportunities for some of the best and wisest writing on education which was published during his century. But it also consumed his time and energy, and made it impossible for him to throw himself as he wished into the composition of poetry. He long persevered in the attempt, and even in the last years of his life kept hoping still to complete poetical designs formed twenty or thirty years before; but actually he wrote less and less with each year after 1851, and very little indeed after 1861.

He did not ascribe his failure entirely to the work with the schools. "We are not here to have facilities found us for doing the work we like, but to make them," he wrote;

and he felt that had he lived in a different age he might
have succeeded in transcending all the difficulties of his
work. But his age was one of a great transition, making
itself felt in social life, in politics, in religion, in every
sphere of thought and activity, while men around him
were blind, if not to the occurrence of change, at any rate
to its nature and its necessity. They closed their eyes to
facts; they were unmoved by surrounding ugliness and
squalor; they were content with mediocrity, with make-
shifts, with nostrums. They lagged far behind the rest of
Europe in their realization of what was taking place, and
in consequence they met new conditions and demands
unintelligently; but, self-satisfied and prosperous, they
spent their time in continual applause of themselves and
in self-gratulation upon their unparalleled virtues. And
thus it was that there existed no clear, undivided current
of national life and faith, such as was necessary to support a great age of literature, but instead endless confused cross-currents of ancient prejudice, of mistaken
belief, of mere stupidity, of triumphant demagogy, of
unbridled desire to marry one's deceased wife's sister—
of what indeed not? Hence men could not know rightly
where they stood or why, and poetry could not flourish,
because a poet might as well attempt to work in a vacuum
as in a chaos of confused and warring elements. So Arnold felt;—he felt that poetry required the stimulus of a
community united in clear vision of things as they are
and in a stirring and confident faith resulting from such
vision.

Balked of his aim and true vocation, then, by the intellectual and spiritual poverty of his age, Arnold turned
to what he could do. With stoical resignation he went
about amongst the schools, and learned to know the life
of the middle and lower classes, while he meditated the
needs of England. And with his election to the chair of

poetry at Oxford in 1857 he began to voice his conclusions. He became a critic of literature, of education, of
society, of politics, of religion; and he endeavoured thus,
if he could not continue with poetry himself, to fashion in
England a fitter home for some poet of the future. He
made himself heard. Under the grateful sunlight of public recognition he grew in strength and confidence, and
he thoroughly enjoyed both his work and his success.

It is not my object to attempt any review of Arnold's
work as a whole, but to inquire into his religious position.
For this a convenient starting-point is afforded by Mr.
Stuart P. Sherman's assertion that Arnold was, "to
begin with, innately and profoundly religious."[1] Mr.
Sherman, at first sight rather oddly, quotes the poem
entitled *The Buried Life* to support his claim. Rather
oddly, because in this poem Arnold, after saying that
there is that in man, his innermost spirit, which, could he
question it, might truly tell him the meaning of life, but
which for ever just eludes him and sends him searching
for the saving truth on a thousand false tracks—after
saying this he goes on to conclude that man may find
his true self most clearly if he has the rare fortune to be
able to read it in the eyes of one who loves him. The poem
is not obviously a religious one, yet Mr. Sherman rightly
presents it as evidence that Arnold, when a young man,
went through a period of what he calls religious disillu-
sionment. Arnold's poetry shows, not that he had any
definite religious faith when we first get sight of him,
but that he keenly felt the lack of it. The pleasures of
Christian certitude he had known, but he had found the
traditional faith ill-based and hollow, so that for a time
he was as one lost in a pathless wild. In *The Buried Life,*
then, we have expressed Arnold's sense of the inevitable

[1] *Matthew Arnold, How to Know Him,* p. 64.

frustration of men's hopes in their search for the truth of their being, with, yet, the possibility somewhat ambiguously held out that this search may at times be rewarded, if anywhere, in a man's sense of unity with one whom he loves. This deeply hidden secret which men unceasingly, yet so vainly, attempt to discover is, of course, just what Christianity, or any other religion, claims to lay bare for us.

Other poems tell the story more explicitly. In *Dover Beach,* as the poet stands gazing at the calm sea through the night air, he hears "the eternal note of sadness" in

> The grating roar
> Of pebbles which the waves draw back, and fling,
> At their return, up the high strand,
> Begin, and cease, and then again begin,
> With tremulous cadence slow.

He recalls that Sophocles heard the same sound long ago, and so was made to think of the "turbid ebb and flow of human misery," while he, standing by the distant northern waves, finds in it another thought:

> The sea of faith
> Was once, too, at the full, and round earth's shore
> Lay like the folds of a bright girdle furled.
> But now I only hear
> Its melancholy, long, withdrawing roar,
> Retreating, to the breath
> Of the night-wind, down the vast edges drear
> And naked shingles of the world.
>
> Ah, love, let us be true
> To one another! for the world, which seems
> To lie before us like a land of dreams,
> So various, so beautiful, so new,
> Hath really neither joy, nor love, nor light,

Nor certitude, nor peace, nor help for pain;
And we are here as on a darkling plain
Swept with confused alarms of struggle and flight,
Where ignorant armies clash by night.

Again, in his *Stanzas from the Grande Chartreuse*, Arnold describes his ascent and the monastery on its Alpine heights, and then turns to ask what is he, that he is in this place?—

For rigorous teachers seized my youth,
And purged its faith, and trimmed its fire,
Showed me the high, white star of Truth,
There bade me gaze, and there aspire.
Even now their whispers pierce the gloom:
What dost thou in this living tomb?

Forgive me, masters of the mind!
At whose behest I long ago
So much unlearnt, so much resigned—
I come not here to be your foe!
I seek these anchorites, not in ruth,
To curse and to deny your truth;

Not as their friend, or child, I speak!
But as, on some far northern strand,
Thinking of his own Gods, a Greek
In pity and mournful awe might stand
Before some fallen Runic stone—
For both were faiths, and both are gone.

Wandering between two worlds, one dead,
The other powerless to be born,
With nowhere yet to rest my head,
Like these, on earth I wait forlorn.
Their faith, my tears, the world deride—
I come to shed them at their side.

Clearly to him who wrote *Dover Beach* and the *Stanzas from the Grande Chartreuse* Christianity was not merely a dead faith, it had been when living a delusion, promising what it could not give. *There* was not certitude, nor peace, nor help for pain; and what Christianity had pretended to offer was in its fulness nowhere to be found. What of ease for his troubled spirit man might gain, he could gain, if anywhere beyond himself, only within the circle of this world in merely human relationships. Clearly, too, Arnold was not sanguine even as to this. In *The Buried Life* his tone is doubtful, his words not wholly unambiguous. In *Dover Beach* and the *Stanzas from the Grande Chartreuse* he speaks more definitely, but less hopefully, and we are told that none of the sons of men can reveal any hidden secrets. Even as we ourselves, men have no final, saving truths to tell; they can only give us the solace that comes of knowing we do not stand alone in our trouble. Elsewhere Arnold returns to the subject of love, disillusioned, without hope for any release of man's veiled and imprisoned spirit. In one of the poems collected under the title *Switzerland* he tells us that men never have more than dreamed that "two human hearts might blend in one" and be "through faith released from isolation without end," for,

> In the sea of life enisled,
> With echoing straits between us thrown,
> Dotting the shoreless watery wild,
> We mortal millions live *alone*.
>
> Like driftwood spars, which meet and pass
> Upon the boundless ocean-plain,
> So on the sea of life, alas!
> Man meets man—meets, and quits again—

while it is ordained by a fate which knows no turning that between men should ever be

> The unplumbed, salt, estranging sea.

Evidently those "masters of the mind," those "rigorous teachers," who seized Arnold's youth, while they took from him the certitude which Christianity had given his forbears, put nothing very positive in its place. It was a kind of naturalism which they offered him, and so completely did it win his acceptance that he wrote as if its absolute truth could be taken for granted, as if it must be self-evident immediately it was presented to the mind. In this sense it was a doctrine positive enough in all conscience, and as final to his mind as any accepted dogmatism to the minds of his ignorant or deluded elders. But, nevertheless, in the beginning at any rate, it put nothing in the place where Christian faith had been, but left its convert feeling himself adrift, without guide and without light. It was not to another world of faith that he turned, it was to wander "between two worlds, one dead, the other powerless to be born." And Arnold wandered disconsolately because, though he did not even slightly hesitate to follow his masters in adjudging Christianity to be no longer possible for a rigorous and sincere mind, still, he continued to be conscious of needs and questionings which had to remain unsatisfied and unanswered.

Whether or not this was a consequence of Arnold's 'innate and profound' religious sense is a question which the character of his later thought must itself answer. Meanwhile it may be asked who were his "rigorous teachers" and what was their quarrel with Christianity? Arnold himself answers these questions, not exhaustively, but sufficiently, in his essay on Heinrich Heine. He tells us that Heine, despite all those faults of character which kept both his life and his work below the level of his inborn genius, was, still, Goethe's most important German successor and continuator in Goethe's most important line of activity. What was this line of activity? Goethe's own words are quoted for an answer: "If I were to say what I had really been to the Germans in general, and to the young German poets in particular, I should say I had been their *liberator*." Arnold goes on to say that modern peoples find themselves the inheritors from a former age of an immense system of "institutions, established facts, accredited dogmas, customs, rules." Their own life has to be carried forward in this system, yet they inevitably feel that it is something not their own, that it fails to correspond with their own actual wants, that, indeed, for them it is customary, not rational. This feeling is the awakening of the modern spirit—a spirit now almost everywhere awake. Almost every one now perceives the want of correspondence "between the forms of modern Europe and its spirit, between the new wine of the eighteenth and nineteenth centuries, and the old bottles of the eleventh and twelfth centuries, or even of the sixteenth and seventeenth." It is no longer dangerous to proclaim this want of correspondence; people, in fact, even begin to feel shy of denying it. And to remove it is beginning to be the deliberate effort of most persons of good sense.

We are told, further, that "dissolvents of the old European system of dominant ideas and facts" all who have any power of working must nowadays be. And Goethe was the grand dissolvent in an age when there were fewer of them than in the latter half of the nineteenth century. Goethe himself is allowed to explain how he proceeded in his task of liberating modern European people from their outworn routine. "Through me," he says, "the German poets have become aware that, as man must live from within outwards, so the artist must work from within outwards, seeing that, make what contortions he will, he can only bring to light his own individuality." This should be thought no impotent conclusion to his declaration that he had been the liberator of the Germans, because it really goes to the heart of the matter. ''Goethe's profound, imperturbable naturalism is absolutely fatal to all routine thinking; he puts the standard, once for all, inside every man instead of outside him; when he is told, such a thing must be so, there is immense authority and custom in favour of its being so, it has been held to be so for a thousand years, he answers with Olympian politeness, 'But *is* it so? is it so to *me?*' Nothing could be more really subversive of the foundations on which the old European order rested; and it may be that no persons are so radically detached from this order, no persons so thoroughly modern, as those who have felt Goethe's influence most deeply.''

In a letter to Cardinal Newman which has been published only recently Arnold said: ''There are four people, in especial, from whom I am conscious of having learnt—a very different thing from merely receiving a strong impression—learnt habits, methods, ruling ideas, which are constantly with me; and the four are—Goethe, Wordsworth, Sainte-Beuve, and yourself.''[2] I pass over for the present the oddness of these juxtapositions—Arnold, of course, himself recognized it—because it seems fair, without implying that the influence of the others named was unimportant, to single out Goethe as the type of those ''masters of the mind'' who formed his thought and gave him his direction. And from the essay on Heine we have seen what that direction was. Essentially it was the exercise of that 'right and duty of private judgement' which in the sixteenth and seventeenth centuries had linked Protestantism, however unwillingly or unconsciously, with the spirit of the Renaissance. It was a re-

[2] The letter was first published in the *Times Literary Supplement* (London), March, 1921. It is printed in *Unpublished Letters of Matthew Arnold* (1923), p. 65.

volt against all external authority, no matter how ancient, august, or widely received. It undermined the foundations of the church equally as well as those of neoclassical criticism. It was the assertion that all institutions, standards, ideas, were within the sphere of individual scrutiny, and were not only subject to change, but to annihilation, at the individual's will.

It is a question how much the quality of Arnold's thought changed as he grew older. Many readers feel a pronounced difference between his poetry and his prose, and when one encounters this feeling one is perforce reminded of the meagreness of our information concerning his earlier years. It is impossible to determine in any final way how quickly, once he had begun, he became genuinely conscious of the direction of his thought. He himself felt that he had matured very slowly, but this alone hardly answers the question.[3] It is highly probable, moreover, on many grounds, that he was to some real extent conscious and self-critical from the beginning; and it is, at any rate, unquestionably true that the difference between his poetry and his prose is almost entirely one of mood, not one of substance. In his earlier period he was conscious chiefly of the negative bearings of those propositions of whose truth he felt assured, and the consequence was a sense of deep oppression, not only because he felt himself loosed upon a pathless wild, but because in the midst of a chaos he could not effectually turn his powers to the uses of poetry. This is illustrated by a remarkable passage in a letter which he wrote to his sister, Mrs. Forster, probably in 1853: "Fret not yourself to make my poems square in all their parts. . . . The true reason why parts suit you while others do not is that my poems are fragments—i.e. that I am fragments, while you are a whole; the whole effect of my

[3] See the *Letters*, edited by G. W. E. Russell, I, 247-248.

poems is quite vague and indeterminate—this is their weakness; a person therefore who endeavoured to make them accord would only lose his labour; and a person who has any inward completeness can at best only like parts of them; in fact such a person stands firmly and knows what he is about while the poems stagger weakly and are at their wits' end.''[4]

Arnold adds that he would not be so frank with every one; and it would appear that in later years he forgot not only this confession, but equally the mood which prompted it. With the passage of time he markedly changed, not as to the substance of his thought, but as to the mood which accompanied it. As he turned from poetry to criticism, and began through this work to win unmistakable public recognition, his sense of oppression gave way to one of genial satisfaction. The tangled forest was after all not so bad a place, and he thought he saw, if not a new path leading on from where the old one stopped, at least a means of effecting a clearing in its midst. As I have said, he grew in strength and confidence. And in 1869 he wrote to his mother: ''My poems represent, on the whole, the main movement of mind of the last quarter of a century, and thus they will probably have their day as people become conscious to themselves of what that movement of mind is, and interested in the literary productions which reflect it. It might be fairly urged that I have less poetical sentiment than Tennyson, and less intellectual vigour and abundance than Browning; yet, because I have perhaps more of a fusion of the two than either of them, and have more regularly applied that fusion to the main line of modern development, I am likely enough to have my turn, as they have had theirs.''[5] This passage has more than once been quoted,

4 *Unpublished Letters*, p. 18.
5 *Letters*, II, 10.

and its substantial truth is, I imagine, becoming more evident with each year that passes. My object, however, is not to discuss that question, but to show at once Arnold's changed mood and, nevertheless, his sense of the continuity of his thought between his earlier years and the period when he lectured on Heine at Oxford and published the lecture in his *Essays in Criticism*.

Clearly he was by that time, at any rate, fully conscious of the nature of his work and of where he stood. He stood on the "profound, imperturbable naturalism" of Goethe. A lengthy parallel might be drawn out between Arnold and Goethe, and it would have many elements of interest, but not the least interesting thing about it would be the point where it would have to stop. Arnold, for instance, wrote an essay on Spinoza. He regarded that philosopher with sympathy and admiration; he even went so far as to say that Spinoza and his work "deserve to become, in the history of modern philosophy, the central point of interest." He regarded Spinoza's attitude of 'cheerful stoicism' as closely akin to his own, and he found much in his *Tractatus Theologico-Politicus* which he converted to his own uses in his writings on religion, but beyond that he did not go. He confined his appreciation to particular points of treatment or of thought and to the personal character of the philosopher; he did not go on to confess himself a disciple, a deterministic pantheist, as did Goethe. And in general Arnold fought shy of committing himself to large positive views. That this was in part a futile effort, as such efforts must be, is true; but, nevertheless, it marks a distinct cleavage between the two men. What Arnold did accept unreservedly from Goethe was his subversive and dissolving individualism, his assertion that man must live from within outwards, his refusal to trust anything on the score of its external recommendations.

This was a method rather than a conclusion, though it of course implied certain definite conclusions, and it was naturalistic because it refused to admit the possibility of anything beyond the regular 'course of nature.' It accepted only that which was within the range of normal human experience and which could, accordingly, be fully tested and verified by one's self. Arnold found his great illustration of this method in the work of Sainte-Beuve. In an obituary notice of the French critic, published in the *Academy* in the fall of 1869, he praised him as a born naturalist, "carrying into letters, so often the mere domain of rhetoric and futile amusement, the ideas and methods of scientific natural inquiry. . . . Man, as he is, and as his history and the productions of his spirit show him, was the object of his study and interest; he strove to find the real data with which, in dealing with man and his affairs, we have to do.'"[6] Sainte-Beuve's long series of literary portraits, then, were to Arnold an example of the true method of gathering the data on which alone trustworthy generalizations about man, his nature and his destiny, could be made.

This was not the method of dogmatic religion, and Arnold's acceptance of it sufficiently explains his abandonment of traditional Christianity. To receive it meant acquiescence in external authority, belief in an infallible church or in an infallible book, and he could believe in neither without denial of his naturalistic principles.

Protestants of an earlier day, exercising honestly the 'right and duty of private judgement,' had been able to subdue their understandings to the Bible because it contained what they thought adequate evidence for its supernatural character. The evidence lay in those prophecies in the Old Testament of the coming of the Messiah which

6 This short notice is reprinted in *Essays in Criticism, Third Series* (Boston, 1910), and in the Oxford edition of *Essays* by Arnold.

were held to have been fulfilled in Jesus in such a manner as to prove their supernatural origin; it lay in those prophecies and also in the miracles recorded in connexion with the life of Jesus, and elsewhere, in the Bible. But for Arnold the force of both kinds of evidence had vanished away. Supernatural prophecy and miracles were quite outside the bounds of contemporary experience, and hence there was a strong presumption that they were outside the bounds of all human experience. At any rate overwhelming testimony was needed to establish their credibility—and such testimony there was not. Critically examined, Arnold held, the prophecies of the Old Testament proved to be very different from what men had once supposed; they supported, in fact, no supernatural claims whatever. All that could be truly said was that, "to a delicate and penetrating criticism, it has long been manifest that the chief *literal* fulfilment by Jesus Christ of things said by the prophets was the fulfilment such as would naturally be given by one who nourished his spirit on the prophets, and on living and acting their words.'"[7]

It was the same with miracles. Men have always been extraordinarily prone to seek for them as a confirmation of what they believe, but in our own day, Arnold concluded, it is the 'Time-Spirit' itself which has undermined the old proof from this source. It does not much matter whether one attacks or defends miracles;—the modern mind, with its increased experience, is simply turning away from them. It is doing so because, as its experience widens, it sees how they come about. It sees that in certain circumstances miracles always do arise, and that they have no more solidity in one case than in

[7] *Literature and Dogma*, p. 103. I quote from the most recent reprint published by Macmillan, New York.

another. Under the stress of appropriate circumstances, wherever men exist there is, as Shakespeare says,

> No natural exhalation in the sky,
> No scape of nature, no distempered day,
> No common wind, no customed event,
> But they will pluck away his natural cause,
> And call them meteors, prodigies, and signs,
> Abortives, presages, and tongues of heaven.

"Imposture is so far from being the general rule in these cases, that it is the rare exception. Signs and wonders men's minds will have, and they create them honestly and naturally; yet not so but that we can see *how* they create them."[8]

This, of course, was simply to say that the real objection to miracles is that they do not occur. Whenever a miracle is reported which can be investigated it turns out that actually it was no such thing; and the modern mind thence concludes, whenever a miracle is reported which cannot be investigated, that actually it also was no such thing. In the presence of this overwhelming and universally-felt probability against miracles Arnold thought that formal argument for them could not be taken seriously and that similar argument against them was superfluous.

There had been, however, in the seventeenth century and later, a third method of proving Christianity true—the proof from so-called internal evidence. It consisted of the rational demonstration of metaphysical propositions concerning the being and nature of God and concerning his relation to man and the world. By this method Christian belief was shown to be completely agreeable with the conclusions of human reason and so an inner correspondency was established between the Bible and

[8] *Literature and Dogma*, pp. 116-117.

the nature of things. The method was conclusive, of
course, only if the metaphysics were sound and impregnable. Arnold rejected them with scornful ridicule. He
was himself no abstract thinker, and he had neither liking
nor respect for those who were. He apparently never
tired of poking fun at logicians and metaphysicians,
though at times he tires his readers. He appears to have
considered metaphysical thought a gratuitous vanity, an
exhibition of their talents by men who were proud of
their dialectical skill and who had no serious employment
to absorb their energies. It is true, however, that, despite
his incapacity to understand his foe and despite his taste-
less blunders, the position he took was not merely the
result of a temperamental reaction, as might be supposed from the form of his attack. For the substance of
his attitude, underneath his cavalier manner, was that
required by his naturalism. By it he was bound to confine
knowledge within the sphere amenable to the methods of
science. He was bound not to go beyond strict induction
from exact observation and experiment. He was bound
to reject all pretensions to transcend the limits of normal, verifiable human experience. This he consistently
did; and many to-day, if not most, would regard sympathetically his attacks on the metaphysician's pretension
to attain absolute knowledge, had he been content to stop
with that. But he was not, for he supposed it possible
and desirable to banish metaphysics completely from the
ken of man. This would be unbelievable were it not that
many men of science and other naturalistic thinkers of
his age took the same position, and that Arnold shared
almost all of their prepossessions. The result, of course,
was simply that an unconscious and largely unexamined
metaphysic was substituted for a conscious one, which
was an advantage from no point of view save, perhaps,
that of journalistic controversy.

Thus it was that Arnold rejected traditional Christianity because he considered its supernatural claims hollow and its metaphysical supports rotten. But the naturalism which took him this far was on its face, as I have said, a method rather than a conclusion. It was primarily an instrument of criticism, or so he came to conceive it as he meditated the needs of England in the light of the ugliness and unintelligence and confusion of standards which he saw around him and in the light of the poverty of integrating ideas which he found within him. He remained, however, as anxious as in his earlier days 'to see life steadily and to see it whole,' which meant, practically, to see it in terms of some absolute conclusion. Hence he was no more able to rest honestly and contentedly in sceptical negations than are other men, perhaps all other men worthy of the name. Truth might be far away and veiled, but he could not suppose her inaccessible and invisible. Her figure was to be discerned, if one only went the right way about it. So he wrote in the Preface to the second edition of *Essays in Criticism:* "To try and approach truth on one side after another, not to strive or cry, not to persist in pressing forward, on any one side, with violence and self-will— it is only thus, it seems to me, that mortals may hope to gain any vision of the mysterious Goddess, whom we shall never see except in outline, but only thus even in outline. He who will do nothing but fight impetuously towards her on his own, one, favourite, particular line, is inevitably destined to run his head into the folds of the black robe in which she is wrapped."

What were the elements of the situation he faced? Goethe's subversive, dissolving naturalism, as has been seen, he accepted unreservedly. Yet, whether he ever fully realized it or not, the fact was that the ugliness, the unintelligence, the intellectual confusion which he saw around him were largely the products of essentially the same modern spirit. The exercise of the 'right and duty of private judgement,' as it worked practically with men as they are in contact with the historical framework of society, produced exactly that 'dissidence of dissent' for whose spirit and workings Arnold felt undying contempt and abhorrence. And as this dissolving spirit of individualism worked in religion, so precisely it worked in other fields, sanctioning everywhere the business of 'doing as one likes,' raising everywhere an immense, impenetrable wave of self-satisfaction. Arnold profoundly deplored the religious, intellectual, and æsthetic anarchy which it had produced, and the political anarchy which he feared it was beginning to produce in his own day, with freedom ever more and more exalted as an end in itself and the *summum bonum* of English life. He fully accepted the dissolving spirit of naturalism, then, but found its consequences intolerable. Hence his problem was really one of discovering, if he could, some method of avoiding those consequences, not by abandoning, but by merely giving a new direction to, their cause.

Such a method he thought he discerned in the naturalistic criticism of Sainte-Beuve. That was the method of knowledge, and knowledge, or science, was the key to life. "I am convinced," he wrote to Mrs. Forster, "that as *Science,* in the widest sense of the word, meaning a true knowledge of things as the basis of our operations, becomes, as it does become, more of a power in the world, the weight of the nations and men who have carried the intellectual life farthest will be more and more felt; indeed, I see signs of this already. That England may run well in this race is my deepest desire; and to stimulate her and to make her feel how many clogs she wears, and how much she has to do in order to run in it as her genius

gives her the power to run, is the object of all I do.'"[9]
Sainte-Beuve's criticism was the application of the
method of science to human life, enabling men to see
human nature as in itself it really is. This meant, of
course, that it really enabled the individual to know his
own nature as it was, in an absolute sense, as is implied
in those subversive questions, 'But is it really so?—is it
so to *me?*' The final truth, only in outline, but, still, sufficient for the purposes of life, was thus discoverable by
each individual for himself if he took the right way of
unlocking the dark and close recesses of his inward being.
But truth!—truth was one, indivisible, universal, always
and everywhere the same. If once each man knew the
truth of his human nature, then would men be even as
gods, perfect in thought and deed, and anarchy of all
kinds would be for ever impossible. All men would be as
one, and perfect, in taste and thought and action; for all
men would implicitly obey the authority of right reason,
felt from within, 'whose prescriptions are absolute, unchanging, of universal validity.'[10]

So Arnold reasoned, and thought his *Essays in Criticism* an illustration of his discovery. He was struck, he
wrote to his mother, on looking through that book by the
admirable riches of human nature brought to light
through his treatment of a small number of writers,
and by the sort of unity the book had to stimulate the
better humanity in us.[11] That is exactly what he had in
mind. Human nature he apparently took to be an absolute entity of some mysterious kind, alike in all and,
so to say, divine, but hidden away variously within
men, there to await their discovery of it, partial or

9 *Letters,* I, 285-286.
10 *Essays* (Oxford ed.), p. 15. (*The Function of Criticism at the Present Time.*)
11 *Letters,* I, 286-287.

complete, as occasion might permit. His name, both for the process of this discovery and for its transcendent results, was culture—a word familiar to all nowadays, thanks largely to Arnold's use of it and to his remarkable success in impressing it upon the mind of a whole generation. He defined it many times and in many connexions, with the tempered but unexhausted fervour of one who was not only its first apostle but, humanly speaking, its embodiment. In the Preface to *Culture and Anarchy* we are told that it is "a pursuit of our total perfection by means of getting to know, on all the matters which most concern us, the best which has been thought and said in the world; and through this knowledge, turning a stream of fresh and free thought upon our stock notions and habits, which we now follow staunchly but mechanically, vainly imagining that there is a virtue in following them staunchly which makes up for the mischief of following them mechanically."

Culture, then, is the study of perfection. Arnold held that study to be synonymous with the effort to see things as they really are, for he also defined culture as the attempt to learn "the true, firm, intelligible law of things." This also is the attempt of the exact sciences, and so far culture and science are one and the same. It is the same instinct or 'power' in human nature which brings both into being, and they are separable only when we come to the study of human nature itself. Arnold was never entirely clear about this distinction, probably because he always tended to take it for granted as obvious, but in his praise of the Greeks he says that they pursued sweetness *and* light, beauty as well as truth, and he lays it down as a mark of their sound insight that they perceived that "the truth of things must be at the same time beauty." Again, in speaking of Greek art he says that it was a fruit of the scientist's effort to see things as they really are, "inasmuch as Greek art and beauty rest on fidelity to nature—the *best* nature—and on a delicate discrimination of what this best nature is."

These statements indicate his position as a humanist more clearly, perhaps, than the distinction he draws out and illustrates in his essay on *Literature and Science.* In this essay he complains that those who wish to give science the chief place in education leave out of their calculations the constitution of human nature. The 'powers' which go to the building up of human life are, on a rough analysis, those of conduct, of intellect and knowledge, of beauty, and of social life and manners. These are not separate entities, for human nature is unitary, and consequently we are continually impelled to relate, for example, "pieces of knowledge to our sense for conduct, to our sense for beauty." But in this science cannot help us; it gives us knowledge, and that is all it gives us; whereas literature touches our emotions and so gives us knowledge *humanized,* related to our sense for conduct, our sense for beauty, and our sense for social life and manners.

Here Arnold is evidently driving at the same point which he suggests in *Culture and Anarchy* when he speaks of sweetness and light in union with each other. It can be defined most clearly by an answer to the question whether the scientist can be said to study perfection, the complete union of truth and beauty and goodness. Obviously he cannot. His concern is with what Huxley called the 'customs of matter,' and his sole effort is to see *them* as they really are. This is the attempt, however chimerical it may be, of the psychologist and the sociologist as well as of the physicist, the chemist, and the biologist. Beauty and goodness are terms of evaluation, and with the world of values the sciences have nothing to do; —they know not of its existence. The scientist does not judge phenomena, or regard them emotionally, as either beautiful or ugly, as either good or evil. As a scientist he accepts phenomena impartially, endeavouring simply to see them as they are. But Arnold, approaching human nature in the same empirical spirit, saw that æsthetic and moral evaluations, which in turn imply standards, are fundamental in it, and he concluded that we cannot get to know human nature as it really is unless we try to learn not merely what we are, but what we may be and ought to be. Hence culture demands that we should get to know what is distinctive in the thoughts and perform-ances of the best and greatest human beings, and get not only to know this but to love it, for which the study of literature and art is a necessity. Thus we may learn to be faithful to nature—the *best* nature—and we may learn how to discern with delicacy and precision what this best nature is.

Culture, being the study of our total perfection, is therefore not content with the partial or fragmentary view of reality which can alone ever be afforded by the sciences. It includes science, but goes beyond it to include much more which to science is not significant. Culture, in fact, includes everything. It is the due nourishment and development of *all* sides of human nature, not separately, but as these exist in us, organically related so as har-moniously to form one unitary being. Moreover, in pro-portion as we are cultured we realize the extent to which our lives are conditioned by the lives of those around us, and come to see that we cannot effectively pursue our own perfection in isolation or in an indifferent environ-ment. As social beings we must not merely seek perfec-tion but seek also to make it prevail, so that culture of necessity aims at general or social betterment. Culture stands or falls with the progress of society towards perfection, with our faith in human progress, and with our desire to labour for this end.

Culture issues in an inward condition of the mind and character which insures one's taking the one right attitude, whatever it be, towards all that one encounters in one's passage through life. It is the disclosure of that mysterious essence of human nature at its best which Arnold saw darkly hidden within each human being. Only when this is duly revealed can one be said to possess one's soul; but then, also, one is possessed by right reason, a principle of absolute authority which is always and everywhere the same. Furthermore, it is not for nothing that Arnold speaks of our 'instinct' for knowledge, our 'instinct' for conduct, and the like, because with him 'right reason' is oddly synonymous with perfection of taste. And when culture frees us from the tyranny of ideas and actions which are customary, not rational, it sets up in their place a principle of perfected taste. When he is called upon to make a judgement or to decide upon a course of action, the cultured man simply allows his consciousness to play freely and spontaneously and disinterestedly upon the subject, with inevitably and absolutely right results. The free, spontaneous play of his consciousness brings him out instinctively on the side of the angels.[12]

Religion, Arnold says, aims at perfection as culture does, but it concerns itself with only one element in our nature and neglects or even contemns the rest. Religion, in its essence and when divested of alien accretions, is merely the attempt to conquer "the obvious faults of our animality." Obsessed with the importance of this aim, it extravagantly and incorrectly tells us that with these faults conquered all other things will be added unto us;

[12] See particularly the concluding pages of the chapter entitled *Our Liberal Practitioners* in *Culture and Anarchy*.

it tells us that this effort is the one thing necessary for our salvation. But for this there is no 'one thing need-ful.' Our problem is not so simple. No one exclusive line of action or of effort can thus be enthroned supernally without disturbing the harmony of our nature, warping it from its true course towards total perfection into an ugly, fanatical one-sidedness which is itself an evil, and which makes impossible our success even in this our one, chosen, exclusive line of advance. 'The man who knows only his Bible cannot know even that.' And religion, which may be defined as "morality touched with emo-tion," takes up only one of the 'instincts' or 'powers' which compose human nature, our 'instinct' for conduct, and tries to work with it alone. Conduct, of course, is of high importance, for it makes up three-fourths of life, and religion has hitherto acted effectively in this sphere on a large scale, so that culture, aiming to see all things justly, grants gladly the weighty place of religion in life. But when religion claims supremacy, the friend of cul-ture cannot grant this, for culture goes beyond religion in its aim at our total perfection. It substitutes for reli-gion's fanatical advocacy of a one-sided development its larger aim after "a harmonious expansion of *all* the powers which make the beauty and worth of human nature."

Arnold agreed that one could not attach too high an importance to morality, but rejoined that one could cer-tainly attach too exclusive an importance to it and that Christianity, more particularly what he called Puritan-ism, did so. So far as it did perform its proper office of aiding us to conquer "the obvious faults of our animal-ity," it was worthy of allegiance and support, but only as, if one may so term it, a single department included within the larger activity of culture. Arnold felt that the dissenting Protestantism of England offered convincing evidence of the harm done by religion when it over-reached itself in its exclusive claims and its hollow pretensions to supernatural sanction. It thus captured the whole-hearted allegiance of many people, only to tell them that all they needed to do in order to fulfil their best and highest selves was to be good, to overcome 'the obvious faults of their animality.' And so they were led to undervalue, or even to despise, beauty and knowledge; and thence issued, not only the ugliness of their chapels and services, but the ugliness, the deformity, the illiberality, the stupid self-satisfaction and contented ignorance of their lives. But this grievous moral plague could be done away by bringing religion down to its legitimate, subordinate place within the sphere of culture.

Soon after Arnold published *Culture and Anarchy*, however, he saw looming up in England a danger opposite in kind to that which it had been written to meet. *Culture and Anarchy* was a vivacious sermon upon the harm done by too much religion, but about 1870 he began to have it forced upon his attention that there was a growing section of the British public for which religion itself was becoming impossible. Science and its implications had begun really to take hold of the popular mind. The opposition between science and the Bible, between science and traditional Christianity, had begun to be widely aired. Scientists like Huxley and W. K. Clifford, and militant atheists like Charles Bradlaugh, had begun to achieve popular success in their attacks upon Christianity and the churches. And Arnold now heard of numbers of men who, learning that the Bible was a merely human product like any other book or collection of books, learning, moreover, that it contained mistakes, doubtful legends, and fairy tales in place of what they had been taught to regard as supernatural proof of its truth, were proceeding to abandon the Bible and its religion alto-

gether. These men concluded that, since the Bible contained much that was not true or that was not what they
had been taught to believe, there was nothing in it of any
significance for them, and they concluded that their
teacher—the Church—was an impostor or a cheat.

In this, Arnold felt, they concluded wrongly. He sympathized with them, in that he considered the theologians
and churchmen to blame for persisting in an absurdly
wrong-headed interpretation and support of Christianity.
But, nevertheless, he felt that they were running into an
extreme which was fully as vicious on one side as was
English Puritanism on the other, and accordingly he
proceeded to set forth the 'simple and natural' truth of
the whole matter in *Literature and Dogma*. All Christian
bodies were agreed as to the importance of the religion
of the Bible; they differed from each other in their interpretation of it; and while they were busily engaged in
acrimonious conflicts amongst themselves over this question, the thing itself, the religion of the Bible, was sinking
into neglect. Arnold came forward in his book as the
devoted friend of true religion seeking to rescue it from
its apparent friends but real enemies, the theologians.
He felt the appearance of inconsistency between his ex-
hortations in *Culture and Anarchy* and those in *Literature and Dogma*, but in fact, as he insisted, there was
between the two books no genuine inconsistency. He
wrote them for different publics, and with objects accordingly different, but that was all. In the latter he wrote
as the friend of true religion, and agreed that too high
an importance could not be claimed for it; but, still, he
wrote as the friend only of religion as he had already
defined it.

We are told that the Bible is to be regarded as a piece
of literature, or rather as a collection of the literature of
the Hebrew people, and that it is mistakenly read if read

as anything else. Its language is "fluid, passing, and literary, not rigid, fixed, and scientific." Its value lies in the fact that the ancient Hebrews apprehended the importance of morality, if not more clearly, at least more passionately than any other people, and succeeded in getting fully into written words their impassioned sense of the worth of the conduct. Hence the Bible is the great classic of the world's literature bearing upon this important side of human nature. But its high position does not make it different in kind from any other literature. It needs, as fully as the literature of any other age or people remote from our own, to be interpreted to us, and this interpretation is a matter of great delicacy and difficulty. It is a work which taxes the ripest culture to its fullest capacity, and which cannot be undertaken without disaster by any one not possessed of the ripest culture. But when the Bible is interpreted by the cultured critic of literature who is alone capable of the task, then we begin to see it truly, and we see that it has more to tell us about the fulfilment of our nature on its moral side than any other book or any other literature.

We discover that the Bible has its basis, not in any unverifiable assumption of a "Great Personal First Cause, the moral and intelligent Governor of the Universe," but in truths of human nature which we can verify in our own experience. God's existence is not a mere assumption, or guess, or hope; it is something we know as genuinely as we know anything; but what we know is simply that God is "the stream of tendency by which all things fulfil the law of their being." This definition is inadequate for purposes of edification, yet it has the inestimable advantage of being a verifiable fact, so that it puts God on "a real experimental basis." It does not go perilously beyond our actual evidence, and so does not involve us in pretences which, when they are

questioned, we are unable to make good. Moreover, since
the law of our being with which religion is concerned is
the law of righteousness, we may fitly term God for religious purposes the 'Eternal Not Ourselves which makes
for righteousness.'

What is the fact about righteousness? The fact, verifiable through experience, is that when we do what we
ought to do and leave undone what we ought not to do we
have a sense of succeeding in life, of going right, of hitting the mark, which brings with it a feeling of peace that
is life's highest satisfaction. The Hebrews had this "near
and lively experimental sense" of the beneficence of
morality which engendered in them the impassioned devotion to it recorded in the Old Testament. The Old Testament is thus calculated to rouse us to the importance
of morality. The New Testament fulfils the Old in the
sense that it tells us, as the Old does not succeed in doing
satisfactorily, how to *be* righteous. The Old-Testament
Jews in the long run tended to lose their intuition of the
importance of righteousness because they sought to embody it in definite rules of external conduct and then
lapsed into the mere mechanical fulfilment of the letter
of their law.

But in the New Testament we are told how Jesus restored the original intuition of the Eternal Not Ourselves
by transforming the idea of righteousness, making it to
consist fundamentally of an inward state of the heart and
feelings. "To do this, he brought a *method,* and he
brought a *secret.*" He "made his followers first look
within and examine themselves; he made them feel that
they had a best and real self as opposed to their ordinary
and apparent one, and that their happiness depended on
saving this best self from being overborne. *To find his
own soul,* his true and permanent self, became set up in
man's view as his chief concern, as the secret of happi-

ness." This was the method of Jesus, and it consisted in that "change of the inner man" which we call repentance, or conviction of sin.

"But for this world of busy inward movement created by the method of Jesus, a rule of action was wanted; and this rule was found in his secret." It was simply self-renouncement. "He that loveth his life shall lose it, and he that hateth his life in this world shall keep it unto life eternal. Whosoever will come after me, let him renounce himself, and take up his cross daily, and follow me." "Thus after putting him by his method in the way to find *what* doing righteousness was, by his secret Jesus put the disciple in the way of *doing* it. For the breaking the sway of what is commonly called *one's self*, ceasing our concern with it and leaving it to perish, is not, Jesus said, being thwarted or crossed, but *living*. And the proof of this is that it has the characters of life in the highest degree—the sense of going right, hitting the mark, succeeding. That is, it has the character of *happiness;* and happiness is, for Israel, the same thing as having the Eternal with us, seeing the salvation of God." We are, moreover, told, on the authority of quotations from Aristotle, Horace, Goethe, Plato, Wordsworth, and, of course, Bishop Wilson of Sodor and Man, that actual human experience has always and everywhere proved that self-renouncement *is* the road to man's true happiness.

No statement, however, of what Jesus brought can be complete which does not include "that element of *mildness* and *sweetness*" in which his method and secret worked. Hence Arnold, after a discussion of this quality, concludes with the assertion that "the conjunction of the three in Jesus—the method of inwardness, and the secret of self-renouncement, working in and through this element of mildness—produced the total impression of his '*epieikeia*,' or sweet reasonableness."

This, then, is true religion, verifiable through experience, placed on a "real experimental basis"—the religion of the Bible, as discriminated by a just and delicate criticism. All things exist in the fulfilment of law. For conscious beings this is happiness. But man's nature is dual, and his fulfilment of the law of his being depends upon intelligent effort. Man has to recognize his lower nature as sinful and to renounce it in favour of his true self, and this brings him a pure happiness secure against all the chances of time and circumstance. This is the moral law; to apprehend it through the emotions so as to act it out consistently day after day is religion—the realization or fulfilment of our nature on the side of conduct. The importance of the Bible is that it states the moral law clearly, in passionate language, and in concrete, literary form, through symbol and myth, so that it brings its contribution of truth to us in a humanized shape which comes home to us and stimulates in us the intense conviction necessary to rouse us to action.

Literature and Dogma is, evidently, an essay in criticism, and one which Arnold wrote under peculiar handicaps. For he already had, when he began, a definition of religion which all religious people, whatever their differences amongst themselves, would unite to repudiate. He was under the necessity of forcing the language of the Bible into agreement with this definition—a necessity which he could only meet by much fanciful and perverse interpretation, by the deliberate repudiation of some portions of the book, and by the total neglect of other portions. He had, furthermore, because of his naturalism, to pretend that virtue can be measured in terms of present earthly happiness enjoyed by each individual—a pretence which, in turn, got him into inextricable difficulties concerning self-renouncement and the Eternal Law which is *not* ourselves. Nor did he, despite all the difficulties he encountered and the sacrifices he made to that end, succeed in inventing a religion which avoided all metaphysic; for his Eternal Not Ourselves remains a metaphysical entity just as certainly whether it be called a law or whether it be called a person, the "moral and intelligent Governor of the Universe."

But, whether a successful one or not, *Literature and Dogma* is, as I say, an essay in criticism, an effort to capture the Bible for literature, an effort to make secure its place as a literary classic full of great poetry in the broad Aristotelian sense of the word. It is a part of culture's search for the best that has been thought and said in the world, and a part of culture's effort to make that best prevail. Hence it is not this newly invented religion of his, but culture, which is to be taken as Arnold's substitute for traditional Christianity. Within his scheme of culture, what he understood by religion occupied a legitimate, even a necessary, but still a subordinate place, and *Literature and Dogma* is not the record of any change in his general attitude. It does, of course, indicate a shift in his thought, which occurred for reasons already mentioned. The 'relaxing and dissolving' influence which he had sought to exert was in fact being exerted by forces far more powerful and subversive than any he could bring to bear upon English society, and with results different from those for which he wished; and *Literature and Dogma* is a memorial of his perception of that fact. He exclaimed in a letter written in 1868, "If we can but dissolve what is bad without dissolving what is good!" That suspicion of a fear, within the short space of a couple of years, grew into the conviction that if religion of any kind was to be more than a memory in the future it must be at once rescued from its tottering guardians and transformed into "morality touched with emotion."

Nevertheless, though he felt uneasy, he was not on the whole displeased with what he saw taking place. In 1881 he wrote to an acquaintance in France that the force which was shaping the future was not with any of the orthodox religions, nor with any of the neo-religious developments which were proposing to themselves to supersede them. "Both the one and the other give to what they call religion, and to religious ideas and discussions, too large and absorbing a place in human life; man feels himself to be a more various and richly-endowed animal than the old religious theory of human life allowed, and he is endeavouring to give satisfaction to the long suppressed and still imperfectly-understood instincts of this varied nature. . . . I think it is, like all inevitable revolutions, a salutary one, but it greatly requires watching and guiding. The growing desire, throughout the community, for amusement and pleasure; the wonderful relaxation, in the middle class, of the old strictness as to theatres, dancing, and such things, are features which alarm many people; but they have their good side. They belong to this revolution of which I speak. The awakening demand for beauty . . . is another sign of the revolution, and a clearly favourable sign of it. . . . The moral is that whoever treats religion . . . as absorbing, is not in vital sympathy with the movement of men's minds at present. . . . The great centre-current of our time is a *lay* current."[13]

In this letter the friend of culture speaks out frankly enough; and in his essay on *The Study of Poetry*, written a little earlier, he sums up in an eloquent passage his enduring position, and at the same time implicitly indicates the real bearing of *Literature and Dogma* as an essay in criticism. "The future of poetry is immense,

[13] *Letters*, II, 220-221.

because in poetry, where it is worthy of its high des-
tinies, our race, as time goes on, will find an ever surer
and surer stay. There is not a creed which is not shaken,
not an accredited dogma which is not shown to be ques-
tionable, not a received tradition which does not threaten
to dissolve. Our religion has materialized itself in the
fact, in the supposed fact; it has attached its emotion to
the fact, and now the fact is failing it. But for poetry
the idea is everything; the rest is a world of illusion, of
divine illusion. Poetry attaches its emotion to the idea;
the idea *is* the fact. The strongest part of our religion
to-day is its unconscious poetry. . . . More and more
mankind will discover that we have to turn to poetry to
interpret life for us, to console us, to sustain us. Without
poetry, our science will appear incomplete; and most of
what now passes with us for religion and philosophy will
be replaced by poetry. . . . Wordsworth finely and truly
calls poetry 'the breath and finer spirit of all knowledge':
our religion, parading evidences such as those on which
the popular mind relies now; our philosophy, pluming
itself on its reasonings about causation and finite and
infinite being; what are they but the shadows and dreams
and false shows of knowledge? The day will come when
we shall wonder at ourselves for having trusted to them,
for having taken them seriously; and the more we perceive their hollowness, the more we shall prize 'the breath
and finer spirit of knowledge' offered to us by poetry.''

What Arnold had to propose, then, as a substitute for
traditional Christianity was culture. He speaks for it,
most men have agreed, surpassingly well. He was, Dis-
raeli told him in 1881, "the only living Englishman who
had become a classic in his own lifetime."[14] And this
flattering verdict has been echoed and amplified by others

[14] *Letters*, II, 219.

of weightier judgement. Yet it remains true that this interpretation of life, summed up in the word culture, still raises, as it did in the minds of serious men when its proponent was living, many questions which Arnold does not answer. And in fact it is something which, it must be said, seems to us clearer and more definite and more plausible than it really is. Consequently Arnold's manner of exposition, so full of charm, so persuasive, so strengthened by its echoes of those great voices from the past which daily spoke to him, his ease and urbanity, his combined lightness and sureness of touch, his freedom from all pretentiousness and pedantry, his obvious good faith and earnest conviction always burning brightly under the surface of his playfulness—all of these qualities, which are the qualities of his greatness as a man of letters and master of effective criticism, still in the end serve us badly when we are carried by them to the point of conversion, and then begin seriously to ask ourselves, what prospect is actually opened up before us, what way of life and what goal of endeavour? For we inevitably discover that these engaging qualities have really acted upon us as a blind, concealing much that is vague or confused and much that is fanciful—fanciful in the sense of being unreal, because unrelated to our actual problems and the possibilities actually open to us.

Frederic Harrison accused Arnold of lacking "a philosophy with coherent, interdependent, subordinate, and derivative principles." For this Arnold poured ridicule upon Harrison, quoting the accusation more than once in order to confess, with mock humility, that it was just. The language used was absurd enough, and no one will wish the ridicule away, yet other contemporaries of more solid parts felt objections substantially similar to the one adumbrated by Harrison which could not be set aside so lightly. Arnold's friend J. C. Shairp was one, and to him no direct reply was ever made. Henry Sidgwick was another. Arnold termed him, with a slight hint of irritation, "an acute though somewhat rigid critic," but did little else to turn the point of his attack. Yet his criticism was thoroughly damaging.[15] He asserted that Arnold treated "of the most profound and difficult problems of individual and social life with an airy dogmatism that ignores their depth and difficulty," and he added that although Arnold was dogmatic he was nevertheless vague, because when he used indefinite terms he did not attempt to limit them, but instead availed himself of their indefiniteness. Sidgwick went on to point out that the root of culture has always been, ethically, a refined eudæmonism. It has been a primarily self-regarding attitude in which thought and feeling have been cultivated because of an exquisite pleasure experienced in refined states of reflexion and emotion. It has encouraged refinement of taste, but it has also encouraged the exclusiveness, the moral indifferency, the dilettantism, and the general smugness of the connoisseur. It has been and is, in short, a 'fair-weather theory of life,' which could not conceivably arise save in a time of exceptional prosperity, and even then only amongst a few individuals amply sheltered from the normal experiences of life— its chances, difficulties, conflicts, and tragic sufferings. And in fact Arnold himself confessed this, or the greater part of this, and it was not culture as it actually is, but a culture idealized, transformed, purified of its smugness and levity and imbued with a devout energy and fire borrowed from religion, that he advocated. But, Sidgwick complained, Arnold talked sometimes of this ideal

---

[15] It is contained in the essay entitled *The Prophet of Culture* in his *Essays and Miscellaneous Addresses*. J. C. Sharp's criticism is to be found in his *Culture and Religion*, a series of lectures first published in 1870 and reprinted a number of times in immediately following years.

culture, sometimes of actual culture, without being able to distinguish them, not knowing of what he spoke. And Arnold illustrated in his attitude towards all but a trifling minority of his fellow-countrymen, and in his attitude towards many current questions, *not* the ideal culture of his dreams and wishes, but the workings of actual culture. He was himself, in fine, the best proof one could want of the impossibility of effecting the transformation of culture for which he wished, and which he saw to be necessary if it was to be adequate to the needs of life.

That Sidgwick's criticism could not be gainsaid Arnold signalized in admitting its acuteness. As for the charge of rigidity with which he qualified his admission, it is clear enough that what he referred to was simply a rigour of analysis which, though modest, offered a marked contrast to his own 'sinuous, easy, unpolemical' manner. It is equally clear, too, that this was the direct cause of whatever acuteness Sidgwick's remarks possessed. Arnold would have done well to emulate it. His refusal to do so made him violate his own counsels in yet another serious way which Sidgwick might appropriately have noticed had he so chosen. For it was one of Arnold's pronounced convictions that his countrymen had a pernicious love of action for its own sake which constantly led them into all manner of mistakes, and it was to be one of the benefits of culture that it would lead men to act, indeed, more effectively than ever before, but not to act hastily or blindly, and not to act at all until they had examined their ideas and aims and, by a just and painstaking criticism, had sifted them and clarified them and made sure that they not only had a worthy source but were intrinsically right. He exhorted them, in the words of his idolized Bishop Wilson, not to exhibit a blind and undiscriminating zeal for making reason and the will of God prevail, but first to make sure that their light was

not darkness. Yet he himself never stopped long enough
in his advocacy of culture to determine clearly what it
was that he preached, and not only failed to distinguish
between its actual and its ideal character, but also between its personal and social aspects, between knowledge
and taste in his scheme, and between culture as a means
and as an end. Into this confusion, moreover, this radical
defect of the critical intelligence, he was led by the workings of culture as it actually is, for he was led thither by
his exclusive, confident reliance upon the oracle of his
own individual taste. Because he fancied that the final
rectification of all things was to issue from the instinctive preferences of perfected taste, he tended to regard
his own instinctive preferences as final and irreproach-
able so soon as he became conscious of them, and forth-
with he pressed them upon the public, without stopping
to make certain that his light was not darkness.

It may be said, however, that, despite all vagueness
and inconsistencies, Arnold's aim was, plainly enough,
the spiritual perfection of humanity, of which perfection
he tried to take a comprehensive view. And this is true,
and the aim was essentially religious. I have quoted Mr.
S. P. Sherman's assertion that Arnold was ''innately
and profoundly religious,'' and this has indeed, particularly since the publication of selections from his notebooks in 1902, become a commonplace of critical opinion,
but the bearings of the fact have not equally been recognized. Arnold's ideal of spiritual perfection he derived
from religion, which is to say, from traditional Christianity. It would not otherwise, moreover, have appeared
before him as a living reality, almost tangible, warm and
colourful enough to be worth fighting for at any risk and
hardship—able, in short, to inspire the most tremendous
actions. Nor could it so have remained for him a real and
vital force had he not continued throughout his life to

nourish his vision on the works of the great Christian
writers. Yet the source from which this ideal came to him
he was constrained by his naturalism to repudiate, and
so, if he was to keep it at all, he had to attempt to trans-
fer it, will he nill he, to some naturalistic theory of life.

It was a thing easier to talk about than to do. Any
naturalistic theory of life which legitimately includes
aims or purposes must have in view some earthly ideal.
It need not be materialistic or sensuous, but it does have
to be, by the nature of the case, an ideal realized or realiz-
able through normal human experience. Perfection of
any sort can only be made a naturalistic ideal by project-
ing it into the indefinite future of the race and resting it
upon belief in human progress. Even then it is impossible to conceive in what sense the word can be used of
beings who, howsoever developed into a fuller and richer
and less fallible humanity, would still be the temporary
creatures of change living amidst storms and earth-
quakes, upon a planet doomed to become uninhabitable
and perhaps itself to perish. But, supposing this crucial
difficulty somehow surmounted, perfection can still be an
ideal only for the race, not for individuals, whose lives
can have only an instrumental value as means to a problematic end not their own and, for all practical purposes,
infinitely distant. Belief in human progress—a different
thing from evolution—has no sort of genuine foundation
in history, science, or reason. It is, as Sidgwick said of
culture, a 'fair-weather theory of life,' the product of a
remarkable epoch of material expansion and spiritual
decadence, and already, after a brief period of efflores-
cence, it has visibly begun to decay. But Arnold wrote
when it was at its optimistic height, subscribed to it himself, and regarded culture as the chosen instrument of
further racial progress. Hence at times he wrote as if he
were attempting only to build for the future, the indefi-

nite future, of the race, to which cloudy mirage individuals were to sacrifice themselves. This was to be an apostle of the 'religion of humanity'; yet Frederic Harrison never converted him to positivism, and usually he did not mean to advocate in culture anything so obviously fanciful and unreal.

Usually he wrote for living individuals and proposed to them something which he asserted to have significance, not simply for their problematic, infinitely remote descendants, but actually for themselves. And then he defined perfection in a special sense and limited it to the individual's spiritual life, assuming, one supposes, this to be so far separable from the individual's body and his strictly physical activities and likewise from his environment with the chances and hardships that issue from it. Within these limits he defined perfection as a certain inward state of being which—judging from what he says in *Literature and Dogma*—gives one the sense of going right, of succeeding, of hitting the mark. It is perhaps significant that he only succeeded in getting thus far with a definition when his subject-matter forced him to try to translate into naturalistic terms the Christian plan of salvation, and it is unfortunate that he then involved himself in the apparent paradox that self-realization cannot be achieved save through self-renouncement. The paradox is, however, only apparent, as he makes it clear that, as his naturalism demands, what he really means to signify by the traditional term is our resignation of our lower selves in favour of our higher selves. How on a naturalistic basis he is able to distinguish absolutely between these two selves is a question he does not answer, and we may for the moment leave it unasked. What we are told is that we have to resign our vulgar tastes in order to enjoy refined pleasures, our love of make-believe in order to achieve the truth, our contentment with ugliness in order to dwell with absolute beauty, and our hankerings for selfish advantage in order to be wholly just. And the reason is that nothing short of this will reward us with an enduring and unmixed feeling of self-satisfaction. Other satisfactions prove to be delusions or snares; they flee our approach or wither in our mouths. Perhaps they do, but one wonders how Arnold can lay it down as a fact. He has himself told us, as has been seen, that man lives from within outwards, and that each one has to make these discoveries for himself and abide by the result steadfastly against all authorities, even against Bishop Wilson if need be. 'Is it really so?—is it so to *me?*'

But, supposing that one makes the 'right' discoveries and does attempt to renounce one's 'lower' self, can one succeed? Christians, of course, have always denied it, have asserted that no efforts of our own can be sufficient to overcome our lower selves, inherently sinful as we are, and must be, while clothed in fleshly bodies; and they have placed perfection in a non-natural, eternal, unchanging world of the spirit which they tell us we may gain only with the help of divine grace, and even with this help not while we remain earthly creatures. But Arnold, necessarily, could have nothing to do with this non-natural world beyond the possibility of human experience, nor yet was he willing to commit himself to the extraordinary paradox that the fulfilment of life can come only through complete devotion to a mere figment of the imagination, an impalpable creation of the fancy which has no real existence anywhere. Hence he was forced to insist that absolute justice and beauty and truth can be realized, actually are realized, within the limits of earthly life.

Is it so? The whole weight of human experience is unitedly and unequivocally against the notion. This world has never yet been the scene of justice, and has not come appreciably nearer that goal within the span of history. This world is not the scene in which is or can be realized any of that company of immaterial values, consciousness of which and all possible devotion to which make up the distinctively human character of life. Nor is this a new discovery. Job's comforters have become a byword amongst us, even though we are always forgetting why the words of Bildad the Shuhite and his companions were displeasing to the Lord. Job, as we all know, was a man altogether righteous, so that the noise of his goodness re-echoed even to the precincts of the Almighty, and yet Job was afflicted with all that is evil in the sight of men, and not the least of his afflictions was the presence of friends who were sure that he was being punished for sins he would not confess. Elihu, Bildad, and the rest were, in other words, of that company who are sure that righteousness is rewarded, that justice is realized upon earth—and they were wrong. And all who believe with them are wrong and, for anything that we can see, must always be wrong. Their number, of course, is large, for probably most of us, if we courageously scrutinize our instinctive judgements, find that there is a certain glamour attaching to worldly success which almost forces our respect, while we feel a suspicion amounting to practical certainty that there must be something wrong with the man who fails to acquire wealth or position, or who is bent by loss or affliction. Yet generally, unless we have the misfortune to be salesmen or efficiency experts, we recognize these instinctive judgements as a weakness and banish them from our serious thoughts. And, indeed, nothing can be more certain to the reflective and informed mind than that injustice and wrong rule the affairs of this world, where in every generation and in every community the wicked, the cunning, the unscrupulous, and the dishonest men flourish, while wise men are neglected or starved and good men are contemned or scorned.

This is a truism, and Arnold was not one in his sober moments to be ignorant of it, but he could not help himself. Yet its consequences are plainly disastrous to his gospel of perfectionism. On the terms he offered not a single effective step can be taken towards the spiritual perfection which was his ideal. For if one proposes earthly satisfaction to men as an end they will seek it where they *can* find it, whether or not it be enduring and unmixed. And in no case, moreover, can one dictate the terms in which such an end is to be conceived, since self-realization or satisfaction is subjective, and men will seek it where according to their own lights it is to be found. Culture may, indeed, refine men's tastes, and cause them to demand that the wine of their delight shall have a ruddier glow, but it will not transform their tastes, while it will bring in return for its gifts its own peculiar vices. Culture as we know it is just that—the education of taste; and, if one may so put it, culture cannot be radically transformed into something else without *becoming* something else.

It is of course not therefore to be despised, but it is the fact that Arnold himself would have been the first to recognize the failure of his attempt to construct a naturalistic theory of life, had he not believed that somehow he could manage to preserve as its keystone or crown a scale of values which came to him from traditional Christianity.

VI

SAMUEL BUTLER

"MELCHISEDEC was a really happy man. He was without father, without mother, and without descent. He was an incarnate bachelor. He was a born orphan." So wrote Samuel Butler, admiringly, for he too was an incarnate bachelor, though this does not mean quite all that the innocent, or the fanatically logical, might suppose. What it does mean can be pieced together pretty completely from his autobiographical novel, *The Way of All Flesh,* from his *Notebooks,* and from the two fat volumes of the memoir written by the naïve, garrulous, devoted Mr. H. Festing Jones. Briefly and in general terms it means that Butler was not so much a responsible sharer and co-worker in the affairs of life as a detached onlooker, pleased to enjoy himself in his own way, unconcerned amidst the fever and toil of those caught in the wheels of circumstance, free to ask embarrassing questions, to utter troublesome remarks and, if he liked, to make faces at the world. He was not forced to obey the rules of the games he played by any obvious or immediately-felt external compulsion, and he had none within him. Fettered by no respect for authority, he light-heartedly ventured to play one game after another, sure that what he called his common sense was a sufficient guide, and content, if he could not do more, at least to have his fun with men of graver and more solid character whom he could not understand and did not care to understand. He contentedly said: "I am the *enfant terrible* of literature and science. If I cannot, and I know I cannot, get the literary and scientific big-wigs to give me a shilling, I can, and I know I can, heave bricks into the middle of them.''

He was right, and for his pains he was once described as the "Galileo of Mares'-Nests.'' The phrase is happy enough, as far as it goes, but it requires not only amplifying, but qualification, in order to a just understanding of Butler's position. His career was a series of escapades, of which probably the queerest was the one which occasioned the descriptive phrase just quoted. This was his theory that the writer of the *Odyssey* was a woman. Not only was he convinced that he had sufficient evidence to establish this, but also to show where she had lived and to identify much of the natural scenery which she must have had in mind in writing the poem. He even gave her a name, insisting that she was Nausicaa, though about this he was not seriously concerned as he was about the rest. What is one to think of this?—what of the competent Grecian who spends much time in carefully working out such a theory, visiting the localities he discusses and attempting to settle his problem with scientific thoroughness? *The Authoress of the Odyssey,* as the book is called, has of course been dismissed by scholars as an instance of misplaced ingenuity, and one who knew nothing else of its writer would inevitably set him down as a mere eccentric. Moreover, Butler's contemporaries, with more or less excuse in different cases, similarly dismissed most of his other books as they appeared, so that, as far as he was generally known at all while still living, he was regarded as a mere eccentric.

Yet this was quite wrong. Butler himself asserted that he never made his books, but that they grew. They came to him and pressed themselves on him with more force than he could resist, insisting on being written and on being such and such. Most eccentrics, I suppose, could say as much for their performances, but Butler also wrote in one of his notebooks, following a list he had made of his 'mares'-nests': "I am not going to argue here that they are all, as I do not doubt, sound; what I want to say is that they are every one of them things that lay on the surface and open to any one else just as much as to me. Not one of them required any profundity of thought or extensive research; they only required that he who approached the various subjects with which they have to do should keep his eyes open and try to put himself in the position of the various people whom they involve. Above all, it was necessary to approach them without any preconceived theory and to be ready to throw over any conclusion the moment the evidence pointed against it. The reason why I have discarded so few theories that I have put forward—and at this moment I cannot recollect one from which there has been any serious attempt to dislodge me—is because I never allowed myself to form a theory at all till I found myself driven on to it whether I would or no. As long as it was possible to resist I resisted, and only yielded when I could not think that an intelligent jury under capable guidance would go with me if I resisted longer."

This has the appearance of candour, and though there is probably a concealed implication in the earlier portion of the passage, it may as a whole be taken for what it seems to be. And what Butler tells us is that, looking merely at common things accessible to all, he continually found questions arising in him concerning their received interpretation. He was ready to entertain any questions that came, yet he never formulated and published a new answer to them until it was forced on him, so powerfully as to make it seem in the end self-evident. He was, in other words, a man of keen, restless, searching mind, who was willing, without preconceptions, in genuinely empirical fashion, to contemplate any possibility. He had no axe to grind. He was not anxious to make the facts mean one thing rather than another. He simply wanted to see what they did mean, and to that end was ready to face impartially in any direction, and was determined not to commit himself until the evidence by its own weight forced a conclusion.

This is something very different from eccentricity, or the love of novelty for its own sake, though in all ages men have been unable or slow to distinguish between the two amongst their contemporaries. And in Butler's case the difficulty was aggravated by several circumstances. His entirely open-minded attitude, as it has just been described, is identical with that which the modern scientist professes to have, and Butler in fact entered as freely into what was thought to be the domain of science as he entered into the realms of literature and art and religion. Yet he himself was not, and never pretended to be, a scientist, nor did he attempt to force his manner of writing into conformity with current and respectable practice when he was dealing with scientific problems. Moreover, he had early in his career, in the only one of his books which became widely known during his lifetime, *Erewhon*, advertised himself as a whimsical observer of society, with an imagination playful but not untinged by malice, who remained to scoff, more or less irresponsibly, albeit with gleams of common sense, where others had come to pray. Who was he, then, this literary upstart, this dilettante, to challenge Darwin concerning evolution, as he began to do in *Life and Habit* and did do more directly in *Evolution, Old and New?* The fact that he did not question evolution itself, nor Darwin's accuracy of observation, or the like, was scarcely a mitigation of his offence. He only questioned, as a thinker, Darwin's interpretation of his data, his hypothesis of natural selection, and, as an historian, Darwin's treatment of his predecessors; but, still, he did question Darwin, and that was enough. It was as if he had set out wantonly to disfigure a great national monument.

He was greeted only with contempt and, as he might have put it, with very little even of that. For the most part he was simply ignored, but he was thus rebuked by the *Saturday Review:* "When a writer who has not given as many weeks to the subject as Mr. Darwin has given years, is not content to air his own crude though clever fallacies, but assumes to criticize Mr. Darwin with the superciliousness of a young schoolmaster looking over a boy's theme, it is difficult not to take him more seriously than he deserves or perhaps desires. One would think that Mr. Butler was the travelled and laborious observer of Nature, and Mr. Darwin the pert speculator who takes all his facts at second-hand."

With the issue thus raised Butler would make no compromise, and in this certainly he was right. He correctly saw a danger to society and a violation of the professed spirit of science in an attitude towards Darwin which Huxley and others were doing their best to encourage. He wrote in a notebook: "Science is being daily more and more personified and anthropomorphized into a god. By and by they will say that science took our nature upon him, and sent down his only begotten son, Charles Darwin, or Huxley, into the world so that those who believe in him, *etc.;* and they will burn people for saying that science, after all, is only an expression for our ignorance of our own ignorance." No one can soberly deny that this danger has existed and still exists, though one may hope that a developing and fully justified popular distrust of the 'expert' will keep things from soon going as far as

Butler feared. On the other hand, Butler's rejoinder to his reviewer was hardly calculated to help either him or his cause. In *Unconscious Memory* he quoted the above passage from the *Saturday Review* and proceeded to comment on it in this manner: "The lady or gentleman who writes in such a strain as this should not be too hard upon others whom she or he may consider to write like schoolmasters. It is true I have travelled—not much, but still as much as many others, and have endeavoured to keep my eyes open to the facts before me; but I cannot think that I made any reference to my travels in *Evolution, Old and New*. I did not quite see what that had to do with the matter. A man may get to know a good deal without ever going beyond the four-mile radius from Charing Cross. Much less did I imply that Mr. Darwin was pert: pert is one of the last words that can be applied to Mr. Darwin. Nor, again, had I blamed him for taking his facts at second-hand; no one is to be blamed for this, provided he takes well-established facts and acknowledges his sources. Mr. Darwin has generally gone to good sources. The ground of complaint against him is that he muddied the water after he had drawn it, and tacitly claimed to be the rightful owner of the spring, on the score of the damage he had effected."

This is a pert rejoinder, and it is unfortunately characteristic of Butler's manner. It illustrates, too, the schoolboyish perversity which was strong in him and which some of his friends were so foolish as to encourage. He, in fact, had a very simple trick which, perpetually repeated, served to start all manner of game, and often did duty with him for candid open-mindedness. He delighted to turn commonly accepted statements upside down and to startle conventional minds with these inverted propositions. "An Honest God's the noblest work of Man." Frequently he went no further than this, but at times he

204 CHRISTIANITY AND NATURALISM

was able to do more with his cheaply-won originality. An
example is the sonnet which he entitled *A Prayer:*

> Searcher of souls, you who in heaven abide,
> To whom the secrets of all hearts are open,
> Though I do lie to all the world beside,
> From me to thee no falsehood shall be spoken.
> Cleanse me not, Lord, I say, from secret sin
> But from those faults which he who runs can see,
> 'Tis these that torture me, O Lord, begin
> With these and let the hidden vices be;
> If you must cleanse these too, at any rate
> Deal with the seen sins first, 'tis only reason,
> They being so gross, to let the others wait
> The leisure of some more convenient season;
>   And cleanse not all even then, leave me a few,
>   I would not be—not quite—so pure as you.

Since Butler's mind was acute, it is not surprising that
in the course of years his simple trick at times served him
well, so that he turned up a number of really important
and fruitful propositions; but neither is it surprising
that these were not immediately assessed at their true
worth, nor that he also turned up a deal of ingenious
nonsense. He could thus fairly claim that all of his
'mares'-nests' lay on the surface and did not require for
their discovery "any profundity of thought or extensive
research," although he meant, perhaps, a little more than
his words at first sight convey. Furthermore, he honestly,
though not always successfully, tried to distinguish his
sense from his nonsense, and the theses which he defended at length and publicly were sincere convictions,
forced upon him after he had tried carefully and impartially to test them. In this matter it is always necessary
to distinguish between his convictions and his manner of
expressing and defending them, as he constantly tended,

even when he was at heart most serious, to give free rein in his method of presentation to his perversity, to his whimsical fancy, and to his vein of malice. In this he was singularly obtuse. Aiming to arrest public attention, he so little understood men and was guilty of such gross faults of taste as to create the impression, in the few who did read his books on their first appearance, that he was a mere mountebank, unscrupulously catching at any notion, howsoever absurd or subversive, in a desperate effort to gain notoriety. The impression was incorrect, and yet not wholly so, for Butler's motives were probably always more or less mixed.

Detached from society, bent on enjoying himself in his own way, the consistent foe of accepted opinion, heaving bricks at the big-wigs, contemptuously rejected or ignored by his contemporaries, Butler was nevertheless a true child of his age and has, besides, taken his place as a not unimportant figure in the history of ideas. Hence his work rewards study, as an outline of the development of his thought will make clear.

The son of an Anglican clergyman and the grandson of a bishop, Butler was expected, after he had received his degree at Cambridge, to take holy orders, and he went from Cambridge to London in 1858 to prepare for ordination by doing parish work amongst the poor. It was not at Cambridge, but while he was engaged in this work, that he was apparently first awakened to any doubts about Christianity and aroused to try to think for himself. His trouble came upon him in a sufficiently odd way. He was led by an accident to the discovery that several boys in his parish had never been baptized, yet he could not see that their lives and characters differed in any way from the lives and characters of others who had been regularly baptized. But what then became of the doctrine of baptismal regeneration? He anxiously extended his inquiries until he was able to compare larger groups of baptized and unbaptized youths, with the result, of course, that his initial doubt was confirmed. He then approached his ecclesiastical superiors with his evidence, only to find that they were unable or unwilling to advance any considerations tending to establish the efficacy of infant baptism—to find, indeed, that they simply regarded his questioning attitude as in itself reprehensible, if not sinful.

Butler's doubts, however, once raised, were not thus to be stilled, and he presently refused to take holy orders. The trouble over infant baptism, one may be sure, was only the gateway, opened to let in other questions. Leslie Stephen has remarked concerning his own abandonment of Christianity: "I did not feel that the solid ground was giving way beneath my feet, but rather that I was being relieved of a cumbrous burden. I was not discovering that my creed was false, but that I had never really believed it. I had unconsciously imbibed the current phraseology; but the formulas belonged to the superficial stratum of my thought instead of to the fundamental convictions."[1] Butler has not said as much, but things must have been pretty well the same with him. The whole course of his life shows that he was not the man to take truth for granted, once his mind was awakened, and shows also that Christian doctrine had never at any time attained any real hold upon him.

In addition, it is known that about this time, or certainly not much later, he began to concern himself over the difficulty or impossibility of harmonizing the accounts of the Resurrection contained in the four Gospels. He was led, in fact, to an independent study of the New Testament, and it would appear that as soon as he had

[1] *Some Early Impressions*, p. 70.

fairly entered on this he began to feel increasingly the weight of all the naturalistic objections to the super-naturalism of Christianity. How rapidly he discovered all that he had never really believed is not definitely known. It cannot be inferred from the dates of his pub-lications bearing on Christianity, as he was in New Zea-land engaged in sheep-farming from 1859 until 1864, and as his time was fully occupied for several years there-after in the study of painting. It is, of course, not a matter of the greatest importance, but it seems probable that his abandonment of Christianity was almost as prompt as it was complete.

He attacked the problem of belief by inquiry into the miraculous elements in the life of Jesus, and of these he came to regard as crucial the event to which his attention had first been called, the Resurrection. If this had oc-curred all of the rest was possible, and acceptance of Christianity followed as a matter of course. As soon as he began to look for it, however, he found that anything even approaching what would to-day be called proof was not to be had, but that, on the contrary, the earliest extant reports of the event were in irreconcilable opposi-tion to each other. This in itself, aside from other con-siderations increasing the probabilities against the Res-urrection, was enough to decide his question, because obviously such an event demanded, for honest belief, the clearest and most overwhelming kind of proof.

He saw, however, that even though he might be cer-tainly correct in rejecting the Resurrection, there was still an historical problem connected with it which de-manded explanation. For it seemed to him just as clear as that the Resurrection had not taken place, that both the immediate disciples of Jesus, and Paul, were con-vinced that it had actually occurred, and that around this one supposed certainty had grown up the whole miraculous legend of the life and ministry of Jesus.[2] Butler found, as he became acquainted with the Biblical scholarship of his day, that Straus endeavoured to clear up this difficulty on a naturalistic basis by supposing that the disciples suffered an hallucination or a series of hallucinations. But he thought this a hopelessly strained and indeed impossible solution. In casting about for one better suited to the probabilities he was led to conjecture that Jesus had not actually died on the cross, and had later recovered sufficiently from his injuries to appear several times before his disciples, who, of course, in that age would not have doubted that he was truly risen from the dead.

Butler elaborated this theory first in an obscurely published pamphlet which appeared in 1865, and then later, hoping to attract more attention to it, he incorporated the greater part of the pamphlet in *The Fair Haven,* which was published in 1873. It was announced on its title-page as "A work in defence of the miraculous element in our Lord's ministry upon earth, both as against rationalistic impugners and certain orthodox defenders, by the late John Pickard Owen, with a memoir of the author by William Bickersteth Owen." In other words, the book was an elaborate piece of irony, planned not for deception, but rather to attract attention to Butler's theory. And the design and execution were so far successful that the book is still readable and still read. The supposed memoir of the supposed author, in particular, is a masterpiece of ironical portraiture.

On the book's first appearance, however, it suffered an

2 In *Erewhon Revisited* Butler illustrated his conception of the origin and growth of Christianity. The book is disfigured by malicious caricature, but is an ingeniously conceived attempt to show how a miraculous legend could swiftly grow up, flourish, and exert a vast influence, although based entirely on delusion and blunder.

odd mischance. A number of people were taken in by it; not only did several religious newspapers commend it as a worthy attempt to defend orthodoxy by meeting opponents of Christianity as far as possible on their own ground, but, besides, some churchmen began recommending it to their friends. Canon Ainger, the editor and biographer of Lamb, sent a copy to a person whom he was attempting to bring back into the fold. Butler had not anticipated such a misfortune. Just before the book was published he wrote to a friend: "I dare say I shall get into a row—at least I hope I shall." And in another letter he said: "I should hope that attacks on *The Fair Haven* will give me an opportunity of excusing myself, and if so I shall endeavour that the excuse may be worse than the fault it is intended to excuse." But alas for the calculations of the unregenerate infidel!—that he would be embraced by the pious he had not dreamed.

He attempted to save the situation by issuing a new edition over his own name, with a preface in which he ridiculed those who had been deceived. The ridicule, whether kind or not, was deserved; it seems now inconceivable that any one could ever have opened the book without seeing its real character. The ostensible defence of Christianity concedes to unbelievers, in the name of scrupulous fairness in argument, every point that was being actively debated when *The Fair Haven* was written. The fictitious Owen, moreover, plainly speaks the author's real opinions in many long passages in which, under the transparent plea of fairness, he summarizes the arguments of opponents of Christianity. And in addition, in the memoir by William Bickersteth Owen, Butler found opportunity not only for much incidental irony, but also for the direct expression of his own views, in passages which tell of a period of scepticism and unbelief through which John Pickard Owen passed before he finally reached the fair haven of a serene belief in a bastard and inverted Christianity.

Readers of this memoir are not likely soon to forget some of the incidents recounted;—such as the story of the investigations which led the two boys to the discovery that a visiting friend of their mother never said her prayers at night unless she thought she was being observed, or as the young John Pickard Owen's grave moral indignation when he found out that women had legs, like men, but deceived all the world by enveloping themselves in a "mass of petticoats and clothes." In these and other incidents Butler did not lose sight of his real purpose, but he achieved a memorable vividness and excellently controlled the tone of his narrative so as to lend the whole an air of verisimilitude. The disguise wore thinner, however, when he began to quote a number of fragments supposed to have been written by John Pickard Owen during his period of scepticism. These fragments, in fact, as far as they go, so clearly express Butler's own settled convictions that it is necessary to pause over some of them.

In one fragment the fabled Owen asks himself why Christians interpret literally all passages in the New Testament about the guilt of unbelief, and insist on the historical character of every miraculous legend, while they become indignant if any one demands an equally literal acceptance of the precepts concerning human conduct. It would be 'visionary,' 'utopian,' or 'wholly unpractical' for him that hath two coats actually to give to him that hath none. He that is smitten on the one cheek is told to hand the offender over to the law, not simply to turn the other to the smiter. Again, we are not really to be indifferent to the morrow, or to neglect ordinary prudence; nor do we pay heed to the Gospel warnings against praying in public. Neither can we strictly inter-

pret any of the parables, except perhaps that of the good
Samaritan, with advantage to human welfare. The parables commonly praised are in reality very bad. The tales
of the Unjust Steward, of the Labourers in the Vineyard,
of the Prodigal Son, of Dives and Lazarus, of the Sower
and the Seed, of the Wise and Foolish Virgins, of the
Marriage Garment, and of the Man who planted a Vineyard ''are all either grossly immoral, or tend to engender
a very low estimate of the character of God—an estimate
far below the standard of the best earthly kings; where
they are not immoral, or do not tend to degrade the character of God, they are the merest commonplaces imagi-
nable, such as one is astonished to see people accept as
having been first taught by Christ.''

As it is with the parables, Owen thinks, so with the
Sermon on the Mount—its teaching is commonplace
where it is not immoral. And he concludes that the admiration freely lavished upon the teachings of Christ is
identical with that lavished on certain modern writers
who have made their reputations by telling people what
they very well knew and were in no danger of forgetting.

The device of quoting supposed fragments enables
Butler to return upon himself and to emphasize some of
his points by repeating them with variations. In a passage following the one concerning the Sermon on the
Mount Owen asks over again his question about the
literal interpretation of one part of the sayings of Christ
while other parts, those which inculcate more than the
ordinary precepts universally accepted as early as the
time of Solomon or perhaps earlier, are interpreted very
freely so as not to cause us undue inconvenience. He de-
cides that we have cut down Christianity so as to make
it suit our own conventions—we have not altered the latter so as to make them harmonize with Christianity. Instead of giving to him that asketh we take care to avoid

him, though if the precept was intended only to encourage liberality it was not needed. The probability is, in fact, that we are naturally inclined to be too liberal in assisting others; and the more indiscriminate liberality we indulge in, the more terrible is the mischief we cause, so that this saying of Christ's, like most of his others, only becomes harmless when we consent to give it merely lip-service. It is, indeed, "only conventional Christianity which will stand a man in good stead to live by; true Christianity will never do so. Men have tried it and found it fail; or, rather, its inevitable failure was so obvious that no age or country has ever been mad enough to carry it out in such a manner as would have satisfied its founders."

Owen proceeds to quote in his support the passage in Swift's *Argument against Abolishing Christianity* where Swift disclaims any attempt to defend real Christianity and says he contends only for the restoration of nominal Christian belief and observance. To offer at the restoring of the former "would be, indeed, a wild project; it would be to dig up foundations, to destroy at one blow all the wit and half the learning of the kingdom, to break the entire frame and constitution of things, to ruin trade, extinguish arts and sciences, with the professors of them; in short, to turn our courts of exchange and shops into deserts." So, Swift concludes, "every candid reader will easily understand my discourse to be intended only in defence of nominal Christianity, the other having been for some time wholly laid aside by general consent as utterly inconsistent with our present schemes of wealth and power."

Yet it is these schemes of wealth and power, and not Christianity, which preserve us from relapsing into barbarianism, which have created and preserved our civilization. "And what if some unhappy wretch, with a serious turn of mind and no sense of the ridiculous, takes all this talk about Christianity in sober earnest, and tries to act upon it? Into what misery may he not easily fall, and with what life-long errors may he not embitter the lives of his children!"

In another fragment Owen says that we do not pluck out our eyes if they offend us, nor cut off our right hands, that we do take heed for the morrow and should be unutterably wicked and foolish did we not, and that in general we do those things which human experience has taught us to be to our advantage, regardless of any precept of Christianity for or against them. Why then do we keep pretending that Christianity is our chief guide? Perhaps it is to compensate for our refusal to take seriously the precepts which have to do with conduct that we rigidly stand out for the letter of the Divine Word in those points which make no demand upon our comfort or convenience. Thus we never conventionalize dogma, but insist most inflexibly upon its literal interpretation. In really practical matters, however, we do say that the teaching of Christ is not to be received according to its import;—why then do we continue to give it so much importance? "Teaching by exaggeration is not a satisfactory method, nor one worthy of a being higher than man; it might have been well once, and in the East, but it is not well now. It induces more and more of that jarring and straining of our moral faculties, of which much is unavoidable in the existing complex condition of affairs, but of which the less the better. At present the tug of professed principles in one direction, and of necessary practice in the other, causes the same sort of wear and tear in our moral gear as is caused to a steam-engine by continually reversing it when it is going it at full speed. No mechanism can stand it."

These fragments written by Owen, evidently, indicate

more than a repudiation of belief in the miraculous elements of Christianity. Christian ethics as well are condemned, and Butler's position is not merely negative, but rests upon an interpretation of life and an ethical system conformed, as one may say, to the ways of this world. In *Erewhon* Butler expresses the same point of view in a different manner. His Mr. Higgs, on his first visit to the land of nowhere, found two religious systems in vogue. There was the ancient respectable religion of the musical banks, which every one professed to believe and treated with great respect, though no one practiced its precepts, and only some of the women even took them at all seriously. But alongside of Erewhonian Christianity there was another cult, that of the Goddess Ydgrun, which no one professed to believe, but whose precepts everybody actually followed, or tried very hard to follow. Ydgrun, of course, is Mrs. Grundy, and her precepts are those of respectability or good form. She tells us to do, as far as we can, what our most favoured neighbours do, and to believe that being in the social swim—which also implies ample financial resources and command of the material refinements of life—is the height of blessedness.

Erewhon, of course, is not a country where everything is as it should be—its analogue is not Utopia but Lilliput —yet in this case Butler's satire is directed against the Erewhonians' hollow profession of beliefs which have no relation to their actual lives, while he describes their secret worship of Mrs. Grundy with approval of them for so far recognizing things as they are and basing their lives on realities.

Butler, then, condemned Christianity not merely because it would ask us—as he somewhere says—to believe that the cow jumped over the moon, but also because he thought it clear that the experience of mankind had demonstrated the absurdity or harmfulness of all of the

distinctively Christian precepts directed to the guidance
of conduct. If the religion was comparatively harmless
in his own day, it was because men's actions were, by so
much, better than their professions. Christian professions men still made, but at any rate they no longer tried
to follow them. Though they remained curiously reluc-
tant to say so outright, by the manner of their lives they
showed well enough that they knew what was good for
them. And it was not the Christian view of life, but one
closer to reality.

Butler's elaboration of the theoretical basis of this
opposed view, closer to reality, would seem, if the order
of his publications be taken as the criterion, to have
come later than his perception of its ethical implications.
And this is almost certainly the case; but, nevertheless,
he had definitely committed himself to a kind of naturalism as early as 1861 or 1862 and, though his naturalism
changed in character with the passage of time, his views
remained no less naturalistic to the end than they had
been in the beginning. Darwin's *Origin of Species* was
published at just about the time when Butler was sailing
for New Zealand. He read the book as soon as he could
obtain a copy after his arrival, and was at once converted. Upon his acceptance of the theory of evolution
he evidently proceeded to reconstruct his mental world
in accordance with it, and he found it an adequate centre
for all he knew of the world of men. This, of course, was
in itself a sufficient change to account for the nature of
his attack on Christianity, and it settled it once for all
that henceforth he was to look upon men empirically and
to define virtue in terms of success and well-being.

As soon, however, as the first flush of Butler's enthusiasm for Darwin's book had passed, he began to look at
it critically, and he found himself dissatisfied. The earliest hint of his dissatisfaction, perhaps at this time felt

rather than fully conscious, but none the less unmistakable, is to be found in a paper called *Darwin among the Machines,* which Butler published in a New Zealand newspaper in 1863. He wrote with characteristic whimsicality. Calling attention to the rapid evolution in recent years of mechanical contrivances, in comparison with the extreme slowness of organic evolution, he professed to be alarmed lest the machines, swiftly gaining on man as they were, might soon achieve primacy over him and enslave him for their own purposes, just as man previously had enslaved the dog, the horse, and the other domestic animals.

But this grotesque fancy is baseless, one may say on reading it unprepared by acquaintance with Butler's other books, for machines do not have purposes of their own as do men. And this was precisely Butler's point. He was already beginning to feel dissatisfied, not with the concept of evolution, but with Darwin's hypothesis of natural selection and the survival of the fittest as the chief means by which it was brought about. He thus was amongst the first, or perhaps was the first, to put his finger on that part of Darwin's work which time has shown to be the least satisfactory. No reputable biologist of the present day, I believe, finds himself able to accept natural selection as Darwin understood it, and some biologists of high attainment are apparently of the opinion that we are no nearer an exact and verifiable knowledge of the method of evolution than men were before the publication of the *Origin of Species.* There has been in recent years, moreover, an increasing tendency to turn to vitalistic hypotheses in explanation of the method of evolution, and all of these go more or less in the direction of Butler's position. What the future will bring in this field no one can know—if, indeed, the subject by its very nature will not always elude strict scientific treatment—but time has at any rate already made evident the cogency of Butler's objection to natural selection and of his alternative conjecture.

Butler's point, then, was simply that men, and all organic creatures, do have purposes of their own—their own at least for the period of their separate existence—whereas machines of whatever degree of complexity do not; and Darwin's way of accounting for evolution *would* account very satisfactorily for the development of machines, but made it impossible to regard organic creatures as purposive beings. In the paper above mentioned, concerning the threatened tyranny of the mechanical creation, Butler gave Darwin's position what he considered to be a perfectly logical development, if it was correct.

Natural selection, of course, so far as it is accepted as the 'efficient cause' of evolution, makes development depend, not upon the creature, but upon its environment. It transfers the factors of development from within the organism to the external conditions acting upon it. Darwin supposed that, of two organisms existing at the same time and almost identical in character, one might be better suited to its environment than the other. Accordingly the former would survive and perpetuate itself, while the latter would not. Thus a given type would become established, not absolutely, but relatively, because it is an ultimate fact that no two organisms are ever absolutely identical, imperceptible variations spontaneously occurring in the case of each one born. The surviving type just referred to, however, would remain relatively constant until a significant new variation occurred; —that is, one enabling its possessor to adapt himself more perfectly to his environment than his friends and relatives. And upon this event he, of course, would become the survivor and perpetuator of his advantageous variation.

Thus it is that natural selection makes environment the determining factor in evolution, the small, constant, spontaneous variations in organisms affording endless differences out of which the surrounding conditions naturally 'select,' on the basis of adaptation, a few for survival. And no trace of purpose or design is to be discerned in the process. It is not only, from the human point of view, incredibly wasteful and cruel, but also wholly blind and objectless. Moreover, the process, impartially comprehending all organic life, of course includes ourselves; and for us it specifically means that not only is consciousness a mere piece of useless ornamentation, without which our lives would go on precisely as they do with it, but also that our purposive view of the world and of ourselves is wholly delusory.

It was this at which Butler balked. It seemed to him that such an explanation of the method of evolution was puerile in its disregard of evidence which any serious hypothesis had to take into account. ''Shall we see something,'' he asked, ''for which, as Professor Mivart has well said, 'to us the word ''mind'' is the least inadequate and misleading symbol,' as having given to the eagle an eyesight which can pierce the sun, but which in the night is powerless; while to the owl it has given eyes which shun even the full moon, but find a soft brilliancy in darkness? Or shall we deny that there has been any purpose or design in the fashioning of these different kinds of eyes, and see nothing to make us believe that any living being made the eagle's eye out of something which was not an eye nor anything like one, or that this living being implanted this particular eye of all others in the eagle's head, as being most in accordance with the habits of the creature, and as therefore most likely to enable it to live

contentedly and leave plentitude of offspring? And shall
we then go on to maintain that the eagle's eye was
formed little by little by a series of accidental variations,
each one of which was thrown for, as it were, with dice?
We shall most of us feel that there must have been a
little cheating somewhere with these accidental variations before the eagle could have become so great a
winner.'"[3]

Butler took his stand in favour of the cheating. He felt
confident that purpose and design there are in the world,
and that most of us instinctively believe this because it is
really so. Moreover, he also considered it inconceivable
that consciousness should be a meaningless, useless reality;—yet a reality it is, and no one denies it. Hence he
felt confident that any hypothesis worth serious attention must take it into account as a significant fact—must
be so framed as to give consciousness work to do such as
we believe actually is effected by our minds. Briefly, he
conceived that phenomena are regulated by an inner
teleology, by a purpose which they carry within themselves, not by a purpose imposed on them from the outside—as, for instance, by a Creator with an independent
existence of his own. Every particle of the universe and
every aggregate of particles from the simplest to the
most complex, such as ourselves, belongs to one family,
all being animated more or less obscurely with what is
essentially one purpose; and this animating principle or
mind resides within the particles of the universe, being,
indeed, one inseparable aspect of them, just as 'matter'
is another. "We shall never get straight till we leave off
trying to separate mind and matter. Mind is not a thing
or, if it be, we know nothing about it; it is a function of
matter. Matter is not a thing or, if it be, we know nothing

[3] *Evolution, Old and New* (ed. of 1911), p. 3.

about it; it is a function of mind.''[4] Ultimately the universe consists of a single vibrating substance, which we may call mind or matter indifferently, or perhaps preferably mind-matter, and the kinds of vibrations going on within it at any given time determine whether it will appear to us ''as (say) hydrogen, or sodium, or chicken doing this, or chicken doing the other.''

Thus the universe makes itself. Taken as a whole, it is the only self-subsistent thing we know, and is what the theologians call God, in whose life we all live and move and have our being. The theologians, however, are wrong in taking, as they always have, a grossly inadequate, one-sided view of God; for God is the sum of all that is. And we are all, from the tiniest, apparently lifeless particle of hydrogen or sodium or the like up to the grandly animated human being, parts not merely of one family, but of one body—the body of God.[5] In appearance so diverse,

[4] *Notebooks*, p. 67. There are further notes on the subject on pp. 74 *ff*. From these the following may be quoted: ''People say we can conceive the existence of matter and the existence of mind. I doubt it. I doubt how far we have any definite conception of mind or of matter, pure and simple. What is meant by conceiving a thing or understanding it? When we hear of a piece of matter instinct with mind, as protoplasm, for example, there certainly comes up before our closed eyes an idea, a picture which we imagine to bear some resemblance to the thing we are hearing of. But when we try to think of matter apart from every attribute of matter (and this I suspect comes ultimately to 'apart from every attribute of mind') we get no image before our closed eyes—we realize nothing to ourselves. Perhaps we surreptitiously introduce some little attribute, and then we think we have conceived of matter pure and simple, but this I think is as far as we can go. The like holds good for mind: we must smuggle in a little matter before we get any definite idea at all.''

[5] In the articles reprinted after Butler's death under the title *God the Known and God the Unknown* he had limited God to the 'organic creation,' the conception being otherwise the same as that outlined above. Later, however, in *Unconscious Memory*, he stated that he had not republished these articles because he had come to see this limitation as untenable and wrong. Thus he ended in a pantheistic naturalism, akin to Goethe's—though there is nothing to show that he was at all influenced by either Goethe or Goethe's teacher, Spinoza. Two passages from *Unconscious Memory* sum-

so discontinuous, so individual, we nevertheless are
united together in the working out of a vaster purpose
than we consciously know, even as are the cells which
form the body of a single organic creature. Our separate-
ness and our differences are delusions if we take them
absolutely—they are *only* appearances, or 'false shows
of knowledge,' in comparison with all that unites us indissolubly each to each.

It follows that, as life and mind are omnipresent in the
universe and are fundamentally one beneath all the
diverse forms they take, in the realm of organic life offspring and parents are literally identical with each other.
A child is literally the continuation of its parents' life,
a link in a chain, and it is illusory to regard it as having
any genuine individuality.

Further, any organism which does not know completely
how to achieve its purpose is endowed with conscious-

ming up his final position may be given here (ed. of 1920, pp. 176, 177):
''I would recommend the reader to see every atom in the universe as living
and able to feel and to remember, but in a humble way. He must have life
eternal, as well as matter eternal; and the life and the matter must be
joined together inseparably as body and soul to one another. Thus he will
see God everywhere, not as those who repeat phrases conventionally, but as
people who would have their words taken according to their most natural
and legitimate meaning; and he will feel that the main difference between
him and many of those who oppose him lies in the fact that whereas both
he and they use the same language, his opponents only half mean what they
say, while he means it entirely.'' ''The attempt to get a higher form of
life from a lower one is in accordance with our observation and experience.
It is therefore proper to be believed. The attempt to get it from that which
has absolutely no life is like trying to get something out of nothing. . . .
A little leaven will leaven the whole lump, but there must be *some* leaven.
. . . We should endeavour to see the so-called inorganic as living, in respect
of the qualities it has in common with the organic, rather than the organic
as non-living in respect of the qualities it has in common with the inorganic.
True, it would be hard to place one's self on the same moral platform as a
stone, but this is not necessary; it is enough that we should feel the stone
to have a moral platform of its own, though that platform embraces little
more than a profound respect for the laws of gravitation, chemical affinity,
etc.''

ness—an instrument which enables it to learn. This is the essence of consciousness, and it may be defined simply as the presence of an unsolved problem of existence. As soon as the problem is solved, consciousness begins to retreat, while habit supervenes, and then instinct. To know that one knows anything is nothing to be proud of; it is a certain indication that one knows it only imperfectly. The moment it is known perfectly it is dismissed from consciousness. An unconscious instinct is the fruit of a successful struggle to solve the problem in question, and its operation is the performance of a perfectly memorized lesson. The instinctive or involuntary acts of animals and human beings are the expression of certain knowledge—of the only certain knowledge they have; they are the expression of what Butler, with the appearance of paradox, called unconscious memory. The things we do we know not why, but because we must, are the best things we do, because they rest on the firmest basis of genuine knowledge. We are not conscious of it, just because we do know it so well, but we remember everything that we ever really learned in the persons of our forefathers—our forefathers who extend through the human race, through the animal and vegetable kingdoms, and through the realm of the inorganic. Hence, to sum it up, the less conscious an organism is—or, more accurately, any particle of matter—the more perfectly it knows what it is about. Animals understand the business and the object of living much better than do human beings—by as much as their consciousness is less.

Paradoxical as this view may seem, it still does do what the hypothesis of natural selection completely fails to do; it does give us a method of evolution which, while it does not violate any of the facts which Darwin took into account, also provides for consciousness a significant place in the process and one in accordance with our own experience of the actual workings of our minds. The eagle, then, *made* its eye, intelligently, knowing what kind of eye it needed for its business, just as the musician, knowing what he needs for his business, intelligently makes his instinctive, though vastly complex, habits of performance. So, too, "a hen is only an egg's way of making another egg."[6] The egg knows perfectly what it is about; the hen knows perhaps not quite so clearly, but still well enough. Man also knows well enough up to a certain point. Man "begins as the primordial cell—being verily nothing but the primordial cell which goes on splitting itself up for ever, but gaining continually in experience. Put him in the same position as he was in before and he will do as he did before. First he will do his tadpoles by rote, so to speak, on his head, from long practice; then he does his fish trick; then he grows arms and legs, all unconsciously from the inveteracy of the habit, till he comes to doing his man, and this lesson he has not yet learnt so thoroughly. Some part of it, as the breathing and oxidization business, he is well up to, inasmuch as they form part of previous rôles, but the teeth and hair, the upright position, the power of speech, though all tolerably familiar, give him more trouble—for he is very stupid—a regular dunce in fact. Then comes his newer and more complex environment, and this puzzles him—arrests his attention—whereon consciousness springs into existence, as a spark from a horse's hoof.'"[7]

From this it is a logical enough conclusion that we are best attending to our real business in life when we are most thoroughly enjoying ourselves. We are then partaking of the essence of life, and the more enjoyment we can secure the better we are. It is, however, not always

6 *Life and Habit*, p. 134.

7 *Notebooks*, p. 55. Succeeding quotations, unless otherwise accounted for, are from the same volume.

an easy matter, and so problems press upon us. With them comes the possibility of mistake, and this is "one of the criteria of life as we commonly think of it. If oxygen could go wrong and mistake some other gas for hydrogen and thus learn not to mistake it any more, we should say oxygen was alive. The older life is, the more unerring it becomes in respect of things about which it is conversant—the more like, in fact, it becomes to such a thing as the force of gravity, both as regards unerring-ness and unconsciousness."

Butler wondered, accordingly, if life was such a force as gravity, still in the process of formation. He apparently concluded that this, or something near this, was the truth of the matter, but at the same time recognized that we now are so far from the end of our problems that we seemingly have an infinite capacity for blundering. And wrong decisions are fatal because, in proportion as they *are* decisions, we inexorably act upon them while life lasts. Consciousness is only an instrument, if, indeed, that word does not go too far in its implication, since, as I have said, it may be defined simply as the presence in the mind of an unsolved problem. The right answer to the problem is enjoyable action or the means to such action, but there is nothing in the nature of consciousness to guide us to this right answer, and we are on the whole unlikely to hit upon it until experience has convinced us that the other possible answers are wrong. But it is of the essence of action to be whole-hearted, and hence when we do make a decision we not only act upon it inexorably but are convinced that everybody else must do so too. Proselytizing and persecution are thus inseparable from life, and appear as vigorously when considerable numbers have gone wrong as when they have gone right.

Butler wrote some fantastic notes on this subject which

he never published, though he said the same thing more soberly in *Life and Habit*. I quote them because they very well illustrate the irresistible temptation he constantly felt to express his thought in an exaggerated, whimsical, grotesque way. No matter how significant and well-considered his thought might be, no matter how seriously he regarded it and wanted others to share his view, he could never get a firm hold on the decent proprieties of illustration and expression, but was always wandering off into trivialities which—appealing though they apparently are to many of his present-day admirers—are often flagrant violations of taste, or masks which effectually obscure, instead of aiding, his real purpose.

Thus he says that the act of eating is really "a kind of proselytizing—a kind of dogmatizing—a maintaining that the eater's way of looking at things is better than the eatee's. We convert the food, or try to do so, to our own way of thinking, and, when it sticks to its own opinion and refuses to be converted, we say it disagrees with us. An animal that refuses to let another eat it has the courage of its convictions and, if it gets eaten, dies a martyr to them. So we can only proselytize fresh meat; the convictions of putrid meat begin to be too strong for us. It is good for a man that he should not be thwarted—that he should have his own way as far, and with as little difficulty, as possible. Cooking is good because it makes matters easier by unsettling the meat's mind and preparing it for new ideas. . . . Sitting quiet after eating is akin to sitting still during divine service so as not to disturb the congregation. We are catechizing and converting our proselytes, and there should be no row. . . . Sea-sickness or, indeed, any other sickness is the inarticulate expression of the pain we feel on seeing a proselyte escape us just as we were on the point of converting it." Indigestion "may be due to the naughtiness of the stiff-necked things that we have eaten, or to the poverty of our own arguments; but it may also arise from an attempt on the part of the stomach to be too damned clever, and to depart from precedent inconsiderately. The healthy stomach is nothing if not conservative. Few radicals have good digestions.'' ''We cannot get rid of persecution; if we feel at all we must persecute something; the mere acts of feeding and growing are acts of persecution. Our aim should be to persecute nothing but such things as are absolutely incapable of resisting us.''

That these observations legitimately spring out of Butler's serious thought is apparent at a glance; and they are amusing—amusing as are the somewhat similar performances of Mr. Harold Lloyd or other professional comedians. There is a place in life for such amusement, but not the place that Butler was always tending to give it. Yet, in truth, Butler was himself a bundle of incongruities, and his exaggerated whimsicality is only one side of a pronounced individualism which he exhibited throughout his life—while he preached a communism more complete than any doctrinaire politician has ever dreamed of!

For, as we see, he arrived at the conviction that the universe is really one immense organism with a purpose towards which it is driving; that what amongst us passes for birth and death is only a process of waste and repair; that we are as old as the universe and shall last as long; that mind and matter are merely functions of each other; that all differences we observe are differences only of degree, our distinctions being useful rather than true; that our immortality resides not in our individualities but in our bodily cells, or, more exactly, in their constituents; and that what we call God is simply the life of the whole viewed as one, the sum of the things that are.

From this pantheistic naturalism Butler made certain

practical deductions which form the basis of his ethical system, if it can legitimately be called such, and which help to give his view-point its distinctive character. In human life, as we have seen, what we call man's natural instincts, as far as they go, comprise his surest wisdom, since they are the sum of what he certainly knows. If instincts sufficed us we should be better off than we are, but even in the best people they do not suffice. We are all constantly confronted with situations which require some conscious decision on our part. What are we to do? By all means, Butler says, avoid thinking for yourself if it is possible. Do not trust your own unaided consciousness, that blundering instrument, if there is any way out of it. To think for yourself is a desperate last resort, and in ninety-nine cases out of a hundred it is not necessary. There is the still small voice of common sense; there is the example of what the best people do, an ever present help in time of trouble. Common sense is the accumulated practical wisdom of mankind, and it is our surest indication of the real values of life and of right courses of action. The best people, as Matthew Arnold complained, are inaccessible to ideas—but why? Because they do not need them; they get along happily as they are. And the almost instinctive deference which we give them is as it should be. It is really nature's way of telling us that these people are the fine flower of humanity whom we would do well to be like as far as in us lies.

Common sense, then, is our surest guide whenever instinct fails us, and the values of life as estimated by common sense are its true values. It tells us to beware of extremes, to avoid the exceptional in thought and conduct, to seek our own welfare. It tells us that Macaulay was right about the acre in Middlesex, that a bird in the hand really is worth two in the bush. It tells us to make the best of our present lives, trusting that remoter possibilities will take care of themselves; and this means that we should seek the maximum of enjoyment consistent with security and the avoidance of consequent illness.

The authority of common sense is self-evident; it is, as was just said, the stored-up wisdom of an infinite multitude, derived from experience. It is thus closer to the divine purpose which animates us darkly than can be the unaided deliberations of any individual. It may occasionally be necessary and right to go counter to common sense, but it is almost certain that the individual who thinks so is wrong, and that his course of action is a blunder. Occasionally it may not be so, but it takes extraordinary and overwhelming evidence to prove that the voice of common sense is not the voice of God.

What the gospel of common sense practically comes to is seen particularly well in *The Way of All Flesh,* and also in many of the published extracts from Butler's notebooks. In the novel, when Theobald Pontifex marries the daughter of a clergyman, Butler turns to the reader and asks, with reference to the latter: "Did you ever have an income at best none too large, which died with you all except two hundred pounds a year? Did you ever at the same time have two sons who must be started in life somehow, and five daughters still unmarried for whom you would only be too thankful to find husbands—if you knew how to find them? If morality is that which, on the whole, brings a man peace in his declining years—if, that is to say, it is not an utter swindle, can you under these circumstances flatter yourself that you have led a moral life?" To lead a moral life, then, is to follow a course of conduct which brings one a sufficiency of means and a mind at peace with itself. "The true laws of God are the laws of our own well-being." When George Pontifex, Theobald's father, dies, Butler remarks that since he lived to be nearly seventy-three years old and died rich he must have been in very fair harmony with his environment. What he had done was "to observe what things do *bona fide* tend to long life and comfort, and to act accordingly"—and doing this he did enough. "All animals, except man, know that the principal business of life is to enjoy it—and they do enjoy it as much as man and other circumstances will permit. He has spent his life best who has enjoyed it most." Butler concedes that George Pontifex's character was not what we call 'exalted,' but points out that common sense has little or nothing to say for people of exalted character. "Homer tells us about some one who made it his business always to excel and to stand higher than other people. What an uncompanionable, disagreeable person he must have been! Homer's heroes generally came to a bad end, and I doubt not that this gentleman, whoever he was, did so sooner or later." A high standard is a luxury, perhaps harmless in the very rich, but sinful in the general run of men. It is like a hothouse plant—something that cannot hold its own in the world.

Right and duty Butler logically dismisses as unsafe guides. "Pleasure . . . is a safer guide than either right or duty. For hard as it is to know what gives us pleasure, right and duty are often still harder to distinguish and, if we go wrong with them, will lead us into just as sorry a plight as a mistaken opinion concerning pleasure. When men burn their fingers through following after pleasure they find out their mistake and get to see where they have gone wrong more easily than when they have burnt them through following after a fancied duty, or a fancied idea concerning right virtue. The devil, in fact, when he dresses himself in angel's clothes, can only be detected by experts of exceptional skill, and so often does he adopt this disguise that it is hardly safe to be seen talking to an angel at all, and prudent people will follow after pleasure as a more homely but more respectable and on the whole much more trustworthy guide.''

Butler's effort here, and in his work as a whole, was evidently to *use* common sense. In the field of conduct he saw men professing respect for Christian ethics but acting for the most part in accordance with very different principles directed towards very different ends. And when he had convinced himself of the hollowness of Christianity's pretensions and had decided that they were based on delusion and mistake, it was an easy and 'sensible' conclusion that men of the world were following a better mode of conduct than they knew. He concluded, as he tells us in *The Fair Haven,* that Christian morality was ''a shoddy morality, which would neither wash nor wear, but was woven together from a tissue of dreams and blunders.'' Violently contradicting common sense, at every point it set at nought the values of this present world for the sake of returns which one could not convert into cash at any bank, and in so doing it demanded a way of life which was a denial of life. That many had been willing to die for Christianity proved nothing;— they had got killed, as a matter of fact, precisely because they were wrong. They were attempting to act—as intelligent people now attempt to act—only on the basis of full and unmistakable evidence, but we now know that their evidence was worthless. Had they been able to know what we know they would never have been so foolish as to become Christians, and no more should we. Fortunately, even when Christianity was at its worst, and was flourishing mightily, many men refused completely to assent to it, and so the race did not perish, and civilization, though scotched, was not killed.

This is plausible, and could be made more plausible than Butler made it, but is it sensible? Christianity is to be condemned because it bids men control or crush natural propensities for the sake of an end to which those propensities do not of themselves lead; whereas in truth, according to Butler, men's natural propensities comprise their surest wisdom. But on his own showing natural propensities are not enough, never have been enough; for consciousness, he says, appears only for a significant work, only when organisms are confronted by genuine problems which baffle instinct or habit. We may, if we like, assent to the paradox that animals have more intelligence than men, because they lead a life untroubled save by external hindrances to enjoyment, but we can only do so by adding that it is the business of leading animals' lives which they so well understand. Ask them to lead men's lives, and you put them up a tree. It is odd, then, that Butler should insist upon the significance of consciousness, as an indubitable indication that we have problems to solve which have never presented themselves to animals, only to turn upon himself and say that we should use conscious intelligence as little as possible because we are likely to come to wrong conclusions— conclusions which do not, as he would wish, bid us try to sink ourselves to the level of animal life. He begins with the 'sensible' conviction that it is foolishness to deny one's self pleasure for the sake of an illusory end, finally to conclude that pleasure is the only object of existence— a conclusion to which only a small number of men has ever been ready to subscribe, and so one which certainly goes counter to common sense. Likewise he begins with the 'sensible' conviction that consciousness has a meaning and a real place in life, to end by saying that it is a horrid burden which we should use simply for the purpose of ridding ourselves of it as fast as we can. We are informed that instead of using conscious intelligence to try to solve the problems which call it into being—and for the solution of which we have Butler's authority for

saying it alone exists—we should use it merely to escape
them, which is neither a logical conclusion nor a hopeful
effort if, as we are told, it is precisely the persistence of
these unsolved problems which makes us men, not
animals.

The fact is, as Butler's work shows clearly, that common sense is an elusive standard, which is always likely
to become a two-edged weapon in the hands of him who
uses it. Its voice is loud and strong upon only a few
elementary questions relating to social cohesion and the
preservation of life; but even concerning these matters
its judgements are of the rough-and-ready kind, are in
need of constant revision, and are often contradictory.
It has no central or well-considered principles, and af-
fords no basis for comprehensive views. Even when its
voice is loudest, moreover, it may be a duty to oppose it
—a duty which is fully recognized by succeeding generations. It is probable that if Butler himself had had more
of it he would have prized it less. And certainly it led
him a strange chase.

For he who so praised common sense and endeavoured
to use it was led step by step from its plain, apparently
impregnable dicta into conclusions not only extravagant
and grotesque, not only contradictory of their own starting-point, but also inevitably self-destroying. What Butler tells us comes to this: that the only certainties of life
are things we do not and cannot know, that we know only
delusions or doubts or unanswerable questions, and that
our aim should be to sink from the immitigable evil of
conscious existence into what for us would be equivalent
to non-existence, or death. To pretend, as Butler does,
that a state of complete unconsciousness would be completely blissful is simply nonsense. Blissfulness is a state
of feeling, and requires for its existence a conscious personality. Butler's goal is either one of sheer annihilation

or it is something utterly unintelligible, to whose meaninglessness he succeeded in blinding himself by a succession of verbal quibbles.

He bids us realize—as, if we were not conscious individuals, we could not—that individuality is a delusion, and that life as human beings can alone know it is a mockery. He bids us worship God, but robs God of all worshipful attributes. He builds his system on the concept of personality but, in order to do so, has to make the concept meaningless by impartially extending it to every atom of the universe and, as well, to the universe as a whole. He tells us to lead a life of enjoyment, but adds that complete enjoyment, like complete knowledge, is inconsistent with human life. By reaction from what he considers the unintelligibility of his contemporaries he leads us into a philosophy whose essence is contradiction and negation and the wholesale, timorous repudiation of life as human beings experience it and know it.

Yet it is not possible to pretend that Butler went about his work of undermining all distinctions, all discriminations, of confounding life in one inchoate mass of some unknowable, inconceivable thinking-substance, out of sheer perversity or love of paradox. Some of his admirers who in their weakness have eagerly caught at his incidental faults of taste and his whimsicality may, doubtless, be thus easily dismissed, but hardly Butler. He was, in truth, forced into conclusions which he did not want any more than we want them, as long as we have left intelligence sufficient to perceive their real drift, because on a naturalistic basis he could go in no other direction. Being a more acute and consistent thinker than either Huxley or Arnold, he so worked out his naturalistic system as to put its self-destroying character in a clearer light than either of them ever did for his own efforts at a constructive view of life, but this is all that can be said for him. In an attempt to find some place for mind and purpose and the divine within the limits of naturalism, he could only succeed by robbing those terms of all meaning, transforming them in effect into synonyms for material substance. He was forced to deny certain of the data of experience more boldly and uncompromisingly than less clear-sighted exponents of naturalism, but even less than they could he avoid the denial of all that can make life significant or give it worth.

VII

THOMAS HARDY

The Dynasts, a recent critic has said, "is the characteristic poem of our age; and characteristic in a profound fashion that has not been lately achieved by poetry among us—in the fashion of its philosophy. . . . In it we have artistic *formation,* definite and explicit, of the reach of man's present consciousness of the world, of his conception of human and cosmic destiny, of mind's chief traffic with the surrounding existence as far as the inevitable and unsurmountable barriers. . . . The relation of known and unknowable is matter for emotion rather than for reason; and what this poem achieves is the presenting to emotion of a metaphysical idea held in some consistent and noble shaping. And this idea is one that underlies most of the intellectual life of our time; though the shaping is altogether the poet's own. . . . We can only say (but of course it must be said without proposing further comparison) that this epic-drama of Thomas Hardy's is, in what may be called its conceptual poetry, akin to the works of Milton and Wordsworth in our literature, and beyond it to *Faust* and *Prometheus Bound.*" These are large claims, but few would now, I imagine, be inclined to dispute them, and they indicate the reason for attempting a study of Mr. Hardy's interpretation of life. This, Mr. Lascelles Abercrombie, from whose volume my quotation comes, has scarcely done. He has not been able entirely to escape it, but he is primarily an artist-critic and his study of Mr. Hardy's works consists chiefly of what in the business-world they term shop-talk.

Large claims have not always been made for Mr. Hardy; on the contrary, in the eighteen-nineties he was subjected to much abusive criticism.[1] He was called, in effect, a scavenger of the lower reaches of life, one who delighted to exhibit human baseness and depravity simply for the perverse pleasure which he and others presumably derived from the spectacle. How far from the truth this was everybody by the present time knows, but even to-day there may be some readers who have been surprised at finding the closing piece in Mr. Hardy's latest volume of verse.[2] There, looking back over the years as he sits before a wood fire, he imagines his own voice speaking from it 'on how he had walked when his sun was higher, his heart in its arrogancy':

> "*You held not to whatsoever was true,*"
>   Said my own voice talking to me;
> "*Whatsoever was just you were slack to see;*
> *Kept not things lovely and pure in view,*"
>   Said my own voice talking to me.
>
> "*You slighted her that endureth all,*"
>   Said my own voice talking to me;
> "*Vaunteth not, trusteth hopefully;*
> *That suffereth long and is kind withal,*"
>   Said my own voice talking to me.
>
> "*You taught not that which you set about,*"
>   Said my own voice talking to me;
> "*That the greatest of things is Charity. . . .*"

[1] Examples may easily be found in the periodicals of the time. A readily accessible instance in a volume published during the period is to be seen in S. L. Wilson's *Theology of Modern Literature* (1899).

[2] Written before the publication (on 13 November, 1925) of *Human Shows: Far Phantasies: Songs and Trifles*.

When a poet speaks, it is generally, if not always, best to suppose that he means exactly what he says; and when we take it in that Mr. Hardy actually set out to acclaim charity as the greatest of things, we find a far-stretching light cast upon some of his best-known work. *Tess of the D'Urbervilles* is the most obvious instance. It is the story of a "pure woman faithfully presented." Tess is no Pamela Andrews, able successfully to calculate her course with a view to worldly advantage, skilfully playing upon and using Alec D'Urberville's passion as a means to obtain wealth and social position along with honourable marriage. She is at once better and worse than this, more honest and finer in grain, while less intelligent and less firm. Her feelings are instinctively pure and right, but she has a soft nature which conspires with chance to bring about the calamitous stages in her life, culminating in her final desperate murder of Alec D'Urberville and her own death upon the gallows. As a girl emerging into womanhood she had yielded herself to Alec, and had borne his child. The episode leads Mr. Hardy into contradictions, but, still, by one means if not by another, he makes his point convincingly. Tess did not give herself to Alec because of moral obliquity, and so after the experience she kept her purity of soul. More than this, the experience actually aided her development. As its result she changed, almost at a leap, "from simple girl to complex woman. Symbols of reflectiveness passed into her face, and a note of tragedy at times into her voice. Her eyes grew larger and more eloquent. She became what would have been called a fine creature; her aspect was fair and arresting; her soul that of a woman whom the turbulent experiences of the last year or two had quite failed to demoralize." Hence she was, if anything, the more fit to make a true wife, and it would have been not charity so much as elementary justice had Angel

Clare been able to see this when, just after he had married her, she told him her story. He was not capable of it. Both temperament and his Christian upbringing united to blind him to the truth and to make him inflexibly hard in judgement. And thence ensued the tragic climax of the tale.

Despite the personal irresponsibility of the characters, this is by general consent one of the few great English novels. It is so because of its high measure of truth, its tragic insight, and its intense, moving power. And in more than one incidental episode as well as in its central theme it is obviously a plea for charity, for a larger tolerance, for a repudiation of narrow, traditional applications of moral principles which sacrifice truth and reality for appearances. It is a plea against arrogance howsoever concealed or sanctified, a plea for the understanding heart, for the right hand of holy love extended freely to all suffering fellow-creatures. All of us alike are caught and twisted by circumstances which we vainly attempt to control, all of us are subject to the freaks and unconscious cruelties of chance, none of us is pure enough to cast the first stone, and this should teach us forbearance and sympathy. Many of the evils of life are inherent in the nature of things, but at least man's inhumanity to man is remediable, through the increase of charity, and here indeed lies the one open path of human progress.

Such would seem to be, briefly, Mr. Hardy's reasoning, exemplified more or less completely in many of his books and poems besides *Tess of the D'Urbervilles*. *Jude the Obscure* is explicable in this light as in no other. One, though only one, reason for the abuse with which the book was greeted on its first appearance was its attack upon the institution of marriage. It was said to be a powerful and deliberate incitement to sexual immorality, the more dangerous because of the deep feeling and mature skill with which it was written. And it may very fairly be urged that simply as an attack upon marriage the book is extremely unjust. But, of course, it is not simply this. Mr. Hardy obviously was moved by a profound indignation at the suffering caused to many individuals by the institution in its present English form,[3] and this suffering is undeniable, hideous, and often grossly immoral in its results. *Jude* is really a plea for a truer morality, for a more generous understanding and sympathy in our social judgements and in the enforcement of our social sanctions. It tells us, more, it shows us, what we well know yet fail to realize in action—that we are not all cast in one mould, nor set amidst identical circumstances, and that our neighbour's life may markedly diverge from our own without being therefore damnable. It is, indeed, a modern homily upon a venerable theme, showing how the letter of the law killeth, whereas the spirit giveth life. Was man made for the Sabbath, or the Sabbath for man?

That Mr. Hardy conceived himself to be persevering in the same lesson even in writing *The Dynasts* is indicated more than once in the unfolding of that gigantic human scene, and perhaps accounts for his giving the last word in it to the Chorus of the Pities as well as for the note of hope which they utter. His consistent endeavour to embody this meaning in his work, consequently, explains his statement in the Preface to *Late Lyrics and*

[3] In a brief statement published in *Hearst's Magazine* (June, 1912) Mr. Hardy wrote: "As the English marriage laws are, to the eyes of anybody who looks around, the gratuitous cause of at least half the misery of the community, that they are allowed to remain in force for a day is, to quote the famous last word of the ceremony itself, an 'amazement,' and can only be accounted for by the assumption that we live in a barbaric age, and are the slaves of gross superstition."

Earlier that he regards himself as an exponent of evolutionary meliorism. He has always repudiated the common charge—if it be a charge—of pessimism, and we can readily see why. If the only hope of human betterment lies in greater charity, and in the changes which that implies, we must at once be forced not only to recognize, but to feel, existing evils as evils. Accordingly the true lover of mankind, seeking to increase the worth of life, is he who feelingly bares its wrongs and forces them into the common consciousness. Many years ago, as he says, he wrote "that if way to the Better there be, it exacts a full look at the Worst," and later he expressed his view clearly in his lines *To Sincerity:*

O sweet sincerity!—
Where modern methods be
What scope for thine and thee?

Life may be sad past saying,
Its greens for ever greying,
Its faiths to dust decaying;

And youth may have foreknown it,
And riper seasons shown it,
But custom cries: "Disown it:

"Say ye rejoice, though grieving,
Believe, while unbelieving,
Behold, without perceiving!"

—Yet, would men look at true things,
And unilluded view things,
And count to bear undue things,

The real might mend the seeming,
Facts better their foredeeming,
And Life its disesteeming.

Many of Mr. Hardy's pieces, whether in prose or in verse, are in appearance simply pictures of the injustice to which we are subject or of the malign elements in human nature itself. They are open to grave misunderstanding—and the more so because of the irony he frequently and effectively uses—unless they are read as fulfilments of a deeply serious purpose, as instances of plain speaking rendered necessary by our sins. A fair example is *The Ruined Maid:*

"O 'Melia, my dear, this does everything crown!
Who could have supposed I should meet you in Town?
And whence such fair garments, such prosperi-ty?"—
"O didn't you know I'd been ruined?" said she.

—"You left us in tatters, without shoes or socks,
Tired of digging potatoes, and spudding up docks;
And now you've gay bracelets and bright feathers three!"—
"Yes: that's how we dress when we're ruined," said she.

—"At home in the barton you said 'thee' and 'thou,'
And 'thik oon,' and 'theäs oon,' and 't'other'; but now
Your talking quite fits 'ee for high compa-ny!"—
"Some polish is gained with one's ruin," said she.

—"Your hands were like paws then, your face blue and bleak,
But now I'm bewitched by your delicate cheek,
And your little gloves fit as on any la-dy!"—
"We never do work when we're ruined," said she.

—"You used to call home-life a hag-ridden dream,
And you'd sigh, and you'd sock; but at present you seem
To know not of megrims or melancho-ly!"—
"True. One's pretty lively when ruined," said she.

—"I wish I had feathers, a fine sweeping gown,
And a delicate face, and could strut about Town!"—
"My dear—a raw country girl, such as you be,
Cannot quite expect that. You ain't ruined," said she.

One further example, *The Pink Frock,* must be quoted, out of many that almost equally deserve it:

"O my pretty pink frock,
I sha'n't be able to wear it!
Why is he dying just now?
    I hardly can bear it!

"He might have contrived to live on;
But they say there's no hope whatever:
And must I shut myself up,
    And go out never?

"O my pretty pink frock,
Puff-sleeved and accordion-pleated!
He might have passed in July,
    And not so cheated!"

Yet, complains Mr. Hardy, not even all his disclaimers and explanations suffice to prevent him from still being called a pessimist. And indeed, considering the looseness of popular language, this should probably be expected by one who writes and publishes many pieces in prose and verse comparable to *The Pink Frock;* but there is a further and more legitimate reason. For Mr. Hardy's work contains elements which his explanation by no means covers, and in fact he has himself also warned his readers not to expect from him a systematic or consistent illustration of any one general view of the world. On the contrary, he has insisted that his works constitute a series of fugitive impressions set down as they have come, with no attempt at coördination. The reason for this, and the extent to which it can be accepted, will be discussed later, though the contention has an obvious ground which must at once be mentioned. For it is a fact that Mr. Hardy has been singularly faithful, sincere, and courageous in the

attempt to follow experience whithersoever it might lead
him. And this in itself merits, as it has increasingly received, high praise. But it can scarcely be allowed that
this is alone sufficient to give him out of hand the supreme
place in modern literature which some in recent years
have claimed for him. The claim is not unnatural in an
age of specialism which has driven perplexed critics back
into the narrower recesses of their field, where they may
talk with some assurance of literature as a problem in
craftsmanship, but, still, it cannot be admitted as legitimate. For an artist's greatness depends in the end, and
always must depend, upon the quality of his experience
as well as upon his honesty and skill in dealing with it.

And this matter of quality is in Mr. Hardy's case rendered doubtful by the fact that his effort to follow impressions wherever they might lead has submerged him
in a fundamental contradiction, strange in its character
though familiar enough in the present age. For he began
his career in mid-Victorian days, living in an atmosphere
charged by a militant and wonderfully confident system
of thought which was supposed to have behind it all the
authority of exact science, and he was no more able than
were others to resist the seeming attractions of the
'mechanical philosophy.' Consequently his observation
of the very aspects of existence which roused his humanitarian fervour and caused him to make deeply moving
pleas for the increase of charity also helped to convince
him that human beings were capable of no responsible
acts whatever. The two things, of course, completely
cancel each other, since unless we have some real freedom it is useless to talk to us about charitable acts or any
other responsible deeds. Yet this is what Mr. Hardy did;
persisting in his humanitarian intention, he nevertheless
came increasingly to interpret life on the basis of a deterministic monism. Even in holding to this, however, he

has not freed himself from a further confusion; for, as we shall see, he speaks much of chance, and at times falls into the indifferentism which logically issues from the view that all things are the product of sheer accident or "crass casualty." He has, none the less, while continuing to the end to hold both views in a somewhat unstable combination, clearly given the predominance to determinism. Hence I shall in what follows make no special effort to disentangle this secondary confusion, if I may so term it, though the evidence for its existence will appear throughout, and I shall presently indicate what appears, at least, to be Mr. Hardy's method of combining these diverse views.

They are expressed plainly in many of his novels and poems, and with unqualified emphasis in *The Dynasts,* where the great pageant of the Napoleonic wars is presented wholly as an example of human irresponsibility and helplessness under the constraining pressure of blind cosmic forces. As is well known, Mr. Hardy has clothed his thought in *The Dynasts* in the language of Schopenhauer, which he has also used in some of his poems and, to a smaller extent, in several of his novels.[4] It seems clear, however, that he did not turn to Schopenhauer quite as to a new evangelist, but rather as to one who, he found, had conveniently provided for him a seemingly

[4] His indebtedness to Schopenhauer has recently been exhibited in detail by Mr. Ernest Brennecke, jr., in *Thomas Hardy's Universe* (1924), and was discussed some years ago by Dr. Helen Garwood in *Thomas Hardy, an Illustration of the Philosophy of Schopenhauer* (1911). Both books are efforts after scholarly exactness, though the former is the more mature piece of work. Both seem to me misleading in their general effect. It may be mentioned that Dr. Garwood received a letter from Mr. Hardy in which, she says, he spoke "of his philosophy being a development from Schopenhauer through later philosophers." There is clear evidence (which no investigator has yet gathered with parallels) of his study of von Hartmann, of whom he himself speaks in the Preface to *Late Lyrics and Earlier.*

adequate and appropriate vocabulary for the expression
of some of his own conclusions. Consequently, though this
influence has an obvious significance and a further meaning which will later be indicated, its importance can
easily be exaggerated. Clearly Mr. Abercrombie is right
in asserting that the ideas embodied in *The Dynasts*
underlie "most of the intellectual life of our time," and
the cause of understanding is not well served by attempts
to narrow unduly the influences which have communicated to Mr. Hardy what may, with as much accuracy as
is possible in such matters, be termed a major 'spirit of
the age.' The thing of primary importance from the
present view-point is the nature itself of the picture presented in *The Dynasts*.

It is foreshadowed in the opening scene, where the
supernatural intelligences—"contrivances of the fancy
merely," as Mr. Hardy tells us—speak to each other
concerning the universe and approaching events upon
the earth. We are informed that the universe can only
be conceived as something fashioned and controlled by a
blind sense or will, working unconsciously, which no force
can swerve from applying its clock-like laws. Says the
Spirit of the Years:

> In the Foretime, even to the germ of Being,
> Nothing appears of shape to indicate
> That cognizance has marshalled things terrene,
> Or will (such is my thinking) in my span.
> Rather they show that, like a knitter drowsed,
> Whose fingers play in skilled unmindfulness,
> The Will has woven with an absent heed
> Since life first was; and ever will so weave.

Amongst the Will's productions are, of course, ourselves, 'flesh-hinged manikins wound up to click-clack off
laws' designed without regard to our happiness or suffer-

ing, life or death. We are puppets whose self-conscious-
ness gives us merely the illusion of responsible and intelligent action. In reality we act we know not why, because
we must, and all our fears and hopes and scruples and
calculations and moral standards are alike meaningless
vanities. This *The Dynasts* illustrates in a long succession of scenes, many of which taken singly are uninter-
esting enough, in many of which the verse is undistin-
guished or distressingly pedestrian, but which in their
cumulative effect are unparalleled in English literature,
perhaps in any literature, for their immense sweep and
sombre grandeur. Yet all the European peoples and their
leaders who enter into this great pageant only unite to
exhibit the unmeaning emptiness and bottomless futility
of life. The lesson is emphasized very early in the drama,
when the Shade of the Earth asks the Spirit of the Years:

What boots it, Sire,
To down this dynasty, set that one up,
Goad panting peoples to the throes thereof,
Make wither here my fruit, maintain it there,
And hold me travailling through fineless years
In vain and objectless monotony,
When all such tedious conjuring could be shunned
By uncreation? Howsoever wise
The governance of these massed mortalities,
A juster wisdom his who should have ruled
They had not been.

SPIRIT OF THE YEARS
Nay, something hidden urged
The giving matter motion; and these coils
Are, maybe, good as any.

SPIRIT OF THE PITIES
But why any?

Spirit of the Years

Sprite of Compassions, ask the Immanent!
I am but an accessory of Its works,
Whom the Ages render conscious; and at most
Figure as bounden witness of Its laws.

Spirit of the Pities

How ask the aim of unrelaxing Will
Tranced in Its purpose to unknowingness?
(If thy words, Ancient Phantom, token true).

Spirit of the Years

Thou answerest well. But cease to ask of me.
Meanwhile the mime proceeds.

The mime proceeds!—turning to the sphere of human life, we behold our fellow-creatures busily engaged in actions they deem purposeful and important. At this moment the British House of Commons is engaged in deliberations which end in a division sustaining Pitt's ministry, whereupon the Spirit of the Pities remarks:

It irks me that they thus should Yea and Nay
As though a power lay in their oraclings,
If each decision work unconsciously,
And would be operant though unloosened were
A single lip!

Spirit of Rumour

There may react on things
Some influence from these, indefinitely,
And even on That, whose outcome we all are.

To which the Spirit of the Years replies, "Hypotheses!" and so dismisses the vague guess. Not even the bare possibility that human beings have any measure of control over their lives and fortunes is to be treated seriously. And of all the thousands who play their parts in the drama only two or three have the slightest inkling of their real situation, while of these Napoleon is the only one who distinctly voices his occasional realization of it, when he says to Josephine:

> Some force within me, baffling mine intent,
> Harries me onward, whether I will or no.
> My star, my star is what's to blame—not I.
> It is unswervable!

After which the Spirit of the Years observes:

> He spoke thus at the Bridge of Lodi. Strange,
> He's of the few in Europe who discern
> The working of the Will.

Napoleon's discernment, which enables him to transgress moral standards without compunction, is later commended by one of the supernatural intelligences, but his freedom from remorse is its only profit to him, as his discernment gives him no foresight and no control over his acts.

Mr. Hardy, then, pictures the universe as a self-sufficient mechanism, or as a single huge organism. Its phenomena are all controlled by an unknowable force immanent in them or, in other words, an integral part of the whole. We may call this, if we like, an impulse or will towards ceaseless ordered movement, but we really know nothing about it. We only know that all phenomena, including ourselves, are basically identical parts of one whole which is moving along its own course. This course has nothing in common with our conscious purposes, desires, or feelings, so that we cannot conceive of it as either conscious or purposive. At the same time, however, we must conceive of our own distinctive traits, such as conscience or remorse, implying as they do responsibility on our part, as delusive. Not only are we really helpless, but all our necessitated actions are, from any human point of view, entirely futile. We are the mere creatures of what, judging by its workings, we can only term blind accident.

It is in this way that Mr. Hardy appears to combine his determinism with the view that all things are the product of sheer chance. As far as we can judge, he seems to say, we are the helpless creatures of accident, yet the necessitated movements of matter follow ordered patterns, and thus have a common character, even though they are not so closely woven together as to form a single coherent whole in which chance can find no place. Hence there is some objective ground for supposing that nature forms a purposive system. Even, however, if she does so, she follows a purpose which we cannot fathom and which has no regard for our happiness, our welfare, or our existence itself. Thus in either case our lives are determined by factors utterly regardless of us their creatures, and practically it is a matter of indifference whether the truth lie in one direction or the other. If, however, we are not to believe that the world and all it supports are simply chaos within chaos—and against this there is the evidence of ordered movement all around us —the only alternative is a deterministic monism. Occasionally, as I have said, Mr. Hardy lapses into the indifferentism which follows from the view that all is accident, but generally, even when he seems unqualifiedly to accept this view, he reacts strongly against it;—that is, he writes as if there were something, an order, a system, a universe, against which to react, and so shows that it is a naturalism, even though somewhat vaguely and paradoxically conceived, which he has predominantly in his mind. In *Hap*, a sonnet written as long ago as 1866, he expressed plainly what has been his prevailing tone, his manner of reaction against the bitterness of the human lot, though at that time, as will be seen, he was apparently content to ascribe all that is to chance alone:

> If but some vengeful god would call to me
> From up the sky, and laugh: ''Thou suffering thing,
> Know that thy sorrow is my ecstasy,
> That thy love's loss is my hate's profiting!''
>
> Then would I bear it, clench myself, and die,
> Steeled by the sense of ire unmerited;
> Half-eased in that a Powerfuller than I
> Had willed and meted me the tears I shed.
>
> But not so. How arrives it joy lies slain,
> And why unblooms the best hope ever sown?
> —Crass Casualty obstructs the sun and rain,
> And dicing Time for gladness casts a moan. . . .
> These purblind Doomsters had as readily strown
> Blisses about my pilgrimage as pain.

While this sonnet on the one hand indicates the hopelessness and bitterness of our situation as the playthings of ''crass casualty,'' on the other it indicates that this is by no means the whole of our misery. For although we are the puppets of real or seeming chance, our feelings and desires are genuine and intense. This it is which gives intolerable poignancy to our situation. Our feelings and desires *are* genuine, yet life pays no heed to them, or rather is bound to frustrate our desires and violate our feelings. And the quality of either makes no difference in the result. It is all one whether a man be a saint or a sinner; these are mere conventional differences with no root in the nature of things. It would be a folly to set up such distinctions could we help it, because, even were we able to determine our courses, there would be really no choice to be made. The feelings of saint and sinner are alike irrelevant to the nature of things, and the desires of both are equally vain and impotent.

Had we been fashioned unconscious manikins, the processes of which we form a part would have been as meaningless as now they are, but at least there could have been no complaint;—there would, indeed, then have been no one to complain. But actually we do have the capacity both to enjoy and to suffer, while only the latter is genuinely satisfied. This is the final, insoluble enigma which confronts Mr. Hardy. Why we should exist, even were we blessedly unconscious of the fact, he cannot see, whereas consciousness simply adds tragedy to what was before incomprehensible. This conviction is voiced in *The Dynasts* and in many of his poems, as well as in *Tess of the D'Urbervilles* and *Jude the Obscure*. In *The Dynasts*, after the Battle of Ulm, the Spirit Ironic says that the "Will Itself might smile at this collapse of Austria's men-at-arms, so drolly done," to which the Chorus of the Years replies:

> Ah, no: ah, no!
> It is impassible as glacial snow.—
> Within the Great Unshaken
> These painted shapes awaken
> A lesser thrill than doth the gentle lave
> Of yonder bank by Danube's wandering wave
> Within the Schwarzwald heights that give it flow!

> SPIRIT OF THE PITIES
> But O, the intolerable antilogy
> Of making figments feel!

> SPIRIT IRONIC
> Logic's in that.
> It does not, I must own, quite play the game.

Again, later, at the death of Nelson the Spirit of the Pities is moved to indignation at the nature of things when contemplating the several hours of useless suffering which intervene between the time when the great admiral is shot down and the moment of his death, and Pity says to the Spirit of the Years:

> Out of tune the Mode and meritless
> That quickens sense in shapes whom, thou hast said,
> Necessitation sways! A life there was
> Among these self-same frail ones—Sophocles—
> Who visioned it too clearly, even the while
> He dubbed the Will "the gods." Truly said he,
> "Such gross injustice to their own creation
> Burdens the time with mournfulness for us,
> And for themselves with shame."[5]—Things mechanized
> By coils and pivots set to foreframed codes
> Would, in a thorough-sphered melodic rule,
> And governance of sweet consistency,
> Be cessed no pain, whose burnings would abide
> With That Which holds responsibility,
> Or inexist.

> CHORUS OF THE PITIES
> Yea, yea, yea!
> Thus would the Mover pay
> The score each puppet owes,
> The Reaper reap what his contrivance sows!
> Why make Life debtor when it did not buy?
> Why wound so keenly Right that it would die?

To such questions Mr. Hardy has no answer. He only says that existence is a mockery or curse, and that it would be better for us to be dead than alive—a proposition laid down and fully illustrated in *Jude the Obscure* and in some of his poems. *To the Moon* is a fairly light-hearted instance:

[5] *Trachiniœ*, ll. 1266-1272. The words are spoken by Hyllus.

"What have you looked at, Moon,
　　In your time,
　Now long past your prime?"
"O, I have looked at, often looked at
　　Sweet, sublime,
Sore things, shudderful, night and noon
　　In my time."

"What have you mused on, Moon,
　　In your day,
　So aloof, so far away?"
"O, I have mused on, often mused on
　　Growth, decay,
Nations alive, dead, mad, aswoon,
　　In my day!"

"Have you much wondered, Moon,
　　On your rounds,
　Self-wrapt, beyond Earth's bounds?"
"Yea, I have wondered, often wondered
　　At the sounds
Reaching me of the human tune
　　On my rounds."

"What do you think of it, Moon,
　　As you go?
　Is Life much, or no?"
"O, I think of it, often think of it
　　As a show
God ought surely to shut up soon,
　　As I go."

Meanwhile, since the show is not yet shut up, we cannot help asking why, nor can we help complaining bitterly
against the nature of things. Mr. Hardy has written a
number of poems in which he tells us what must be the
character of any deity we can imagine as the creator of

ourselves and the world we inhabit. They are not flattering. *New Year's Eve* may serve as an example:

"I have finished another year," said God,
  "In grey, green, white, and brown;
I have strewn the leaf upon the sod,
Sealed up the worm within the clod,
  And let the last sun down."

"And what's the good of it?" I said,
  "What reasons made you call
From formless void this earth we tread,
When nine-and-ninety can be read
  Why nought should be at all?

"Yea, Sire; why shaped you us, 'who in
  This tabernacle groan'—
If ever a joy be found herein,
Such joy no man had wished to win
  If he had never known!"

Then he: "My labours—logicless—
  You may explain; not I:
Sense-sealed I have wrought, without a guess
That I evolved a Consciousness
  To ask for reasons why.

"Strange that ephemeral creatures who
  By my own ordering are,
Should see the shortness of my view,
Use ethic tests I never knew,
  Or made provision for!"

He sank to raptness as of yore,
  And opening New Year's Day
Wove it by rote as theretofore,
And went on working evermore
  In his unweeting way.

In another poem, *God's Education,* the deity is imagined as being gradually taught to improve his moral sense by listening to the admonitions of man; while in *A Plaint to Man* God asks why man ever had to create him as an object of prayer, because, since then,

> The doing without me has had no play
> In the minds of men when shadows scare;
>
> And now that I dwindle day by day
> Beneath the deicide eyes of seers
> In a light that will not let me stay,
>
> And to-morrow the whole of me disappears,
> The truth should be told, and the fact be faced
> That had best been faced in earlier years:
>
> The fact of life with dependence placed
> On the human heart's resource alone,
> In brotherhood bonded close and graced
>
> With loving-kindness fully blown,
> And visioned help unsought, unknown.

In *God's Funeral* the dwindling deity is at length finally discredited and buried; but this consummation in no wise lightens the weight of Mr. Hardy's bitterness against the nature of things, as can be seen in *The Blow:*

> That no man schemed it is my hope—
> Yea, that it fell by will and scope
>   Of That Which some enthrone,
> And for whose meaning myriads grope.
>
> For I would not that of my kind
> There should, of his unbiassed mind,
>   Have been one known
> Who such a stroke could have designed;

Since it would augur works and ways
Below the lowest that man assays
    To have hurled that stone
Into the sunshine of our days!

And if it prove that no man did,
And that the Inscrutable, the Hid,
    Was cause alone
Of this foul crash our lives amid,

I'll go in due time, and forget
In some deep graveyard's oubliette
    The thing whereof I groan,
And cease from troubling; thankful yet

Time's finger should have stretched to show
No aimful author's was the blow
    That swept us prone,
But the Immanent Doer's That doth not know

Which in some age unguessed of us
May lift Its blinding incubus,
    And see, and own:
"It grieves me I did thus and thus!"

The burden of Mr. Hardy's indictment against life or against the nature of things comes down to this: that since everything in our lives is necessitated by something outside of our own sense of purpose and beyond our control, and since this entails upon us real but meaningless suffering, the source of our being can only be described by us as unconscious and without purpose. It follows that there is unescapable injustice in our having consciousness at all and, much more, intolerable injustice in our being endowed with "the disease of feeling." No one can fathom any reason for our existence and no one can deny its combined suffering and futility.

Mr. Hardy tells us that he began life as a believer in

Christianity. His works do not indicate clearly the path which led him far from the orthodox fold, but, nevertheless, his general course can be traced with a degree of certainty. The dates affixed to some of his poems show that such Christian beliefs as he once had must have become impossible for him about the time he reached manhood or very shortly thereafter. He did not relinquish these beliefs gladly, but with sorrow and with at least some tendency to condemn himself for his inability to find in Christian faith the reality or solace which others found there. At the same time, however, he felt a certainty of being in the right of it which soon overtopped his mood of humility, though it perhaps did not so quickly drown his regret at what he had lost.

What caused this initial change? It was apparently a combination of experience and philosophy, each seeming to reinforce the other. He doubtless had been taught that Christianity was a miraculously revealed body of truths and, for the rest, his belief seems largely to have consisted in the propositions that everything had been providentially arranged for man's convenience and that justice was the fundamental law of life. Unfortunately it is not at all incredible that this should have been so. But, of course, it took only the slightest reflexion upon experience to show that there were fundamental difficulties in such beliefs. Man's life was in reality an unceasing struggle against both his natural and his human environments, and a struggle conditioned by many factors—such, for instance, as heredity, parentage, social customs—for which he was in no way responsible and yet which always influenced and sometimes predetermined the outcome. There were factors both of personal circumstances and of temperament which greatly facilitated such disillusioning discoveries. And, as has already been said, Mr. Hardy, who was born in 1840, reached manhood at a time when naturalistic thought was undergoing an immense revival of prestige through the progress of the exact sciences and particularly through Darwin's seeming proof of the evolution hypothesis. To one who could not be indifferent to philosophical and religious questions, naturalism at this time appeared to offer with all the authority of exact science an unifying conception embracing the whole round of reality and likewise completely accounting for the very facts of experience which had unsettled a comfortable theistic faith. And the result was Mr. Hardy's conversion to a deterministic monism.

The change, however, opened up new difficulties in place of those it had resolved. For their understanding something must first be said of naturalism as it has usually developed by way of reaction from religion. The naturalistic point of view has always had the implicit support of common sense and has always had a strong attraction for men of secular, sensuous temperament. There has been from the beginning, as far as can be known, a practical dualism in human nature, exemplified by standards of conduct, based on religious sanctions, which have been hard to live up to. There has ever been a war within ourselves; impulses have pulled us in contrary directions, and we have ventured to ascribe a divine origin to some of these, while others we have stigmatized as base, wrong, or sinful. In general these evil impulses are strong and universal, their satisfaction gives an unmistakable, immediate pleasure, and we share a number of them with the rest of the animal kingdom. Good impulses, on the other hand, are generally weaker and may be almost absent from many men, their satisfaction usually does not result in immediate pleasure and may even be painful, and they are almost exclusively peculiar to humanity. It may be said that what is good tends on the whole to promote human life;—that is, it is either advantageous to the community of which we are a part, although it may be painful to us as individuals, or it tends to develop and make predominant what is specifically human in us as opposed to those other elements in our nature which we share with other animals.

Occasionally some man has had so overwhelming a sense of the importance of these good or specifically human elements in our nature and so clear an insight into their meaning and character as to be able to impress his conviction regarding our situation and needs upon a whole nation or group of nations. But these are not obvious matters, and we are peculiarly liable to make mistakes about them. In this direction we are pioneers feeling our way towards the opening-up of a wholly new path. And even the wisest man, or rather any man just in proportion as he is wise, if he ventures to talk to others, is limited by what they can be made to understand. Consequently new standards or ideals are the more likely to be overlaid with falsehood and superstition the more widely they are received. They are supported with blind and indiscriminate zeal, or with the wrong reasons, or they are clothed in symbolic language which itself becomes sacred and inviolable, though actually it was intended only as a makeshift whose usefulness depended on its relevance to the surrounding conditions of those for whom it was framed. Nor is this all, for concrete applications of standards and ideals become similarly sacred and inviolable. Yet man's environment is constantly changing and so demanding what never takes place soon enough—the equally constant revision of the language in which standards and ideals are stated and supported, and of the codes of conduct which embody their practical applications.

Hence there have always been periods when it has been extremely easy for a self-confident man of sensuous temperament and limited insight to conclude that the religious sanctions of good conduct are a mere sort of make-believe; and thus far even religious men may perforce have agreed with him, because they could not help seeing that the current religion was an outworn shell, a relic of the formalism of a past age;—or because they could not help seeing that, as has sometimes happened with decayed religions, it actually was preserving beliefs and practices which did violence to the moral sense. But of course the self-confident man would not stop here. Revolting from palpably superstitious beliefs, he concludes not only that there are no elements of truth underlying them, but also that the conduct connected with them is harmful. In some respects, moreover, this may really be so, because, as was said, conduct, like language, is a relative matter; it must needs change with changing conditions. Conduct which once was right may now be evil, or *vice versa*, because of the discriminating application, under varying conditions, of one unchanging principle. It is not, however, in the interest of a wise and careful revision of the 'commandments' that the revolt being described takes place. This is a difficult and delicate work, requiring for success extreme pains and patience, while the rebel against pious usages has no motives impelling him to such a task. On the contrary, he has powerful reasons for denying or remaining oblivious of its possibility. For his quarrel is really with difficult conduct as such, and he merely seizes for his own purpose on some practical rule left exposed to his onslaught by blind religious conservatism.

This the rebel does because he is, like the rest of us, troubled by the dualism of human nature and longs to do away with it, while he has little either inside himself or around him to aid him in understanding its character. Hence he concludes that this troublesome and dark conflict within our members is not inherent in human nature, but is imposed by some men on others for interested reasons;—our fears and scruples are played upon by priests for the sake of maintaining and enhancing their own power and welfare. Thus he appears as the true friend and liberator of mankind when he proceeds to announce that men's irrational beliefs and the painful or, as we say, unnatural conduct accompanying them are not good, but absurd and injurious. Human nature, he says, is one, not dual, and we are all members of one body; our only goddess is our ancient mother, Nature herself, the kindly nurse of all her children great and small, and she has given us in our natural impulses all we need in order to our welfare. Can she have done less for us than she has for the cattle of the field and the beasts of the forest? Surely not! We ought, then, to trust our strongest, universal impulses, forsaking all mere man-made laws, and, so doing, we shall return to the good heart of things from which we have strayed, and shall regain that golden unity of nature which it is unalloyed happiness to possess—a happiness only known to us hitherto in tragically brief, stolen moments of elemental ecstasy, in which the voice of conscience was hushed and the weary battle forgotten.

To many thoughtful people in the latter half of the nineteenth century a variety of considerations, including the discoveries of science, and particularly those bearing on evolution, seemed imperatively to call for this naturalistic conclusion, and Mr. Hardy was amongst them. In one of his infrequent essays he stated that his purpose in his novels was the handling of tragic motives in terms of modern knowledge, and that he sought "to show Nature's unconsciousness not of essential laws, but of those laws framed merely as social expedients by humanity, without a basis in the heart of things"; and he added that he aimed to give his material "treatment which expresses

the triumph of the crowd over the hero, of the commonplace majority over the exceptional few.'"[6] In several of
his novels, including notably *Far from the Madding
Crowd, The Return of the Native,* and *The Woodlanders,*
he sought in greater or less degree to submerge his characters in their natural surroundings and so to exhibit the
oneness of man and nature. Men were to be regarded as
outgrowths of the soil, like trees or brambles, the mobile
products of vast germinative forces, with no independent
powers properly to be called their own. And in *Tess of
the D'Urbervilles,* after Tess's irregular union with Alec
D'Urberville and the birth of their child, he attempted
to make credible her continuing purity of character
partly by explaining that what she had more or less will-
ingly done was not unnatural, was indeed simply what in
the world of nature would be taken as a matter of course,
and that she was 'guilty' only of violating man-made
laws 'framed as social expedients and without a basis in
the heart of things.'

Mr. Hardy could not, however, rest in this position.
Impressively as contemporary discoveries and thought
seemed to point to the basic unity not only of all organic
creatures but of the whole universe of phenomena, still,
evolutionary doctrine also exhibited the processes of
nature as full of savage cruelty and ruthlessness. Nature
was, in fact, 'red in tooth and claw,' and to return to her
bosom was to return to something worse than barbarism,
to a world dehumanized, necessitated in all its workings
by forces wholly indifferent to, if not at all points opposed to, everything in life valued by human beings.
This, Mr. Hardy, with his sensitiveness and honesty of
feeling, could not help but perceive, and accordingly in
the three earlier of the above-mentioned novels he showed

[6] *Candour in English Fiction* (*The New Review,* January, 1890).

himself to be by no means unconscious of certain malign aspects of the natural world, while in *Tess* this conscious-ness at length appeared with unqualified strength, and at a heavy expense in congruity. For *Tess* contains a number of passages which make up a bitter indictment of the fair-seeming order of nature. Portions of the same indictment are repeated in a number of his poems, and an illuminating instance is the one entitled *In a Wood*, where a few lines of mere observation of fact contained in *The Woodlanders* are amplified and given a quite new meaning:

> Pale beech and pine so blue,
>   Set in one clay,
> Bough to bough cannot you
>   Live out your day?
> When the rains skim and skip,
> Why mar sweet comradeship,
> Blighting with poison-drip
>   Neighbourly spray?
>
> Heart-halt and spirit-lame,
>   City-opprest,
> Unto this wood I came
>   As to a nest;
> Dreaming that sylvan peace
> Offered the harrowed ease—
> Nature a soft release
>   From men's unrest.
>
> But, having entered in,
>   Great growths and small
> Show them to men akin—
>   Combatants all!
> Sycamore shoulders oak,
> Bines the slim sapling yoke,
> Ivy-spun halters choke
>   Elms stout and tall.

Touches from ash, O wych,
  Sting you like scorn!
You, too, brave hollies, twitch
  Sidelong from thorn.
Even the rank poplars bear
Lothly a rival's air,
Cankering in black despair
  If overborne.

Since, then, no grace I find
  Taught me of trees,
Turn I back to my kind,
  Worthy as these.
There at least smiles abound,
There discourse trills around,
There, now and then, are found
  Life-loyalties.

One might suppose that a man who had made this discovery, who had the courage to face it, and who was honestly seeking the truth, would have come to the obvious conclusion that after all naturalism was in the wrong of it. Naturalism, one might think he would have seen, was merely one more attempt to comprehend the universe in a generalization based on man's very limited experience and, moreover, based on only an arbitrarily selected portion of it, illegitimately leaving out of the account as it did the data of experience which pointed to a fundamental divergence between man and the natural world. And consequently he might have been forced back on the conclusion that human nature was inherently dual in character; man was an animal, certainly, and in his animality was firmly linked to the world of phenomena, and so far was wholly one with beasts, or even with the beech-tree and the pine-tree; but man was at the same time something other than an animal, extending his being to the experience of something beyond the phenomenal world, to the experience of something no less real to him in the world of values—the world where, somehow, "smiles abound," and, "now and then, are found life-loyalties."

Actually, however, Mr. Hardy did nothing of the sort. Naturalism he had espoused, and to it he still gave his undivided allegiance, even though this now caused him extraordinary difficulties. His insight and honesty forced him to repudiate the optimistical cosmic dreams of many of his contemporaries, but could not force him to forgo the vanity of cosmic dreams themselves. In his prefaces he has exhibited symptoms of the 'fear-of-giving-himself-away disease' but, nevertheless, has not obscured the fact that a monistic world he was bound to have, whatever the cost. Accordingly, his formulation of his experience was subject to this prejudice. He concluded, as has been shown, that the phenomenal world, of which we are a part, is a non-moral, purposeless, meaningless complex of appearances exhibiting a single gross anomaly, probably the result of blundering accident, in human consciousness. The inner world revealed by consciousness—the world of feeling, values, and purpose—he pronounced unreal. It is unreal, not in the sense that we do not actually have feelings and desires and aims, but in the sense that these are merely subjective excitations not corresponding to objective reality, so that they are doomed to be violated and frustrated at the hands of the indifferent world.

> I sat. It was all past;
> Hope never would hail again;
> Fair days had ceased at a blast,
> The world was a darkened den.

The beauty and dream were gone,
And the halo in which I had hied
So gaily gallantly on
Had suffered blot and died!

I went forth, heedless whither,
In a cloud too black for name:
—People frisked hither and thither;
The world was just the same.

This unreality to which we are subject is that which causes a division between us and the phenomenal world and which makes life a burden to us—a burden the more real and terrible both because we do sometimes snatch delusive joys from life but cannot keep them, and because we endure all our unescapable pains and hardships for no conceivable end. Consequently the one blessing we can look forward to and possess is the oblivion of death.

This suggests the question how Mr. Hardy can have come to such a conclusion with the confidence, and even pride, which he evidently feels in it. The obvious answer is simple enough: that he has fearlessly attempted to be faithful at any cost to his own experience, as the one immediate certainty accessible to him. This may be granted; it is not likely that there is any one more honest than Mr. Hardy, and his honesty gives a certain value to his work of which no other consideration can deprive it. But faithfulness to experience is not the simple matter which it is often taken to be and, in addition, any one man's experience is bound to be extremely limited, may be extraordinary, and may indicate that the man himself is no true protagonist of humanity.

Nor is this all, for it is not easy to see how a man can attribute any value to his own thought who regards human beings as mere cunning machines, regulated by a

non-human force which renders all their ideas illusory.
If this be so, how can any of us discover it? The man who
pretends to do so must, if he knows what he is about,
consider himself an unique phenomenon, different in kind
from the rest of humanity. There is that in Mr. Hardy's
manner at times which almost suggests that he does make
so audacious a claim. As Lionel Johnson remarked, his
"novels are not written for a purpose, to prove the truth
of something; but with the prejudice, that it is a proven
truth."[7] Nevertheless it is incredible that this should be
the explanation of Mr. Hardy's self-assurance, so that it
must be sought elsewhere.

In the first place, then, faithfulness to experience is not
a simple matter because impressions can never be expressed or communicated directly, but only through some
medium. This always offers difficulties of its own. Impressions have to be translated into ideas and pictures,
and these in turn have to be communicated through
words and rhythms. Thus limitations of logical grasp, of
imagination, of language, and of music all go together
to obstruct faithfulness to experience. We all have to
learn sooner or later that even in our simplest tasks our
reach somehow exceeds our grasp, so that what we accomplish falls short of what we intended. And commonly
our deepest impressions are those which most strenu-
ously resist expression. Hence even gifted men often in
sheer impatience and desperation fall back upon a language or a system of thought not their own which says
things, as it were of its own independent force, that they
do not wish to say; or again, attempting as best they may
to express individual perceptions and impressions in
terms of the prejudices and dominant conceptions of
their own age, they say against their will what others

[7] *The Art of Thomas Hardy* (ed. of 1923), p. 172.

have succeeded in imposing on them. Of course, this is true, as has just been indicated, in more or less important ways of all men, so that we properly enough disregard it for the most part, and only recall it now in the face of a very extraordinary and awful view of the human scene. And it suggests that perhaps Mr. Hardy has at times said more than he has meant to say, or has at least not succeeded in conveying his meaning with the shades of doubt or reservation which he may himself feel, so that to him his estimate of life may properly seem a less extraordinary and difficult one than to us.

This is possible. It does account for Mr. Hardy's unfortunate and somewhat confusing use of the language of Schopenhauer, but perhaps it does little more. For it is probable that the ground of Mr. Hardy's self-confidence lies rather in another meaning which the ideal of faithfulness to experience may have. That phrase is not merely a cumbersome synonym for honesty, but denotes also what may be called a characteristic boast of naturalism. In this use it is a literary equivalent of the inductive method of science, and, in addition, it implies that the man of letters makes the same claim as the scientist regarding the scope of his work. Both propose, they tell us, to deal with what is real and with what alone is real. They engage disinterestedly to concern themselves with the world of actual fact, admitting nothing because men would like to believe it, banishing all that is merely imaginative, and eagerly facing the worst so it be that thus they can reach the truth. They imply that not only is the truth their aim, but that they alone aim solely at the truth, with no preconceptions, no mixed desires, and no concessions to powerful or respectable authorities already in the field. Whence comes solace, asks Mr. Hardy, whence comes renewed courage to face the battle of life?

Not from seeing
What is doing, suffering, being,
Not from noting Life's conditions,
Not from heeding Time's monitions;
   But in cleaving to the Dream,
   And in gazing at the gleam
   Whereby grey things golden seem.

Thus do I this heyday, holding
Shadows but as lights unfolding,
As no specious show this moment
With its iris-hued embowment;
   But as nothing other than
   Part of a benignant plan;
   Proof that earth was made for man.

Thus he allowed himself to think on a holiday, while he rested from the severe pursuit of reality; yet even then he scarcely succeeded in deceiving himself, but remained inwardly faithful still to what he took to be the meaning of the literal aspect of phenomena. And this, unqualified submission to brute fact, is the ideal compressed into a phrase. The writer endeavouring to realize it aims to act, not as the interpreter, but as the mere reporter of impressions. These he wishes to let speak for themselves, he being regarded as a passive and impersonal collector of data. Thus Mr. Hardy wrote, in the Preface to *Poems of the Past and the Present:* "Unadjusted impressions have their value, and the road to a true philosophy of life seems to lie in humbly recording diverse readings of its phenomena as they are forced upon us by chance and change."[8]

---

[8] In his essay entitled *The Science of Fiction* (*The New Review*, April, 1891) Mr. Hardy speaks of selection and omission, "with an eye to being more truthful than truth (the just aim of Art)." At first sight this might

This, I believe, goes far to explain Mr. Hardy's confidence in his conclusions. He has felt completely sure of the rightness of his method, and it is of the essence of this method that it is to be followed without any regard whatever to the conclusions it opens up at the end of the road. This in itself makes a powerful appeal to men, akin to the ideal of justice administered without fear or favour, and Mr. Hardy's confidence in his method is not at all surprising in view of what has already been said about the period when he reached manhood and began to think for himself. Nevertheless it is surprising that he should have retained it through the years, without spot or blemish, not only in the face of his conclusions, but also in the face of increasingly general knowledge of the real character of scientific method.

It is impossible to suppose that Mr. Hardy is or has been at all disingenuous in pretending to disinterested impartiality in following a process of pure induction, but, if he is not disingenuous, he has been deceived. For he has not ever succeeded in doing what he has claimed to do, and for the best of reasons. We are commonly told that induction is the corner-stone of modern science, though it is also said that no single scientific discovery could ever have been made solely through the inductive method. What is more, both statements are true. Fruitful scientific work depends upon the formulation of hypotheses, or likely guesses, by means of which experimentation is controlled to definite ends—either the rejection,

appear to contradict what has just been said and his own words quoted above, but in reality Mr. Hardy is dealing with a different question in *The Science of Fiction*. He is speaking, not of the gathering of material, but of the artist's work of construction—of his task, once he has found his material, of giving it coherence, proportion, and emphasis. He is speaking, in other words, not of impressions, but of the artist's work in dealing with their details, their component parts, so as to convey impressions truly.

modification, or acceptance of the hypotheses in question. In other words, the scientist is never a mere collector of data, but one who uses the data of experience for his own purpose, which is the discovery of 'the habits of matter,' or of the so-called laws of nature which enable us to predict future occurrences and so to take practical advantage of our knowledge. To this end the scientist rigidly selects and controls the experience to which he binds himself to be faithful. His experience is doubly selected and controlled, first by the hypothesis which he is seeking to test, and secondly by the fact that he can test it only through the quantitative measurement of phenomena. Induction is thus of incalculable value as a limiting norm, but practically it means, as far as I am aware, only this: that it limits the sphere of scientific activity to that portion of experience which is quantitatively measurable. Hence experience and hypothesis mutually control each other, while both are controlled by the limitations of experimentation. Science can deal with only a fractional part of the world in which we live and, within its sphere, one may say that fancy is controlled by fact, but that the facts are selected by fancy.

So much as this, every one now knows about the processes of science, but its bearing upon the claim of a novelist or poet that he deals faithfully with his experience, in the sense that he acts simply as an impersonal and impartial collector of data, is obvious and destructive. Not only is the individual's experience limited in extent but, within the field of possible experience, it is further limited by the selective or purposive activity of the subject. There is no way in which the subject can avoid this; so we are made. No writer or artist has ever simply held a mirror up to nature. To do this, one would have to be a mirror instead of a subject or, in other words, a reflecting thing instead of a conscious human being. As far as can be known, consciousness itself would not exist were it not for unrealized aims present in us as problems. It takes an inner as well as an outer stimulus to rouse and fix our attention. We take cognizance of those matters only in our environment which seem significant to us, and we are indifferent to or oblivious of the remainder.

Hence it is that the man who attempts to act as a mere recorder of data can never achieve his aim. The fact that he has such an aim itself indicates that his mind has already taken up a definite attitude towards life; and this means that he has already to some extent determined the kind of experience he will record, and that he already has at least a tentative meaning to attach to his experience. Since, however, in the present case the aim is an attempt to elude this necessity, what he actually does is to place himself at the mercy of his unregenerated temperament. Instead of consciously exercising some measure of control over his experience for definitely conceived purposes, he allows himself to drift on the sea of change surrounding him. But this does not mean that he has succeeded in converting himself from a human being into a machine—it means only that he has given up as far as possible one kind of control for the sake of allowing free sway to another. He has forgone conscious, deliberate control in order to be guided by the relatively blind complex of spontaneous feelings and desires which continually surge up in him from the centre of his being. It is difficult to see how any reader of Mr. Hardy's novels and poems can avoid being struck by the fact that this is what has happened to him. Objective as his work is in method, it is in substance a singularly exclusive reflexion of his own unregenerated temperament.

It has been said that though Mr. Hardy's mind "has been impregnated with modern ideas, his temperament is essentially rustic, primitive, pagan.'"[9] What I have just sought to indicate is how modern ideas have served, not to curb, but to give free rein to this native disposition. It now remains to define it more exactly. In *A Conversation at Dawn* Mr. Hardy makes one of the characters exclaim,

> No God intends
> To thwart the yearning He's father to!

He means, of course, that no god should do this, that if it is done, from whatever cause, it is wrong. We are made with certain feelings and desires; we are not responsible for their existence within us, but so we are fashioned without our advice or consent; hence if we are to discern any goodness in the world or in the nature of things it must be through the satisfaction of these natural wants of ours. A grievous outrage has been inflicted upon us if we have been given these wants only to find that they are not to be satisfied. Nor is there any ground for discriminating between our various feelings and desires, terming some good and some bad. The only thing to be considered is the fact that they are all equally real, and hence all equally deserving of satisfaction.

This kind of reasoning, which issues legitimately and indeed inevitably from Mr. Hardy's naturalistic premises, of course opens up a profound basis for endless complaint against the universe, of which, as we have seen, he has taken full advantage. Moreover, since he admits no qualitative standard of judgement, but only the quantitative one of intensity, it follows that he values chiefly those impulses and desires which arise from our animal nature. To what most men call the higher values

[9] *Thomas Hardy, Poet and Novelist,* by Professor Samuel C. Chew, p. 143. Lionel Johnson had said the same thing: "Modern though he be, and even of an 'advanced' modernity, his writings have a primitive savour, a tang of antiquity, an earthy charm, an affinity, a comradeship with nature." (*Post Liminium,* p. 142.)

of life he has remained almost, if not completely, blind;
and there is no indication that it has ever entered his
head to inquire whether or not the very conditions of
life which he so deplores might favour the realization of
those higher values. His idea of Paradise, were he to
permit himself to play with the idea at all, would be very
Mahometan. In fact, in a poem which gathers together
the implications of many others, he explicitly exalts a
group of pleasures which will be recognized as closely
related to the traditional sacred trinity of the sensual
man:

> Sweet cyder is a great thing,
>   A great thing to me,
> Spinning down to Weymouth town
>   By Ridgway thirstily,
> And maid and mistress summoning
>   Who tend the hostelry:
> O cyder is a great thing,
>   A great thing to me!
>
> The dance it is a great thing,
>   A great thing to me,
> With candles lit and partners fit
>   For night-long revelry;
> And going home when day-dawning
>   Peeps pale upon the lea:
> O dancing is a great thing,
>   A great thing to me!
>
> Love is, yea, a great thing,
>   A great thing to me,
> When, having drawn across the lawn
>   In darkness silently,
> A figure flits like one a-wing
>   Out from the nearest tree:
> O love is, yes, a great thing,
>   A great thing to me!

Will these be always great things,
  Great things to me? . . .
Let it befall that One will call,
  "Soul, I have need of thee":
What then? Joy-haunts, impassioned flings,
  Love, and its ecstasy,
Will always have been great things,
  Great things to me!

But these great things of life are usually denied us or,
if they are given, are given grudgingly, insufficiently,
capriciously. If we do succeed in getting what we want
it is straightway snatched from us; and if by chance we
regain it we are only led to the discovery that what
charmed us once charms us no longer. We can command
neither things around us nor our own moods. Though
we chase the most corporeal delights, the most intensely
felt pleasures, still, even these we find are will-o'-the-
wisps, and this is Life.

Coomb-Firtrees say that Life is a moan,
  And Clyffe-hill Clump says "Yea!"
But Yell'ham says a thing of its own:
    It's not "Grey, grey
    Is Life alway!"
    That Yell'ham says,
  Nor that Life is for ends unknown.

It says that Life would signify
  A thwarted purposing:
That we come to live, and are called to die.
    Yes, that's the thing
    In fall, in spring,
    That Yell'ham says:—
  "Life offers—to deny!"

Mr. Hardy's hedonism is integral to his naturalism,
and, though he has clung to both, in his utter disillusion-

ment he has found only emptiness in both. His conclusion that life offers what *he* seeks merely to deny it is, I think, irrefutable, and I should wish not to combat it, but to emphasize it. For most people, I should suppose, life is not really much happier or more joyful than Mr. Hardy would have us believe. There are few, of course, who share his unrelieved, profound despair; but there are probably also few who, though they find life worth living, do not value it chiefly for the enjoyment or happiness which they hope to obtain, rather than for that which they have obtained in the past or at present possess. Of these there are certainly many. It would appear, indeed, that the number of people who frankly make earthly or temporal happiness their life's aim is far greater than it has been in some preceding ages, or perhaps in any preceding age of which we know anything. It does not follow, however, that they are succeeding in their pursuit. This is a peculiarly difficult question to answer. About the whole subject of happiness a great deal of nonsense has been written and spoken, and about it there is also much self-deception, both unconscious and, strangely enough at first sight, conscious and deliberate. This deliberate self-deception is not really so strange, however, in the light of the fact that very many people of this age have come to the conclusion that temporal happiness is all that life can offer them. Belief in its possibility is with them a counsel of despair, as their only other alternative is the outlook of Mr. Hardy.

Venturing briefly to suggest some considerations bearing on the pursuit of happiness, I should say, in the first place, that the multiplication of mechanical contrivances designed for comfort or distraction does not materially promote it, since desires multiply and fluctuate at least as fast, and since in general both multiply faster than our incomes. And probably the general prosperity of a community or a nation has very little bearing on it, or, it may be, an adverse effect. Certainly the American business men who are excitedly telling the labouring classes, the ignorant foreigners, and some college professors how un-American they are in refusing to be contented with their lot, are not an illustration of the doctrine they preach, since they are obviously actuated by an acute, nervous anxiety which knows few scruples and occasionally seems to approach insanity. The boat which cannot be rocked is hardly a very seaworthy craft, and I do not think that many examples of secure and unalloyed happiness are to be found amongst its higher officers.

Happiness, moreover, being subjective, can never be unmistakably inferred from any of the external conditions of life. Our least doubtful information on the subject comes from ourselves, and when each of us consults that oracle he is very likely to discover that he cannot at present call himself happy, though he sees many other people who are, and he still hopes that presently he will be. As far as careful observation of others can take us, it appears that in general the happiest people are the most bovine and stupid. If one is able to learn from experience, if one is sensitive, imaginative, and reflective, one's chances of happiness are lessened. A man of sense cannot continue blindly to indulge a hope perpetually deferred; and if a man's lot does happen to be fortunate he must be singularly blind and callous to avoid uneasiness for his own future, and distress over the multitude of loathsome social and personal ills which surround him and form the background enabling him to call himself fortunate. Such a man, too, must be equally somnolent in order to rest contentedly in his present state, whatever that may appear to be in the eyes of others. Furthermore, the volume of palpable, unmistakable human distress and suffering is so great that we are in the habit of attributing good fortune to others on very slight and often entirely negative grounds.

I should not think of suggesting, of course—and no more does Mr. Hardy—that the great majority do not have moments of happiness, real and sometimes considerably prolonged, though generally paid for at a high rate. I do not mean at all to suggest, either, that genuine and permanent happiness is impossible of achievement; but it is, I fancy, rare, and it is not likely to be recognized for what it is by any one save the man who is achieving it. For the truth is that happiness is a by-product, never to be won by him who deliberately seeks it for its own sake. It is a mood of satisfaction which comes with the successful pursuit of some purpose or end which the subject regards as worthy in itself; and its quality and permanence depend upon the character of the end one is pursuing. If one's end is ephemeral or is found to be valueless as soon as it is attained, one's happiness is bound to be equally fleeting, and one will look back upon one's deeds and their rewards as alike vain and delusory.

How common this experience is need hardly be asked. Only he who has never done anything can have wholly escaped it, and it is Mr. Hardy's greatness that he has thus far seen life truly and has had the courage and skill to picture it honestly and vividly as he has seen it, despite all misunderstanding and sneers and abuse from his public. The creations of his sympathetic and powerful imagination live and will long continue to live in the minds of men because, even against our will, they force home to our saddened consciousness the tragic necessities in which we are enmeshed, the vanity and emptiness of our little lives, the utter indifference of the vast phenomenal universe to all our concerns, the malignity of human nature itself, which shows that our enemy flourishes even within our most retired strongholds, and the

implacable if not completely hopeless warfare we wage
for our souls' safety, attempting to conquer outer nature
to our purposes while, failing to examine those purposes
themselves, we leave the subtler enemy within to entrench
himself ever more and more firmly. Mr. Hardy has also
shown deep and true insight in insisting that life's tragic
aspect is not touched, and cannot be touched, by our
material progress, which at the most changes only the
fringes and appearances of our lives, while their substance remains what it has been. And he has succeeded,
too, in achieving what neither Sophocles nor Shakespeare
ever attempted or, as far as one knows, would have
thought of attempting. For he has written of the common
lives of common men; he has brought tragedy down from
the princes and their courts of elder days to live amongst
the ignorant, the obscure, and the mediocre. I hardly need
add that of course he has not been the discoverer of the
sufferings of the lowlier sons of earth, and that he has
not been the first to feel them sympathetically; I mean
only that he has, most notably amongst modern English
writers, succeeded in doing what long had been thought
impossible, in giving them tragic significance.

It has to be said, however, that this is an equivocal
achievement. For in thus making his humble figures and
their elemental passions symbolic of the drama of all
existence, he has robbed that drama of a meaning which
alone gave it, not merely dignity, but worth. He has
attained the necessary effect of vastness and universality
only by submerging his characters in their surroundings,
making them as a result wavering symbols of indifferent,
non-moral, non-human natural forces. He has not merely
vulgarized life in basing his complaints on the difficulty
or impossibility of man's satisfying his desire for enjoyment, but also, in cutting off man's conscious life from
reality and in robbing man completely of freedom, he has

deprived life of significance. He has so, indeed, managed to contrive a new thing, if it was worth contriving—what one may call a cosmic, rather than a human, tragedy. And this, because it is something new in kind, it is profoundly misleading to link, as he himself has ventured to link it, with the theme of Greek tragedy and of the Christian Gospels. Here, moreover, if I may say so, lies Mr. Hardy's own tragedy. His naturalistic philosophy has conspired to reinforce a native tendency, so that he has steadfastly, even truculently, remained blind to life's higher values. Attempting an original treatment, in terms of modern thought and knowledge, of life's fundamental issues, he has been misled by pretentious hypotheses into the creation, not of protagonists of humanity, but of mere helpless puppets and manikins. Confusing the primitive and elemental with the real, he has been led to concentrate his attention upon those aspects of life wherein we are most completely the creatures of instinct and circumstance. Despite his insight and honesty he has been led into hopeless contradiction by his effort at any cost to force the fruit of human experience into the narrow mould of a deterministic monism, which itself he has been unable to hold without further confusion. Faithfully obedient to this paradoxical and confused guess—a guess made in the light, not of human, but of physical data—he has in effect resigned his humanity.

He remains, indeed, at one with the highest wisdom alike of Greece and of Christianity in insisting upon the immitigable evil inherent in our divided, phenomenal existence. But he is a whole world apart from those venerable authorities, invoked in his Preface to *Late Lyrics and Earlier,* in his failure to grasp the significance of that deep division in man's nature which has led him to his own bitter and rebellious condemnation of the universe and which has led him, despite the complete contradiction of his philosophy which it implies, to conceive his own work as a plea for increased charity between men. For through this division within ourselves a new world is opened up to us, a world not phenomenal in its nature but timeless and changeless, a world of qualitative values, whose existence is as real in our experience as that of the phenomenal world in which we also live, and a world which we can and do make progressively more and more our own in proportion as we learn the true lessons of experience. Much in our lives is hopelessly beyond our control, in many directions we are helpless in the clutch of circumstance, but here there is a region of freedom which all men may win. We are born with nothing that is ultimately valuable for its own sake except a fighting chance—not for honour or reputation or earthly power, whether over nature or other men, nor for enjoyment—but a fighting chance to create a free human spirit. This alone it is which gives meaning and dignity and worth even to such existences as ours. And, we know not why, we know only from experience that so it is that, as we go into life, our hardships, our crosses and disappointments and sufferings, do actually open up to us the pathway to eternity. Mr. Hardy has felt this no less than the rest of us—all of his writing is the expression of it—yet in persisting in his blindness to its only possible meaning he has failed to give an even intelligible account of the same enduring facts of life which have stood before his predecessors in tragic art and which they have turned to noble use.

VIII

NATURALISM AND CHRISTIANITY

NATURALISM, as was said in the first of these essays, is as old as philosophy, and it will probably continue to manifest itself in ever new forms as long as men attempt to construct philosophical systems. The secret of its perennial strength lies on the surface of our Western civilization. For naturalism takes its origin from the desire to know, from men's desire to visualize their environment in simple comprehensive terms, from the desire somehow to grasp reality as an order, a system of regular law. In its beginnings it is a critical effort of the understanding, directed against crude, contradictory, and incomplete explanations of the universe and life drawn from traditional sources. As such it not only deserves to be welcomed by all true friends of humanity, but it has again and again vindicated itself in ways whose impressiveness and fruitfulness for civilization none can deny.

Perhaps the case for naturalism has not often been more clearly and sanely stated than it was by William Wallace in his second course of Gifford Lectures, in which he reviewed and criticized the Earl of Balfour's *Foundations of Belief*. Naturalism, he pointed out, like the rationalism of the eighteenth century, has been a protesting force, a creed subsisting by opposition to prevalent notions thought to be erroneous and injurious. In its origin it was the protest, "not against the supernatural in itself, but against a supernatural conceived as arbitrary, incoherent, and chaotic: it was the protest against the idle profanity which thinks it has explained an event, when it has said, with pious gesture, that it is the work of God—as if aught were not the work of God." The protest was made in the name of knowledge, and implied that man can understand the universe and his own place in it by the exercise of his eyes and his reason. But, the Earl of Balfour had asked, what would be a world which we should understand, or which we had thoroughly understood? "A world, clearly, without interest; the den of listlessness and dumb despair: or rather the ice-age of humanity, when to be and not to be would for once be absolutely alike. But, on the other hand, what were a world which we did *not* understand, had not in any measure understood? A world full of fears rather than hopes: a perpetual uncertainty, a grisly mystery, which made darkness cover the earth, and gross darkness its peoples. The world which reason claims is one where she may go for ever on and never die: a world where nothing can be called utterly unknowable, though much may remain for ever unknown: a world where, as humanity accumulates more and more its intellectual and spiritual capital, we shall move about more and more freely, *i.e.*, more and more wisely, as becomes those who are called to inherit the kingdom. The world which the genuine Naturalist desires is not different. It is a world of law.'"[1]

We all know the generous fulfilment which time and the efforts of men have brought to this desire. The search for a world of law has been wonderfully rewarded in terms of useful knowledge which has brought into being a new civilization of high complexity and vast wealth. And thus, as I say, the secret of the perennial strength of naturalism lies on the surface of our Western world. To put it vulgarly, it has paid, paid marvellously in coin exchangeable in the market-place; and as long as it does

[1] *Lectures and Essays on Natural Theology and Ethics,* pp. 96, 97. Quoted by permission of the Oxford University Press.

so it will appeal irresistibly to common sense. Our benefits have not been confined, moreover, to changes in the
material aspects of our lives, because we have also been
freed from many irrational fears, imaginary dangers,
and 'grisly mysteries.' This is not the place to describe
it at length, but our debt to the impulses which have produced naturalism is incalculable; and, as Wallace has
pointed out, even the faults of naturalism have sprung
from the creditable ''desire to be honest, to say only what
you can prove, to require thorough consistency and continuity in the whole realm of accepted truths.''

But, though these desires are creditable, so mixed are
the conditions of life and thought that the gravest of
faults have sprung from them. For while naturalism
begins in a critical effort, as a movement of opposition
to what is felt to be superstition or error, it also requires
for its beginning a mood of audacity or, if one likes, of
human self-confidence, which apparently knows no limits
once it has made its appearance, though in itself it is
blind and may without warning lead men into the deepest
of pitfalls. Naturalism implicitly makes the claim that
human intelligence can learn the essence and reasons of
things, and so can achieve an understanding of the universe as it actually is. Assuming that we do live in, and
are ourselves parts of, a universe, the naturalist regards
the phenomena about him as fleeting embodiments of one
vast process of orderly change. By observation and experiment he begins to learn the 'habits of matter'; he
discovers 'laws of nature'; he finds himself able to master
nature, within limits, for his own purposes. But, then, by
virtue of his creditable desire to 'say only what he can
prove, and to require thorough consistency and continuity in the whole realm of accepted truths,' the naturalist
begins to deny whatever is not in harmony with his own
discoveries and so sets up a positive system or theory

which pretends to completeness and finality. Thus naturalism has come to mean any system of thought which merges all 'appearances' in one common 'nature,' or process of change.

This may seem innocent, as it is certainly 'natural,' but it has extraordinary consequences. For the unified conception thus obtained on the basis of objective study inevitably involves the sacrifice of human nature, and hence the destruction even of the 'knowing' naturalist who has conceived the picture. It can be achieved only by a process of abstraction in which the special, the exceptional, the individual, is thrown aside as insignificant, while the common elements that remain are taken to constitute the objects' essential nature. Thus rocks and trees and human beings are merged into one nature at the expense of their several natures, and all things take place in necessary sequence, obedient to universal law.

In this way a mental picture of a conceivable universe is obtained. And such pictures have during the last seventy-five years acquired not only a new definiteness and an astonishing wealth of detail, but also the value and authority associated with truth. The unconscious artists who have drawn them have found their assumptions supported year by year ever more convincingly by the discoveries of science, so that the naturalistic view is by many no longer regarded as one amongst several possibilities, but as the only view consistent with present-day knowledge.

And not merely our intellectual environment but our physical environment also at present impels us towards naturalism. As I have said, we are partakers in a new civilization. We live in a world which has been transformed—how greatly only a few of us really know—by the powerful union of business and applied science, a world in which most of us are the helpless creatures of the advertising man, the banker, and the technical expert, a world which has materialized our lives, confused our standards, and dulled our spiritual natures. The complexity of our social organization forces us together in vast herds and makes us dependent on each other for almost all things, whether great or trivial, so that we are merged, or even drowned, in our environment and rendered well-nigh helpless against its defects. We cannot live complete lives, nor exercise free choices, nor learn the lessons of rounded experience, not merely because the crowd is ever upon us, pressing in relentlessly, but also because we are all ourselves in effect involuntary employees of a vast corporation. Upon conformity our own livelihoods depend, and equally they depend upon the success of a general system which nobody has planned or foreseen and for which nobody is responsible. The corporation, indeed, impersonal, soulless, and relentless, working its will like a veritable force of nature, is a characteristic creation of our time and may serve as the typical illustration of those large and blind forces which pull us hither and thither and make us their creatures, until we become the unconscious slaves of routine thought and action;—either that or the slaves of a blind, anarchical spirit of rebellion.

So it is that we are made ready for some naturalistic gospel. Yet even amidst our externalized, convenience-ridden, routine lives we can hardly remain long blind to the remarkable paradox inherent in a gospel invented by human beings for the sake of denying their own humanity. For this sums up the character of naturalism. It is a product of human imagination, as certainly and truly as is the *Divine Comedy* or *Hamlet* or *Faust,* and it represents a personal evaluation of life which must stand or fall by the test of common human experience. For it has behind it no peculiar authority which enables it to escape this ultimate test of all beliefs or creeds.

We have been asked to accept naturalism on the authority of the exact sciences, but, though many may continue to be taken in by this supposed authority, there is no longer the excuse for it that once there was. It is clear that exact science, working as it must with objective data such as are susceptible of quantitative measurement, can deal with human beings only so far as they are animals and things, while it must remain silent about their specifically human characteristics. During a brief space this silence was taken, both by scientists and by philosophers, as equivalent to denial, but that time has quickly passed. For it is now generally realized that by no means all of the data of experience are susceptible of scientific treatment, so that we no longer feel obligated, from loyalty to the cause of knowledge, to shut our eyes to certain of the experienced facts of human life, or to attempt to explain them away by vehemently asserting that they 'must' have arisen from causes which bear no resemblance to them.

And not only have we become aware that science is competent to deal merely with a limited portion of the field of experience, but we have also been almost violently forced in recent years to recognize the provisional character and subjective colouring of such 'science' as we do have. "To judge from the history of science," says a contemporary writer upon scientific subjects, "the scientific method is excellent as a means of obtaining plausible conclusions which are always wrong, but hardly as a means of reaching the truth."[2] The face of science, in other words, is constantly changing, because of discoveries which are not simply new but revolutionary. The

---

[2] J. W. N. Sullivan, *Aspects of Science,* a volume of brief essays written with competence and unusual charm.

same writer goes on to say: "In the Victorian age the
main lines of everything were settled; the chief features
of the universe were known. There were matter and
energy, and there was, of course, the æther. The astro-
nomical and geological scales were known in broad outline,
and a first survey of the march from amœba to man had
been taken. The work of future ages was to fill in the
details. The universe of the Victorians was a large and
rather grand affair, but it was sombre. Those emotional
barometers, the poets, in so far as they were aware of
the scientific outlook, either 'transcended' it or were
crushed by it. Jules Laforge furnishes an excellent example of the effect of the Victorian scientific outlook on an
intelligent and sensitive mind. His reaction was to compose funeral dirges on the death of the earth and the
extinction of mankind. The universe of the Victorians
was objective, indifferent, tracing a purposeless pattern
in obedience to 'iron' laws." But in the space of only a
few years physical science has been compelled to change
its primary assumptions, so that it has not merely been
extended, but has become a radically new thing, "and
there are very good reasons for supposing that it is
going to change still more. . . . The total effect of the
new ideas is to make the universe of physics less objective; to an unsuspected extent this indifferent universe,
with its iron laws, is a product of our own minds."

It is fair, then, to say that science lends only an ambiguous and doubtful support to any kind of philosophy.
The system-maker who builds on the provisional science
of yesterday is very likely to find his constructions discredited at their source almost as soon as they are published. And the large pictures of reality which we draw
with the aid of science are pictures only, structures of the
mind, with no peculiar or sacred right to represent the
truth, and with at best, indeed, a partial validity whose

extent no one can measure and whose genuineness no one can assess. Naturalism, consequently, cannot properly claim the powerful support from science which has been its chief mainstay in recent years, while, judged on its own merits, it can only be regarded as a maleficent when not a self-destroying falsehood.

These are strong words, but not, I believe, too strong; and they are, I hope, sufficiently substantiated by the preceding essays. A philosophy, after all, is only the reflective statement of a gospel, of a personal evaluation of life, and has to be judged by its truth to general experience. No interpretation of life ever offered to men has succeeded in taking equally into account all the facts of experience, it is true, but this failure is more disastrous in some cases than in others because all the facts are not equally significant. And the trouble with naturalism is that it wholly neglects the facts of experience which characterize us as human beings in order to emphasize other facts which link us with the animal and inorganic worlds. These other facts are not to be denied, and when they are denied the forces which make towards naturalism have a critical task of the utmost importance, which deserves grateful acknowledgement, in drawing us back to a due recognition of them. But it is an entirely different thing to go over to the opposite extreme and to deny our specifically human nature itself, and it is this that naturalism inevitably does. "A too ardent assault upon superstition," it has been well said, "may itself become a superstition, and a baleful one, for its champions."[3] And such a baleful superstition naturalism becomes whenever it presumes to erect itself as a positive interpretation of the universe. From the dawn of European thought to the present day it has again and again

[3] W. Wallace, *Lectures and Essays*, p. 96. Quoted by permission of the Oxford University Press.

proved its usefulness as an instrument of criticism, but
it has never attained autonomous expression without
exhibiting its utter incompetence to deal with the significant facts of human life.

For this the reason is clear, and it has in part been
already indicated. Man is certainly an animal, linked with
the 'animal creation,' and even with the 'vegetable creation,' as the doctrine of evolution teaches us. Thus far
man is purely a product of, or a part of, the natural
world, and thus far we are all nowadays in agreement
with the contention of naturalism. But at the same time,
whether it is explicable or not, man is obviously, indubit-
ably something more and other than an animal, and it is
this difference, this otherness, in terms of which he char-
acterizes himself as a human creature, and which to him
is the crucially significant fact about himself. Hence in
this fact any interpretation of life and of man's relation
to the universe which has the slightest claim to credence
must centre itself. Yet it is precisely this fact which naturalism can make nothing of and must even attempt to
deny in order to exist. And consequently it is impotent
the moment it is asked to answer pertinent questions.

Probably the most enlightening illustration of the incompetence of naturalism is afforded by the modern
efforts, extending from the Renaissance to our own time,
to construct a naturalistic ethics. They have been many,
and they have uniformly ended in self-contradiction, in
paradox, in the justification or praise of immorality, or in
more or less baleful absurdities. This is a sweeping
charge, but it cannot be seriously disputed. The most
careful and dispassionate effort, so far as I know, which
has been made in our time to examine the ethics of naturalism is the work of Professor W. R. Sorley. In discuss-
ing the theory of evolution he points out that the
tendency has been to evade or ignore the properly ethical

question, and to substitute for any discussion of it an
attempted historical treatment of the development of
moral feelings and standards. "But this is not the question before us when we ask how good is distinguished
from evil, or what the worth of things or conduct is, or
how the ideal of life or ethical end is to be conceived.
The question thus expressed in different forms implies
a new point of view, and no amount of history can answer
it. It is an irrelevant answer to the question 'What is
good?' when we are given a mere record of men's ideas
about what is good and of the way in which these opinions arose. We ask about the validity of moral judgements, and are put off by speculations concerning their
history."

And when we press the really ethical question we discover that there is a very good reason for the attempt to
evade an answer. For the only ideal for conduct which
evolution can reach is simply "the realization—or,
rather, continuation—of human nature as it has been and
is—with this formal modification, that, while the various
impulses are, so far as possible, to have free play given
them, they should be developed in a harmonious manner. It seems doubtful, however, how far this tendency
towards harmony is properly suggested by, or consistent
with, evolution, which has implied a ceaseless struggle of
opposing forces. At any rate, evolution does not seem
competent to give any sufficient principle of relative sub-
ordination between the various impulses, such as might
add reality to the formal principle of harmony." It in
fact simply sets up as our ideal "conformity to human
nature as it is, or to the tendencies in it which are strongest and most persistent."

Professor Sorley concludes that the theory of evolution is resultless in ethics. He sums up the outcome of
his inquiry by saying: "The further we go in examining

any naturalistic theory of ethics, the clearer does it become that it can make no nearer approach to a solution of the ethical question than to point out what courses of action are likely to be the pleasantest, or what tendencies to action the strongest; and this it can do only within very narrow limits both of time and accuracy. As to what things are good it can say nothing without a previous assumption identifying good with some such notion as pleasant or powerful. The doctrine of evolution itself, which has given new vogue to Naturalism both in morality and in philosophy generally, only widens our view of the old landscape. By its aid we cannot pass from 'is' to 'ought.' . . . The naturalists seem to be in the same difficulty as Dr. Johnson was when Boswell plagued him to give a reason for action: ' "Sir," said he, in an animated tone, "it is driving on the system of life." ' In their case too, the strength of the answer lies in its 'animated tone.' "[4]

Indeed, the whole history of the human race exhibits on every page the folly of naturalism's attempt to merge man in his surroundings and to confound ethical with impulsive or unreflective action. Civilization is, it may be said, simply the record of man's unceasing attempts to thwart, to oppose, to control nature—both his own nature and external nature—for purposes of his own. Dr. E. E. Slosson candidly says in a recent book: "Admire Nature? Possibly, but be not blinded to her defects. Learn from Nature? We should sit humbly at her feet until we can stand erect and go our own way. Love Nature? Never! She is our treacherous and unsleeping foe, ever to be feared and watched and circumvented, for at any moment and in spite of all our vigilance she may wipe out the human race by famine, pestilence, or earth-

[4] *The Ethics of Naturalism*, 2d ed., pp. 320-321, 302-303, 309, 326-327.

quake and within a few centuries obliterate every trace of its achievement."[5]

In the last century John Stuart Mill, with his usual clarity and vigour, gave almost classic expression to the same patent fact of history and experience in his essay on *Nature*. "Conformity to nature," he says, "has no connexion whatever with right and wrong." "The duty of man is the same in respect to his own nature as in respect to the nature of all other things, namely not to follow but to amend it." He thus summarizes his conclusions: "The word Nature has two principal meanings: it either denotes the entire system of things, with the aggregate of all their properties, or it denotes things as they would be, apart from human intervention. In the first of these senses, the doctrine that man ought to follow nature is unmeaning; since man has no power to do anything else than follow nature; all his actions are done through, and in obedience to, some one or many of nature's physical or mental laws. In the other sense of the term, the doctrine that man ought to follow nature, or in other words, ought to make the spontaneous course of things the model of his voluntary actions, is equally irrational and immoral. Irrational, because all human action whatever, consists in altering, and all useful action in improving, the spontaneous course of nature: Immoral, because the course of natural phenomena being replete with everything which when committed by human beings is most worthy of abhorrence, any one who endeavoured in his actions to imitate the natural course of things would be universally seen and acknowledged to be the wickedest of men."[6]

This undying opposition between man and his natural environment, between man and his own 'natural' self,

[5] *Creative Chemistry*, p. 10.
[6] *Three Essays on Religion*, American ed., pp. 62, 54, 64-65.

needs, I should suppose, only to be recalled to our attention in order to be admitted as the truth. The proof of it is all around us and within us, transparent and unescapable. And it is clear that for the sake of what at bottom is an æsthetic motive—the desire for a simple, comprehensive, and symmetrical unity—naturalism is content outrageously to deny the fundamental truth about human nature. For no necessary or compelling reason it thus seeks to stultify life, it becomes the agent of tragic confusions, and it serves as the justifying gospel of weaklings and sentimentalists. Huxley himself, in his last years when he was endeavouring by reading and reflexion to make good some of the defects of his early education, found it necessary to admit the opposition between man and nature, despite the difficulties the admission brought upon him. This has been discussed above, in connexion with the lecture in which he stated his conclusions, the Romanes Lecture on *Evolution and Ethics.* In another essay written subsequently and published in the *Fortnightly Review,* but never reprinted, Huxley explained the sense in which he used to assert that the Romanes Lecture was a very orthodox discourse on the text, "Satan, the Prince of this World": "It is the secret of the superiority of the best theological teachers to the majority of their opponents that they substantially recognize [the] realities of things, however strange the forms in which they clothe their conceptions. The doctrines of predestination, of original sin, of the innate depravity of man, and the evil fate of the greater part of the race, of the primacy of Satan in this world, of the essential vileness of matter, of a malevolent Demiurgus subordinate to a benevolent Almighty, who has only lately revealed himself, faulty as they are, appear to me to be vastly nearer the truth than the 'liberal' popular illusions that babies are all born good, and that the example of a corrupt society is responsible for their failure to remain so; that it is given to everybody to reach the ethical ideal if he will only try; that all partial evil is universal good, and other optimistic figments, such as that which represents 'providence' under the guise of a paternal philanthropist, and bids us believe that everything will come out right (according to our notions) at last.'"[7]

These lists are somewhat curious, but the important thing is that Huxley in the end came to see the evil impossibilities of naturalism and admitted that the best theological teachers have substantially recognized, as other men have not, the realities of things. And this is the enduring worth of historic Christianity. Though the forms in which its substance is clothed have grown strange to modern eyes, and though it does not answer all the questions which, as the proverb has it, any fool can ask, still, historic Christianity does recognize the enduring facts of life and does give them a sound meaning, and its estimate of human existence and its possibilities, when tried by the test of common experience, shows itself solid and true at the centre.

Matthew Arnold once said that Cardinal Newman's religion was "frankly impossible." As we have seen, he regarded Newman with a feeling akin to veneration, yet he considered that in embracing the Roman faith Newman had set himself down as a victim of transparent delusion and of gross superstition, and had taken a step impossible to one who was not either ignorant of, or culpably indifferent to, well-nigh the whole realm of modern knowledge. Most would agree with this verdict, without pausing to examine the paradox which it involves. But it is at least curious and worthy of remark

[7] *An Apologetic Irenicon, Fortnightly Review,* November, 1892. The above paragraph is quoted in Leonard Huxley's *Life* of his father, II, 322.

that out of this stronghold of delusion, superstition, and ignorance there came forth sweetness and light. For by universal consent Newman was not only himself a man of high and noble character but was also one who understood human nature almost miraculously. If anything is obvious, it is obvious that he knew the workings of the human heart, the springs of character, the motives of action, the subtle and various turnings of the spirit upon its restless course. Here he stood an acknowledged master, and the magic voice which held all Oxford spellbound year after year still speaks its deep and sobering message from the volumes of his sermons. What he understood so well was nothing new, but precisely that which, underneath the ceaseless change of our ways of life, endures at the centre of human nature and forms the stuff of man's abiding thoughts, and problems, and hopes, and achievements in the gaining of inner freedom and peace, and in spiritual growth. We may pause for a moment to listen to him who speaks better for himself than others can speak for him. Our "sense of the nothingness of human life, impressed on us by the very fact that it comes to an end, is much deepened, when we contrast it with the capabilities of us who live it. Had Jacob lived Methuselah's age, he would have called it short. This is what we all feel, though at first sight it seems a contradiction, that even though the days as they go be slow, and be laden with many events, or with sorrows or dreariness, lengthening them out and making them tedious, yet the year passes quick though the hours tarry, and time bygone is as a dream, though we thought it would never go while it was going. And the reason seems to be this: that, when we contemplate human life in itself, in however small a portion of it, we see implied in it the presence of a soul, the energy of a spiritual existence, of an accountable being; consciousness tells us this concerning it every moment. But when we look back on it in memory, we view it but externally, as a mere lapse of time, as a mere earthly history. And the longest duration of this external world is as dust and weighs nothing, against one moment's life of the world within. Thus we are ever expecting great things from life, from our internal consciousness every moment of our having souls; and we are ever being disappointed, on considering what we have gained from time past, or can hope from time to come. And life is ever promising and never fulfilling; and hence, however long it be, our days are few and evil.'"[8]

I quote this passage almost at random, one out of very many, but it is not necessary to 'prove' what all have admitted from the days when Newman was preaching in St. Mary's Church to the present time. This conceded fact, however, does itself prove that there must at least be important elements in Newman's religion which should be excepted before one agrees that it is "frankly impossible." I am not at all concerned to try to deny, or to gloss over, those portions of Roman Catholic belief and practice which most outside of that church would now regard simply as the unholy relics of a past age of ignorance or relative barbarism. I should myself agree that Roman Catholicism is at present so encumbered with these survivals as to make it an 'impossible' religion for honest and enlightened men and women. Yet at the same time it seems obvious that a simple rejection of Catholic Christianity is made also impossible by such a witness as Newman, whom I instance alone not because he stands alone, but merely because he is in this pre-eminent amongst Englishmen of the nineteenth century. The religion in which he was nurtured, in terms of which he thought and acted and learned whatever he knew, must

[8] *Parochial and Plain Sermons*, IV, 215-216.

contain within it fundamental and enduring truths, else it could never have ministered fruitfully to such insight as his nor have helped him to such knowledge as he showed of man's inner life, its meaning and issues. I am, I hope, no fonder of delusion and superstition and ignorance than others, and I should wish to throw all my strength against them wherever they show their heads, yet it seems to me that only a blind and wilful prejudice can refuse to acknowledge that these children of darkness did not prevent Newman from knowing what men should know about themselves, and that, indeed, a religion which many would now call a tissue of falsehood from beginning to end actually developed and brought to maturity in him precisely the kind of knowledge most significant for us as human beings. To candid minds this must be an arresting and disturbing fact. And when one reflects that the modern knowledge because of which many have repudiated Christianity is a 'knowledge' whose inevitable tendency is to belittle and obscure our humanity and its significance, it becomes—if one cares to put it paradoxically—a nice question whether this 'knowledge' is as beneficial to us as Newman's delusions and ignorance were to him. No human belief is unmixed with error, as Newman knew better than some who consider themselves more enlightened, and it is a real question whether Newman's errors, now seemingly so patent, were as serious as those of our contemporaries who know so much more about their kinship with beasts than with angels.

It is told of Bossuet that, when he was once asked if he did not think there were interesting things to be learned from following the scientific speculations of his day, he replied that he had no doubt of the interest of those speculations but that he considered it beneath the dignity of a bishop to pay serious heed to them. The story is two-edged, and it would be better for all of us had he and others like him been of a different mind; but, on the other hand, there is profound truth in Bossuet's reply if it be taken to mean that exact knowledge of material phenomena, important and useful as it is, may still not be the most important and useful knowledge for men, and may lead them widely and tragically astray if it blind them to their real vocation on the battle-field of their inner lives. The truth which is always being forgotten and which must ever be rediscovered by the individual, if it is rediscovered, through the hard lessons of experience, is that the exact sciences cannot of themselves give us anything that is ultimately valuable. They are means, not ends, and they are means, moreover, only to the use of the kind of material with which they can deal. He who loses himself in them, and attempts to limit his life by their limitations, loses himself indeed in a deathlike unmeaning flux.[9]

And in fact men half-consciously know this. It was a very common belief amongst contemporaries of Arnold and Huxley that not only Christianity, but religion, was destined presently to disappear from the earth and no

[9] Some sentences may be quoted here from an article by W. H. Mallock, *"Cowardly Agnosticism"* (*Fortnightly Review*, April, 1889). The article was addressed to Huxley but he, with his usual skill in choosing opponents, never made a public reply to it. It is vitiated by faults which enter more or less into all of Mallock's writings, but it is acute, and deserves to be read in its entirety. ''Theologic religion does not say that within limits the agnostic principle is not perfectly valid and has not led to the discovery of a vast body of truth. But what it does say is this: That the truths which are thus discovered are not the only truths which are certainly and surely discoverable. The fundamental principle of agnosticism is that nothing is certainly true but such truths as are demonstrated or demonstrable. The fundamental principle of theologic religion is that there are other truths of which we can be equally or even more certain, and that these are the only truths that give life a meaning and redeem us from the body of death. Agnosticism says nothing is certain which cannot be proved by science. Theologic religion says, nothing which is important can be. . . . Here is the dilemma which men, sooner or later, will see before them;

longer to cloud our atmosphere. The belief was so completely mistaken that no one can now be found who persists in it, and men, whether they like it or not, are ready to agree that religion will never disappear. It will not do so because, ultimately, it is the embodiment of man's enduring conviction that life *is* significant and does contain 'intimations of immortality.' The real question is what kind of religion we are to have. There is no magic to prevent our having a bad or perverted religion. Religions, like other institutions, are affected by the societies amidst which they exist, and may so become corrupt, decadent, and even vicious, just as religion in America to-day on the whole reflects the ignorance, the shallowness, the prejudice, and the specialism characteristic of our culture and education. Is it still possible that Christianity should serve us in the future as once it served men in a very different age, guiding them to their true vocation with no uncertain light and confidently opposing the plausible and attractive forms of naturalism? It is perhaps not impossible, and one would need to examine the very considerable efforts now being made to reconstruct or revive Christian belief before venturing upon an answer.[10] But this at least would appear to be certain: that no existing form of Christianity as it now stands can greatly help us or look forward to a large future, and yet that no religion of the future can hope to achieve true

. . . and they will then have to choose one alternative or the other. What their choice will be I do not venture to prophesy; but I will venture to call them happy if their choice prove to be this: To admit frankly that their present canon of certainty, true so far as it goes, is only the pettiest part of truth, and that the deepest certainties are those which, if tried by this canon, are illusions. To make this choice a struggle would be required with pride, and with what has long passed for enlightenment; and yet, when it is realized what depends on the struggle, there are some at least who will think that it must end successfully.''

[10] I hope to deal with this question in a later volume.

success which does not substantially embody the interpretation of life, its meaning, possibilities, and rewards, which historic Christianity has presented to past generations.

Christianity as it now stands is moribund, as practically every one sees. And it is moribund not so much from the 'wickedness of the people,' though they are wicked enough, as from its own internal failures. Gradually since the Reformation it has sunk lower and lower in the scale of existence, until it has so nearly severed all intelligence and enlightenment from itself as to make men wonder how its few great outstanding figures can have honestly and sincerely taken up the cross. Attempting to iron out differences by the tyrannical method of exclusion, it has only multiplied sects and damned good men until it has dispersed its one-time strength almost, if not quite, irremediably. Even Rome itself has more and more taken on the character of an exclusive sect, so that it shares many of the worst traits of its revolted children and has exaggerated some of them. Newman's conception of a living church is, it would seem, the only possible one, and there is the whole sad story of his later life to show that Rome can no longer pretend even to understand it, much less to embody it. The excommunication of Tyrrell[11] and M. Loisy, moreover, proves the fact beyond the possibility of doubt. Not that I should contend that the doctrines of Tyrrell and M. Loisy should have been formally accepted, for I do not see how Rome could have accepted them without ceasing to be Christian; but there is a world of difference between intelligent opposition

[11] Perhaps accuracy demands the qualification that Tyrrell suffered only the minor excommunication and that his case was still, ostensibly at least, under consideration at Rome when he died. He was, however, denied burial with Catholic rites.

and the mere stupid, self-betraying assertion of infallibility.

But if there are few notes of a living church in Rome,
there are fewer still in the ranks of Protestantism—the
one possible exception being the Anglican Church. This,
however, subsists only on the basis of illogical expedients
which must be a standing amazement to any one not an
Englishman and not brought up within the bosom of
that strange fold. And for the rest it is sufficient here to
say that Protestantism by its very nature is, what its
whole history amply and unmistakably shows, a subversive, anarchical, self-destroying force. Very probably
Luther and Calvin will come to stand out in the pages of
history as the wilful, headstrong destroyers of Christianity;—perhaps with some injustice, as the corruption and
decadence of Catholicism at the beginning of the sixteenth century was manifest and hideous, and called for
heroic measures. But if nothing short of separation and
the creation of sects could have sufficed, it is by now clear
enough that the remedy was as bad as the disease, and
that the Reformation should in this case be regarded
simply as the first overt stage of an inevitable disintegra-
tion. And indeed the real character of Protestantism was
not unapparent even in the beginning to Luther himself
and to some of his co-workers. We have ''a painful series
of confessions of disappointment with the moral results
of their work on the part of the Reformers themselves,
and especially of Luther. It is difficult to give an idea of
the weight of this evidence [except by the accumulation
of quotations. But] in passage after passage Luther declares that the last state of things was worse than the
first; that vice of every kind had increased since the
Reformation; that the nobles were greedy, the peasants
brutal; that the corruption of morals in Wittenberg itself
was so great that he contemplated shaking off the dust of

his feet against it; that Christian liberality had altogether ceased to flow; and that the preachers were neither
held in respect nor supported by the people. Towards the
close of his life these complaints became more bitter and
more frequent. Sometimes the Devil is called in to account for so painful and perplexing a state of things.'"[12]
Possibly the Devil did have a hand in it, but at any rate
what Luther saw were the earliest symptoms of a disin-
tegration of spiritual and intellectual forces which
Protestantism has steadily, if always unwillingly, continued to promote.

The fundamental tragedy of Christianity is its persistence in holding to relatively external forms, and its regarding these as final and inviolable and essential, while
it has neglected the inner substance of its message. That
inner substance is imperishable and will not vanish from
amongst men, nor cease to oppose itself to all forms of
naturalism, but perhaps those who in the future bear
witness to it will not be Christians. For as Christianity
now is, it has become a necessity, in the name of honesty,
in the name of truth to the spirit, in the name of religion
itself, for those who are most alive to its abiding verities
to remain outside of its doors. It may not always continue
so, but change, if change there is to be, will have to come
from the pious upholders of use and wont. Perhaps they
may yet remember one of the luminous sayings of Coleridge: "My opinion is thus: that deep thinking is attainable only by a man of deep feeling, and that *all truth is a
species of revelation.*" Perhaps they may yet remember
that 'in a higher world it is otherwise, but that here below
to live is to change and to be perfect is to have changed
often.'

However this may be, it is not doubtful that men will

[12] *The Reformation of the Sixteenth Century, etc.*, by Charles Beard,
fifth ed., pp. 145-146.

continue to see life as Christians in the past have seen it. It is not doubtful, because the Christian view of man is simply the summation of lessons of common human experience which all may learn whose eyes are open and whose hearts are honest. "Life is ever promising and never fulfilling." "We still crave for something, we do not well know what." "You must either conquer the world or the world will conquer you." "The world may seduce, may terrify, may mislead, may enslave, but it cannot really inspire confidence and love." The world "has no substance in it, but is like a shade or phantom; when you pursue it, when you try to grasp it, it escapes from you, or it is malicious, and does you a mischief. We need something which the world cannot give." How can these aphorisms be gainsaid? We need only acquaintance with ourselves to know that man is a fearful compound of grandeur and misery. He is an animal, and often enough a beast, yet he wonderfully transcends the phenomenal world and finds his true home in a far region of immaterial reality. He learns to know himself and to rise beyond himself through struggle, through disappointment and suffering and even defeat, at least as certainly as through the experience of good fortune and the taste of earthly enjoyment. All experience can teach him heavenly truths, yet none teaches him anything whatsoever unless it points beyond itself and preserves him from being enslaved by the world in a stupid contentment which is the death of the spirit. The probationary character of life, the fact that man, animal though he inexplicably be, is yet a spirit, fighting his way towards freedom in the realm of immaterial reality—these are truths which time does not wither.

INDEX